OTHER BOOKS BY WILLIE SNOW ETHRIDGE

You Can't Hardly Get There From Here
I Just Happen to Have Some Pictures
There's Yeast in the Middle East
Let's Talk Turkey
Going to Jerusalem
It's Greek To Me
This Little Pig Stayed Home

STRANGE
FIRES

Willie
Snow
Ethridge

STRANGE

The
Vanguard Press Inc.,
New York

FIRES

The True Story
of
John Wesley's
Love Affair
in
Georgia

Manufactured in the United States of America by
H. Wolff Book Manufacturing Company, New York

Library of Congress Catalogue Card Number: 77–170902

SBN 8149–0693–1

Designer: Ernst Reichl

For
LILLA HAWES
Director of the Georgia Historical Society
not only because she is warm, resourceful,
and encouraging,
but also because I am more deeply indebted to her
than to all the other wonderful librarians
and their assistants in the United States and England
who so generously helped me
with this book

For
LILLA DANES,
Director of the Georgia Historical Society
not only because she is warm, resourceful,
and encouraging
but also because I am more deeply indebted to her
than to all the other wonderful librarians
and their assistants in the United States and England
who so generously helped me
with this book

INTRODUCTION

My interest in John Wesley had its beginning when I was a student at Wesleyan College in Macon, Georgia, which is only one of the innumerable colleges, universities, churches, leagues, foundations, missions, and males named for that amazing founder of Methodism, although he himself died a rector of the Episcopal Church. Though my grandfather on my paternal side was a Methodist preacher and my father was a member of that denomination until my devout mother won him over to the Baptist fold, I had never given Mr. Wesley any particular attention until that time. My interest wasn't stirred sufficiently, however, for me to do anything about it until a number of years later when I discovered, while doing research on James Oglethorpe preparatory to writing a historical novel about him, that John, when he had accompanied my hero on his second trip to Georgia, had fallen passionately in love with an eighteen-year-old girl, Sophy Hopkey. This love affected profoundly, if not completely, John's life and the history of the Christian world.

9

There were contributing factors to this metamorphosis, but Sophy was the catalyst. I decided then that someday I would write a book about John and the great love of his life. And it would have to be fact, not fiction. The romance was too unbelievable to be put into a novel.

Yet, as astounding as John's and Sophy's love story was, it has been only recently that it has been possible to get at the true details of the affair. For almost two hundred years, the heart of the secret was locked in John's Georgia Diary, a baffling complex of shorthand, abbreviations, and ciphers that, like his other diaries, was devised to conceal his thoughts and actions and, incidentally, to save time and space. Furthermore, this pertinent volume, containing the significant events of his Georgia days, was never included in the Colman Collection, a collection that contained all of John's other diaries and many of his other writings. Indeed, it was referred to as "lost."

It was not until July, 1903, when an article by the late Bishop Eugene R. Hendrix appeared in the *Methodist Review*, that the Georgia Diary's mysterious history became known to a limited few in this country.

When John died in 1791, he willed all his works to Dr. Thomas Coke, Dr. John Whitehead, and Henry Moore "to be burnt or published as they see good." Among the works was the Georgia Diary, a tiny volume, six and a half inches long by four inches wide, stoutly bound in calf, and containing one hundred and eighty pages of "superior" note paper. Each page was given over to a single day in John's Georgia stay and each line to a single hour, except for those days when he was battling storms as he traveled between Savannah and Frederica and Savannah and Charleston. The entries were usually written in John's clean hand, but were indecipherable because of the code.

In 1817, Mr. Moore, according to the inscription on the fly leaf, gave this little Diary to Miss Elizabeth Taylor of Carmarthen and she bequeathed it in 1847 to the Reverend

John Gould Avery, a distinguished Methodist minister, in whose family it remained secure and, no doubt, dusty for fifty years. Then, in 1897, Mr. Thursfield Smith of Salop, England, purchased it for his collection of Wesleyana, the largest such collection owned by a private individual in the British Isles. Mr. Smith set great store by his acquisition— he pronounced it "the most precious Wesley document in existence"—and refused all offers for it until Bishop Hendrix, when he was fraternal messenger to the British Wesleyan Conference in the early 1900's, persuaded Mr. Smith that, since it had been written in Georgia, it should be returned to America. It is now in the library of Emory University in Atlanta.

However, before it left English soil, the Reverend Richard Green, the late Governor of Didsbury College and author of *The Wesley Bibliography*, had the loan of it for six months for intensive study. Though he was unable to break the code, he was successful in interpreting some of the abbreviations John had used. The abbreviations were, for the most part, somewhat similar to those used today for taking down lecture notes in institutions. For example, among the Reverend Mr. Green's interpretations were "p.p." meaning "private prayer," "Lr.br.," "Letter to brother," "Br.B.," "Breakfasted on bread," "Lr.O." or Wr.O," "Wrote letter to Oglethorpe," "Rp. x," "Read prayer and examined," and "Ntw.," "Interview." The one difficult translation achieved by the Governor was that "y" stood for "hearers."

Thus the curious, deeply moving details of John's ardor for the young girl in Georgia remained hidden until a red-letter day between the publication of the Hendrix article in 1903 and November, 1909, when the code was actually broken and the Georgia Diary was published in Volume 1 of *The Journal of John Wesley*. After years of arduous labor, the feat of decoding was accomplished by the late British army chaplain, the Reverend Nehemiah Curnock, with the help of several "experts."

Though Mr. Curnock, to my knowledge, never recorded the date of this break-through, he did write about the long, intricate decoding process; indeed, it is much too intricate to describe here. It is sufficient to say that the first clue leading to the break-through was revealed to Mr. Curnock, according to his own account, in a dream. He had discovered in John's first Diary—the Oxford Diary—a place where the colon sign ":" could mean only "12." This was of no help, however, until in a dream he saw that "2" stood for "a." As he triumphantly proclaims, "This was the first ray of light" in "years of reasoned inference and testing."

But even with the code broken and the publication of *The Journal*, the absorbing facts of John's romance were all but buried in page after page of his hour-by-hour and frequently minute-by-minute report of his activities, of long Biblical quotations, of extracts from sermons, of exhaustive theological dissertations, of snatches of hymns in the process of composition, as well as by reams of footnotes of the very articulate, opinionated, erudite Editor Curnock.

Nevertheless, the facts are there in John's own words for those patient enough to mine them and, coupled with other evidence from early Colonial records, journals, and letters of the time, prove without doubt that John's all-encompassing love for Sophy led to one of the greatest transformations in character ever recorded.

Willie Snow Ethridge

STRANGE FIRES

ONE

It was on Sunday morning, March 7, 1736, that John Wesley preached his first sermon in Savannah. Already spring held Georgia in the palm of its sweet-smelling, colorful hand. In the nearby woods, jasmine vines swung clusters of tiny gold bells of bloom in the steeple-tall belfries of the pines; wild honeysuckle sprouted geysers of pale pink petals; violets ran blue as rinsing water, and the new, fuzzy, curled-up leaves of the magnolias nudged against their older, more hardened, brassy-bright brothers.

However, inside the little building used both as courthouse and church—located on the corner of Bull, the main street of the three-year-old town, running from north to south and dividing it in half, and Bay Lane—there was no hint of spring. The air was still musty and dank as winter twilight.

John Martin Bolzius, the minister and "chief director" of a small settlement of a religious sect of Germans called Salzburgers, at Ebenezer, approximately twenty miles from Savannah, gave in his diary a most dismal picture of the struc-

15

ture that he and his flock were "privileged to use" on first landing in Georgia: "It is roughly built of clapboards, has neither windows nor choir and is nothing more than a shelter." The dimensions were twelve feet by thirty feet; nevertheless, it held about one hundred persons. This Sunday every seat was taken.

A tremor of excitement and curiosity ran through the hundred as John Wesley stood behind the crude, hand-hewn pulpit to read the rules by which he intended to conduct his ministry. Though small of stature—just five feet, four inches tall and weighing at the most one hundred and twenty pounds—he had a commanding presence. His head, held gracefully erect, was in perfect proportion to his body and his features were cleanly chiseled: a broad, high brow; a straight, thin, aristocratic nose, slightly curved at the tip; a full-lipped mouth with a Cupid's bow; lean jaws and a firmly rounded chin that cupped a deep dimple.

Indeed, all these features were so delicately cut and harmonious that the Rt. Hon. Augustine Birrell, K.C., in writing about John, claimed there was a "touch of femininity about his face" and in support of his assertion pointed out that Adam Clarke, "who knew well the whole family, said that, except for his clothes, John was indistinguishable from his sister, Martha." But there was nothing "in the least derogatory about this circumstance," argued His Honor, "for Martha Wesley was a strong minded woman. . . ."

Besides these nearly perfect features, John had a clear, healthy complexion that testified to his love of the out-of-doors and made him look somewhat younger than his thirty-three years minus four months. His eyes, however, attracted the most attention. Rather narrow and minnow-shaped, they were so lively, so alert and piercing, that no one ever thought to mention their color.

On this significant Sunday, John was no doubt wearing the conventional dress of the Anglican Episcopal church: the two white, stiffly starched bands at the neck; the long, slim

16

black cassock like a Roman toga, and over it the ankle-length white surplice; the badge of his Master's degree, a narrow, black silk scarf; and even the powdered wig with the tight cork-screw curls touching the shoulders. At the beginning of his ministry he wore the wig on all ecclesiastical occasions. Later he abandoned it almost entirely, as he disliked the expense of keeping it dressed and, besides, preferred appearing with his own fairly long auburn hair uncovered, parted exactly in the middle, and brushed to a silky sheen.

That morning John mentioned by name only two members of the congregation: John Brownfield, who, according to *A List of Early Settlers of Georgia*, was a former servant of James Oglethorpe (this does not necessarily mean he was a domestic; considering that he became register of the Colony, it seems more than likely he had been a secretary or clerk); and Baron Freidrick George von Reck, the leader of the first group of Moravians to settle in Georgia.

However, there were also doubtless present Thomas Causton, the First Bailiff, who, with a second and sometimes third bailiff and a recorder, formed the ruling body of Savannah, known as the Magistrates; his wife Martha; her eighteen-year-old niece, christened Sophia Christiana, but almost always called Sophy, Hopkey; the Caustons' young son, also named Thomas, but nicknamed Jacky; the soon-to-be Second Bailiff, Henry Parker, and his wife Anne; the Recorder, Thomas Christie, a bachelor; and Samuel Quincy, whom John was replacing as minister.

To John's surprise, many congregants were extravagantly dressed—that is, extravagantly dressed considering that one of the chief reasons for Georgia's establishment was to relieve the sickeningly crowded debtors' prisons in England of their less culpable inmates and to rescue others on the brink of imprisonment. On his arrival in Savannah, John had been told by a "gentleman" that he would "see as well dressed a congregation on Sunday as most he had seen in London," but he had not believed it. Now, realizing the truth of the statement, he made a mental note to expound on "those Scriptures which related to dress." In the future he wanted to see neither "gold in the church, nor costly apparel," but only "plain clean linen or woolen." (A little more than a year later, on April 4, 1737, a law was read at a meeting of the Georgia Trustees in London "against the use of gold and silver in apparel and furniture, in Georgia, and for preventing extravagance and luxury.")

Today, however, there were other matters to which John must give his attention. First, the reading of the rules by which he intended to conduct his ministry. He wanted to make them clear at the very beginning so that every parishioner would be fully acquainted with them. (Could he have seen so early the grave consequences that would befall him because of one of them?)

Deliberately and solemnly he read:

"Number One: I must admonish every one of you, not only in public, but from house to house

"Two: I can admit none to the Holy Communion without previous notice

"Three: I shall divide the morning service on Sunday in compliance with the first design of the Church

"Four: I must obey the Rubric by dipping all children who are able to endure it

"Five: I can admit none who are not communicants to be sureties in Baptism

"Six: In general, though I have all the ecclesiastical authority which is entrusted to any in this Province, I am only a servant of the Church of England, not a judge, and therefore obliged to keep her regulations in all things."

John waited for the meaning of these rules to sink in. In spite of the flashes of finery, the overwhelming majority of his parishioners were simple, illiterate, unsuccessful tradesmen: carpenters, barbers, butchers, bakers, woodcutters, cobblers, bricklayers, peruke (wig) makers, linen drapers and other day laborers, and their wives and children. They needed time to comprehend what John had said.

Continuing the service with the reading of the eighteenth chapter of Luke, the twenty-ninth and thirtieth verses, John was struck by their peculiar applicability to his own situation. Jesus had said: ". . . Verily I say unto you, 'There is no man that hath left house or parents or brothers, or wife, or children, for the kingdom of God's sake, Who shall not receive manifold more in this present time, and in the world to come life everlasting.' "

Though John had neither wife nor children, he had left home and parents and brethren for the sake of the kingdom of God. Indeed, he had left a most doting mother, a loving father, and close, affectionate brothers and sisters. He was one of nineteen children of Susannah and Samuel Wesley, ten of whom reached their majority. He had been born on June 17, 1703, at Epworth in Lincolnshire, a low-lying section of England cut by rivers and canals, where Samuel was Episcopal rector for almost forty years.

While practically still in his mother's arms John was imbued with a strong belief in rules and order. Susannah raised him, as she did all her children, in a strict, businesslike manner. From his first birthday he was expected to get up, to go to bed, and to eat at appointed hours. He never ate more than three times a day and behaved like a little gentleman as soon as he was able to sit at the table. Even at this early age he stood in awe and fear of the rod and understood he was never to display a show of will power. Susannah argued that a child with a will of his own had the devil himself within him, whom only frequent floggings could exorcise.

Before John could talk, he learned to ask by signs the blessing at mealtime, and, just as soon as he could talk, he learned the Lord's Prayer, which he repeated morning and evening. Susannah taught him to read when he was five, the age at which she taught all his sisters and brothers. She fol-

19

lowed a regular method of instruction: The day before a child was to have his reading lesson, she set the house in order, assigned duties to all the other children, and warned them not to interrupt her and her pupil between the hours of nine and twelve and two and five. She allowed only one day for a child to learn the alphabet; each of them succeeded except two of the girls, Molly and Nancy, who took a day and a half. As soon as a child had mastered his letters, he was taught to spell and then to read.

Samuel, the oldest brother, was held up as an example for John and the others. In just a few hours Samuel knew his letters and began to read the first chapter of Genesis. He learned to spell the first verse, after which he read it over and over until he could do it without faltering; then, on to the second chapter until he was able to take ten verses a day for a lesson. Within two months, he was reading the Bible quite well.

Though John was not as quick as Samuel, Susannah lavished more attention on him than on any of the other children because she believed he was destined for a special service to God since, when he was five, he had escaped burning to death in what she considered a miraculous fashion.

She gave the graphic details of the fire in the following letter to a neighboring clergyman:

"Epworth, Aug. 24, 1709

"On Wednesday night, February the ninth, between the hours of eleven and twelve, some sparks fell from the roof of our house upon one of the children's (Kitty's) feet. She immediately ran to our chamber, and called us. Mr. Wesley, hearing a cry of fire in the street, started up: (as I was very ill, he lay in a separate room from me) and opening his door found the fire was in his own house. He immediately came to my room and bade me and my two eldest daughters rise quickly and shift for ourselves. Then he ran and burst open the Nursery-door, and called to the maid to bring out the

20

children. The two little ones lay in bed with her; the three others in another bed. She snatched up the youngest, and bade the rest follow, which the three elder did. When we were got into the hall, and were surrounded with flames, Mr. Wesley found he had left the keys of the doors above stairs. He ran up, and recovered them, a minute before the staircase caught fire. When we opened the street door, the strong North East wind drove the flames in with such violence that none could stand against them. But some of our children got out through the windows; neither could I get to the garden-door. I endeavoured three times to force my passage through the street door, but was as often beat back by the fury of the flames. In this distress I besought our blessed Saviour for help, and then waded through the fire, naked as I was, which did me no further harm than a little scorching my hands and my face.

"When Mr. Wesley had seen the other children safe, he heard the child in the nursery cry. He attempted to go up the stairs, but they were all on fire, and would not bear his weight. Finding it impossible to give any help, he kneeled down in the hall and recommended the soul of the child to God and left him, as he thought, perishing in the flames.

"But the boy, seeing none come to his help, and being frightened, the chamber and bed being on fire, he climbed up to the casement, where he was soon perceived by the men in the yard, who immediately got up and pulled him out, just in the article of time that the roof fell in and beat the chamber to the ground."

John also gave his version of this near-tragedy, beginning at the moment his father sank to his knees to pray. He wrote:

"I believe it was just at that time I waked; for I did not cry as they imagined, unless it was afterwards. I remember all the circumstances as distinctly as though it were but yester-day. Seeing the room was very light, I called to the maid to take me up. But none answering, I put my head out of the curtains, and saw streaks of fire on the top of the room. I got up, and ran to the door, but could get no farther, all the floor beyond it being in a blaze. I then climbed on a chest, which stood near the window: one in the yard saw me, and proposed running to fetch a ladder. Another answered, 'There will be no time, but I have thought of another expedient. Here I will fix myself against the wall: lift a light man, and set him on my shoulders.' They did so and took me out at the window. Just then the whole roof fell in: but it fell inward, or we had all been crushed at once. When they brought me into the house, where my father was, he cried out, 'Come neighbors! Let us kneel down: let us give thanks to God! He has given me all my eight children; let the house go: I am rich enough!'

"The next day, as he was walking in the garden, and surveying the ruins of the house, he picked up part of a leaf of his polygot bible on which just these words were eligible, 'Vade; vende omniaque habes attolle crucem sequere me.' 'Go; sell all that thou hast; and take up thy cross and follow me.' "

Dr. Thomas Coke and Henry Moore, in their book, *The Life of the Rev. John Wesley, A.M. Including an Account of the Great Revival of Religion in Europe and America of Which He Was the First and Chief Instrument*, published in 1792, one year after John's death, make a significant accusation in connection with this fire. They say that all writers on this subject before them had supposed the fire to be an accident; but, according to the account they had from John, it was due to "the wickedness of some of his father's parishioners, who could not bear the plain dealing of so faithful and resolute a pastor." Furthermore, they point out that "the incendiaries had twice before attempted to burn the house." The accusation seems especially cogent in view of the traits John displayed in Georgia—traits he evidently inherited from his father.

Accident or no, Susannah was convinced that the lives of all of them and especially John's, had been preserved by divine design. And so, in devout gratitude, she addressed herself to God thusly through the pages of her diary:

"I would offer Thee myself and all that Thou hast given me: and I would resolve, O give me grace to do it, that the residue of my life shall be devoted to Thy service. With the soul of this child that Thou hast so mercifully provided for I do intend to be more particularly careful than ever I have been; that I may do my endeavour to instill into his mind the principles of true religion and virtue. . . . Lord, give me grace to do it sincerely and prudently and bless my attempt with good success."

From that day forth, in weekly sessions, Susannah discoursed privately with John on religious subjects (she did the same with the others, though not so painstakingly) and, as soon as she thought he could comprehend doctrinal fundamentals, she took them up with him in long, formal epistles.

John, who was a serious, thoughtful, intelligent child, listened attentively to all that his mother said and absorbed all that he read; but he accepted exasperatingly little without serious debates with himself. Even when bread was passed to him at the table, he was unable to decide whether to take some until he had argued the matter out in his mind.

"Child," his father said impatiently to him one day, "you think to carry everything by dint of argument; but you will find how little is ever done in the world by close reasoning."

Then, turning to his wife, he mourned, "I profess, sweetheart, I think our Jack would not attend to the most pressing necessities of nature unless he could give a reason for it."

Having little respect for the prevailing methods of instruction in the common schools, Susannah continued to teach John until he was nearly eleven, when he entered Charterhouse School in London.

Here his religious life underwent a partial change.

"Outward restraints being removed," he wrote a friend some twenty-four years later, reviewing his long road to salvation, "I was much more negligent than before and almost continually guilty of outward sins, which I knew to be such, though they were not scandalous in the eye of the world.

However, I still read the Scriptures and said my prayers morning and evening. And what I now hoped to be saved by was (1) not being so bad as other people; (2) having still a kindness for religion; and (3) reading the Bible, going to church and saying my prayers."

From Charterhouse, on June 24, 1720, just a week after his seventeenth birthday, he entered Christ Church College of Oxford University. That fall he was ordained, and the following spring he was elected a Fellow of Lincoln College. On entering upon his duties, he "executed" a resolution that he considered of the utmost importance: he shrugged off all his "trifling acquaintances." To screen those worthwhile, he closely observed the temper and behavior of all who called upon him, and when he judged they did not truly love and fear God, he did not return their calls.

He also began to appreciate acutely the value of time and to apply himself more conscientiously and systematically to his studies. Monday and Tuesday he gave to the Greek and Roman classics, and to poets and historians; Wednesday, to logic and ethics; Thursday, to Hebrew and Arabic; Friday, to metaphysics and natural philosophy; Saturday, to oratory and poetry; and Sunday, to divinity. In his free hours he perfected his French, which he had begun to learn two or three years before; worked on experiments in optics and in mathematics; and studied Euclid, Keil, and Sir Isaac Newton. His method of making a book his own was to read it through, then to copy into a notebook the passages he considered important and beautiful.

It was about this time, too, that he acquired the habit of diary writing—a habit that was to continue throughout his life.

While a Fellow of Lincoln, he returned twice to Lincolnshire to serve as curator in Samuel's twin parishes of Epworth and Wroot. There is a very charming, human record of the first visit, which lasted from April to September, 1726, in his Number 1 Diary, which Mr. Curnock summarizes.

"John worked in the old garden at Wroot," the Doctor writes, "made arbors . . . gathered roses and elder flowers for his sisters, cut stakes, shot plovers in the fenland that then lay between the two parishes, wrote sermons for himself and his father, drank tea here and there, swam on summer mornings in the fen river, and went to every village fair within reach; transcribed letters . . . ; explored a hermit's grave, covered by a great stone; as to one whom hard reading had become easy, he pursued his classical and theological studies, read and collected Spenser's FAERIE QUEENE, indulged in THE SPECTATOR, in plays and other light literature; discussed points of doctrine or moral philosophy with his learned mother, carefully noting her opinions in his Diary; laboriously copied out DISSERTATIONS ON JOB for his father; read to his sisters as they sat working in the arbour, stood godfather to sister Nancy's baby . . . preached severely to the people of Epworth, not sparing their sins, especially their gossip and scandal, visited their sick, and buried their dead. Mindful of the voice that called him to the devout life, he 'writ' his Diary, and gave himself to prayer and self-examination. . . ."

Then, after a dozen or more lines in which the Reverend Mr. Curnock deserts John's Diary to do some editorializing on his own, he gives us this estimation of John during this, his twenty-third summer:

"He is gentlemanly, refined, familiar with the best literature of the day, a congenial companion; to some extent worldly, yet standing absolutely clear of grossness, though not of what he so frequently calls 'levity'; not exempt from temptation, but 'buffeting' his body, and bringing himself under the iron rule of law and resolution. All the while he honestly strives to be a Christian disciple—an Israelite indeed, in whom there is no guile.

". . . We follow this little, handsome, clean-living parson as he rides about the fen lands in immaculate attire—cheery, conversational, adored by his sisters, the ever-welcome companion of his scholarly mother; and apart from [a] miracle, we have difficulty in realizing that this man, a few years hence, will be one of the Church's greatest evangelists."

John's second visit to Lincolnshire, when his father was sixty-five and Susannah was in failing health, lasted for two years; then the rector of Lincoln College called him back to fulfill his duties as a Fellow.

Returning, John found that his brother Charles, who was five years his junior and now at Oxford, and two fellow Oxonians, William Morgan and Robert Kirkham of Merton College, had formed a small Society to encourage themselves and others of like mind to regular attendance at Holy Communion, a strict observance of the rules of the Anglican Episcopal Church, the earnest study of the classics and the Holy Scripture, and the spread of philanthropic deeds.

Contrary to general belief, John had no part in the origin of the Society; he returned to Oxford when it was already in bud if not in full flower. He did, however, immediately join and straightway take over its operation. A letter written to a friend by the Reverend John Gambol, who knew John at Oxford, gives the most vivid picture of the Society's zealous leader and of its many activities.

"Mr. John Wesley was always the chief manager, for which he was very fit," he wrote. "For he had not only more learning and experience than the rest, but he was blest with such activity as to be always gaining ground, and such steadiness that he lost none. What proposals he made to any were sure to charm them, because he was so much in earnest; nor could they afterwards slight them, because they saw him always the same. What supported this uniform vigour was the care he took to consider well of every affair before he engaged in it, making all his decisions in the fear of God, without passion, humour, or self-confidence; for though he had naturally a very clear apprehension, yet his exact prudence depended more upon humility and singleness of heart. To this may I add that he had, I think, something of authority in his countenance; though, as he did not want address, he could soften his manner, and point it as occasion required. Yet he never assumed anything to himself above his companions; any of them might speak their mind, and their words were as strictly regarded by him as his were by them."

Mr. Gambol was also greatly impressed by John's dedication to prayer ("I have seen him come out of his closet with a serenity of countenance, which was next to shining," he declared), by his emphasis on the "appointed improvement of the present minute," and by his nature ("always cheerful, but never triumphing, he so husbanded the secret consolations which God gave him that they seldom left him . . .").

Still not satisfied with these paeans of praise he had heaped upon his youthful hero, Mr. Gambol went on lyrically:

"I have heard his brother say(to comfort me who was not so happy) that he thought he (John) had never exceeded in eating or drinking for some years. When he was just come home from a long journey, and had been in different companies, he resumed his usual employments, as if he had never left them. . . . Much less was he discomposed by any slanders or affronts. . . . He used many arts to be religious, but none to seem so. . . . The first thing he struck at in young men was that indolence which would not submit to close thinking. Nor was he against reading much, especially at first . . . he earnestly recommended to them a method and order in all their actions. After their morning devotions— from five to six being the time, morning as well as evening —he advised them to determine with themselves what they were to do all parts of the day. . . . By fasts, visiting poor people and coming to the weekly Sacrament . . . they would cut off their retreat to the world. . . . He taught them . . . to take an account of their actions in a very exact manner, by writing a constant diary; in this they noted down

in ciphers, once if not oftener in the day, their employments.
. . . Mr. Wesley had these records of his life by him for
many years back. . . ."

The members of the Society were accustomed to meet
either at John's chamber or at one of the others'; say prayers, usually on the subject of charity; eat supper together
and read aloud from some book. The main business, however, was to go over what each member had done that day to
promote the Society's common design and to decide what
steps should be taken next.

Their projects included talking with young students to
save them from bad company and instill in them a desire for
a sober, studious life; visiting the prisons, especially the
nearby Castle and Bocardo in the old North Gate of the City
of Oxford; instructing poor families, and taking care of the
parish workhouse and school.

"When they undertook any poor family," Mr. Gambol recorded, "they saw them at least once a week, sometimes gave
them money, admonished them of their vices, read to them
and examined their children. The school was, I think, of Mr.
Wesley's own setting up; however, he paid the mistress and
clothed some, if not all of the children. When they [the Society members] went thither, they inquired how each child behaved, saw their work (for some could knit or spin), heard
them read or their catechism, and explained part of it. In the
same manner they taught the children in the workhouse, and
read to the old people as they did to the prisoners."

They also had a fund, to which many of their friends con-
tributed, to use for the release of prisoners who were confined
for small debts and to buy books, physic, and other neces-
saries for those who needed them and could not afford them.

Naturally, these activities of the Society—especially when
for brief periods its number grew to thirty or more—greatly
shocked fellow Oxonians, who gaped at its members with

astonishment, discussed them *ad nauseam*, and called them all manner of names.

"Some of the men of wit in Christ Church entered the lists against us," John said in a letter to a clergyman, "and between mirth and anger made a pretty many reflections upon the Sacramentarians, as they were pleased to call us. Soon after, their allies at Merton changed our title and did us the honor of styling us the Holy Club."

Others dubbed them Bible Moths, the Godly Club, Bible Bigots, Enthusiasts, and the Reforming Club. They were also called the name that has stuck to John's followers through the centuries: Methodists. John's contemporary biographers, Dr. Thomas Coke and Henry Moore, claim, "This last title was given them by a fellow of Merton College, in allusion to an ancient College of Physicians at Rome, who were remarkable for putting their patients under regimen and were therefore called Methodists."

John disliked the name. In a letter to the father of William Morgan, after that young man's death, he wrote:

"As for the name of Methodists, Supererogation Men and so on with which some of our neighbors are pleased to compliment us, we do not conceive ourselves to be under any obligations to regard them. . . ."

At first John used for the original group at Oxford, and for similar groups he organized later in Georgia, only the title Our Company or Our Little Society; but finally he succumbed to the point where he referred occasionally to this mother organization as "The Oxford Methodists."

TWO

John first heard the call to Georgia in the summer of 1735. His father, Samuel, had died in June of that year and his mother had broken up the home and gone to visit among her married daughters. For a brief period John found himself at loose ends. He did not want to return to Lincoln College; he felt too old (he was thirty-two) to mingle with the students in any role except that of master, and somehow he was in no frame of mind for mastership or even for Oxford.

The idea that he should go to Georgia was suggested to him by Dr. John J. Burton of Corpus Christi, Oxford. He was an old friend of John's, but, of more significance at this juncture, he was a member of the Board of Trustees for the Establishment of Georgia and also of the Society for the Propagation of the Gospel. He and his co-workers believed the little new province offered a golden opportunity for missionary endeavor. Savage Indian tribes bordered it to the north and west, and many unsavory characters who belonged to no church, much less to the Church of England, inhabited

30

the town of Savannah and the small settlements surrounding it. On August 28, Mr. Burton met John in Ludgate Street and first mentioned Georgia to him.

Sometime later, so John wrote in his Journal, he had "a conference or two" with James Oglethorpe. Astoundingly, that is every word John put down about this meeting (or meetings) with the man whose name was on practically every tongue in London.

James Oglethorpe looked every inch the famous English gentleman he was. Stolidly built, his head sat confidently, even jauntily, on broad shoulders. He was not handsome in the accepted fashion of the times: his features were too sharp. He had an extremely thin, patrician nose; a high forehead beneath a tightly curled wig; shaggy brows that sprouted quickly upward above deep-set, hazel eyes; long, lean cheekbones and a forward-thrusting chin; but there was about him an aura of alertness, good breeding, and intelligence.

(He never lost his good looks, according to the historian Joseph Bancroft. "Even in the last year [of his life]," Bancroft wrote, "he was extolled as the finest figure ever seen, the impersonation of venerable age; his faculties were as bright as ever, and his sight undimmed: ever heroic, romantic and full of old gallantry.")

At this period, he was forty years old; a bachelor; a well-to-do landowner; a war hero of some distinction, having, when still in his teens, joined Prince Eugene's expedition against the Turks, and, as his aide-de-camp, fought through the bloody, epochal battle of Belgrade; a member of Parliament; a friend of Queen Caroline and King George II, and the governor in actuality, if not in name, of Georgia. It was he who originally conceived the founding of the Colony as a haven for debtors and religious refugees from middle Europe, and, at the same time, as a barrier between South Carolina, occupied by the English, and Florida, occupied by the Spaniards.

After two years in the New World, struggling against terrific odds to establish this philanthropic Colony, he was back in England to raise more money and more men for the undertaking. He needed laborers, artisans, tradesmen, soldiers, and ministers.

Before saying either yea or nay to James Oglethorpe's and Dr. Burton's proposal, John received a subtly flattering, follow-up letter from the doctor:

". . . Your short conference with Mr. Oglethorpe has raised the hopes of many good persons that you and yours" [it is believed that Dr. Burton had hopes in the beginning of securing for Georgia all the active members of Our Little Society] "would join in an undertaking which cannot be better executed than by such instruments. I have thought again of the matter, and upon a result of the whole cannot help again recommending the undertaking to your choice. . . ."

Naturally, before John could take such a drastic step, he had to confer with everyone whose opinion he valued. His mother was ecstatic—if she had twenty sons she would send them all; and Charles was so enthusiastic that he agreed to go both as Secretary for Indian Affairs in Georgia and secretary to James Oglethorpe.

When John finally said yes, Dr. Burton wrote him another letter, advising him about the locale and conduct of his ministry.

"You come to a people some ignorant and some disposed to licentiousness," he explained. "Your good offices will be required at Savannah Town at first, which is but a few miles distant from the Indians. The magistrates will authorize your access to every family, and the young will be under obligation to receive instructions . . . you'll find abundant room for the exercise of patience and prudence as well as piety. The generality of the people are babes in the progress of their Christian life, to be fed with milk instead of strong meat. The wise householder will bring out of his stores food in proportion to the necessities of his family."

The minutes of the meeting of the Board of Georgia Trustees on October 10 made no reference to Indians, but pointed out that John was "to perform the duty of clergyman in the room of the Rev. Mr. Samuel Quincy" as well as to "perform all religious and ecclesiastical offices" in the new town that James Oglethorpe was planning to establish on the Southern frontier. Nevertheless, John labored under the impression that his main ministry was to be to the Indians. Writing to Dr. Burton the very same day the Trustees were meeting, he set out "the grounds" of his "design of embarking for Georgia":

"My chief motive to which all the rest are subordinate is the hope of saving my own soul. I hope to learn the true sense of the gospel of Christ, by preaching it to the heathen. They have no comments to construe away the text, no vain philosophy to corrupt it, no luxurious, sensual, covetous, ambitious expounders to soften its unpleasing truths. . . . They are as little children, humble, willing to learn and eager to do the will of God, and consequently they shall know of every doctrine I preach whether it be of God. . . .

"A right faith will, I trust, by the mercy of God, open the way for a right practice, especially when most of those temptations are removed which here so easily beset me. Toward mortifying the desire of the flesh, the desire of sensual pleasures, it will be no small thing to be able, without fear of giving offence, to live on water and the fruits of the earth. This simplicity of food will, I trust, be a blessed means, both of preventing my seeking that happiness in meats and drinks which God designs should be found only in faith and love and joy in the Holy Ghost, and assist me—especially where I see no woman but those which are almost of a different species from me—to attain such a purity of thought as suits a candidate for that state wherein they never marry nor are given in marriage, but are as the angels of God in heaven."

Those last lines in which John expresses his longing for that state "wherein they neither marry nor are given in marriage, but are as the angels of God in heaven" are most significant in light of the coming events in Georgia. In the next paragraph, he even predicts he will be "delivered" from the "lust of the eye"; but in this, too, his expectations are doomed to be shattered—as we will see, he will be bound by passion. John continues:

"Neither is it a small thing to be delivered from so many occasions as now surround me, of indulging the lust of the eye. They here encompass me on every side; but an Indian hut affords no food for curiosity, no gratification of the desire of grand or new, or pretty things. . . ."

Benjamin Ingham, who had been a member with John and Charles of the Little Society at Oxford, agreed to accompany them. He was an impetuous, godly, industrious young man, just turned twenty-three. John Toltschig, who knew him well in Savannah, described him as "a very young man . . . who has many good impulses in his soul and is much awakened."

Benjamin had a face as oval as an egg, with features almost too delicate for a man. His upper lip had a deep Cupid's bow; his nose was straight and long and ran evenly, with no indentation at the bridge, between fairly small, close-set eyes under a prominent forehead, usually framed by a wig of tight ringlets.

The challenge presented by the heathen Indians played some part in Ingham's decision to go to Georgia, though in the end his going was brought about almost fortuitously. After talking one evening to John Wesley, he found his heart so moved that, almost without thinking, he said, "If neither Mr. Hall nor Mr. Salmon go along with you I will go." As Mr. Hall, the Wesleys' brother-in-law, and Mr. Salmon, a gentleman of Brazenose College, Oxon, had announced their intention of accompanying John and there seemed no probability of their withdrawing, Benjamin thought he was making an empty offer. Yet, practically on the eve of sailing, both men withdrew and Benjamin was trapped. He accepted the outcome, however, as an act of God.

One other young man joined the group—Charles Dela-

motte, the twenty-one-year-old son of a London sugar merchant. He wanted so badly to make the journey that he refused his father's offer to set him up in business and vowed
he would serve as a servant if John could use him in no other
capacity.

On Tuesday, October 14, the four—John and his brother
Charles, Benjamin Ingham, and Charles Delamotte, whom
John called Delamotte to prevent confusion with his own
brother (as we shall) took boat at Westminster for Graves-
end. They reached there about four in the afternoon and immediately went on board the ship called the *Simmonds*. Two
cabins in the forecastle were allotted to them by James Oglethorpe. The Wesleys had one and Benjamin and Delamotte
the other. The Wesleys' was fairly large, enabling the four to
meet there together to read and pray.

Also on board the *Simmonds* were twenty-six Moravians,
journeying to Savannah to join sixteen of their brethren who
had sailed approximately a year before to prepare for their
coming a communal house, cabins, and gardens. The Moravian passengers were under the direction of David Nitschmann, a bishop of the Moravian Church. He was sixty years
old and, so the Reverend Mr. Curnock writes in a footnote
in the Wesley *Journal*, "a sufferer for conscience sake."

The Moravians already in Georgia and those on the way
were to become almost as close to John as his brother
Charles, Benjamin Ingham, and Delamotte. John lived with
them; he read and prayed and sang with them; and he sought
their advice at the most critical point in his Georgia life. Benjamin also admired them extravagantly. Even during the
shipboard days he wrote this glowing letter:

"The Moravians are a good, devout, peaceable and heav-
enly-minded people, who were persecuted by the Papists and
driven from their native country. They were graciously received and protected by Count Zinzendorf, a very holy man,
who sent them over to Georgia. Discipline is strictly exer-
cised without respect of persons. They all submit themselves

to their pastors, being guided by them in everything. They live together in perfect love and peace, having, for the present, all things in common. They are more ready to serve their neighbors than themselves. There are twenty-six of them on our ship and almost the only time that you could know they were in the ship was when they were harmoniously singing the praises of the Great Creator, which they constantly do in public twice every day, where they are."

The acceptance of the Moravians for Georgia was not as simple as Benjamin made it sound. At first the Trustees didn't favor the idea at all. The fact that they spoke no English and had vowed never to go to war, or even to lend a hand in any kind of defensive undertaking, made the Trustees reluctant to take them. Finally, though, the Count persuaded the Trustees to grant him personally a five-hundred-acre tract on which he agreed to pay an annual rental of five pounds, beginning eight years from the date of the grant.

Delamotte, in his admiration of the Moravians, was no less fervent than were Benjamin and Charles. In fact, he later became a member of the sect.

Among the *Simmonds'* other passengers—most of whom were bound for the new settlement on St. Simons Island, which James Oglethorpe planned to name Frederica after the Crown Prince Frederick—was a small quarrelsome group consisting of a surgeon, Dr. Thomas Hawkins, and his wife Beata; John Welch, a carpenter, and his wife Ann; and Mr. and Mrs. Richard Lawley. Both Ann Welch and Mrs. Lawley were pregnant, as were several other passengers. Indeed, so many were in a delicate condition on the *Simmonds* and the *London Merchant*, which accompanied the *Simmonds*, that three passengers were left behind, according to a touching item in the *Colonial Records* of Georgia:

"Mr. William Bradley, Son, and Mr. John Robinson were left behind by the London Merchant, who went ashore at Portsmouth to engage a midwife to go to Georgia for some of the Women Passengers near their time on the London Merchant and Simmonds. (As Bradley had a cradle on ship, his wife must have been expecting.)"

At last the wind, for which James Oglethorpe and his captains had been longing for more than six weeks, sprang up and, like the tides, waited on no man.

Long before that wind, however, John and his Little Company, as he now referred to his three companions and himself, organized their lives into a schedule that they followed meticulously unless illness prevented. They began their day at four o'clock in the morning (John had discovered at Oxford that he did not need all the hours for sleep he had been allotting for that purpose. He found himself waking every night about twelve or one o'clock and he soon realized this was because he "lay a-bed longer than nature needed." So he secured "an alarum" that aroused him the next morning at seven, an hour earlier than he was accustomed to rising. The next night, however, he still lay awake, so he set the "alarum" to rouse him at six; when he still lay awake, he set it for five and then, still lying awake, he set it for four. From that morning on, wakefulness was unknown to him. "Taking the year around," he boasted, "I didn't lie awake a quarter of an hour together in a month").

So now all the members of the Company got up at four and spent each day, so John's Journal set out, thusly:

"From four in the morning until five each of us used private prayer. From five to seven we read the Bible together, carefully comparing it (that we might not lean to our own understandings) with the writings of the earliest ages. At seven we breakfasted. At eight were the public prayers, at which were present usually between thirty or forty of our eighty passengers. From nine to twelve I commonly learned German, and Mr. Delamotte, Greek. My brother writ sermons, and Mr. Ingham read some treatise of divinity or instructed the children. At twelve we met to give an account to one another what we had done since our last meeting, and what we designed to do before our next. About one we dined.

The time from dinner to four we spent with the people partly in public reading, partly in speaking to them severally, as need required. At four were the evening prayers, when either the Second Lesson was explained—as it always was in the morning—or the children were catechized and instructed before the congregation. From five to six we again used private prayer. From six to seven I read in our cabin to two or three of the passengers, of whom there were about eighty English on board, and each of my brethren to a few more in theirs. At seven I joined with the Germans in their public service, while Mr. Ingham was reading between the decks to as many as desired to hear. At eight we met again, to exhort and instruct one another. Between nine and ten we went to bed, where neither the roaring of the sea nor the motion of the ship could take away the refreshing sleep which God gave us."

On November 3, the ships still lying at anchor awaiting the wind, the Little Company took a walk on the mainland and, after considerable discussion, agreed upon the following resolutions:

"In the name of God, Amen,

"We whose names are here underwritten, be fully convinced that it is impossible, either to promote the work of God among the heathen without an entire union amongst ourselves; or that, such an union should subsist unless each one will give up his single judgement to that of the majority, do agree by the help of God—

"First, That none of us will undertake anything of importance without first proposing it to the other three

"Second, That whenever our judgements or inclinations differ, any one shall give up his single judgement or inclinations to the others

"Third, That in case of an equality, after begging God's direction, the matter shall be decided by lot

"John Wesley
"C. Wesley

"B. Ingham

"C. Delamotte"

(Several of John's and Charles's biographers claim that the Moravians taught the Wesleys the practice of divination by lot, or sortilege, as it is frequently called; but, judging from these resolutions, it is apparent that the Wesleys were familiar with this practice before their intimacy with the members of this sect.)

It was well that the four members of the Little Company had such a good understanding among themselves, for soon their lives were not moving as smoothly as they had planned. On November 23, John felt impelled, so he wrote, "to get a boy well whipped by Mr. Oglethorpe's orders for swearing and blaspheming. Private admonition had no effect upon him, so I was forced to have recourse to public correction."

Almost immediately afterward, both Charles and John encountered rude rebuffs that should have warned them they were now in the midst of people who were completely indifferent, if not actually antagonistic, to their ministry. A fellow passenger, the son of Robert Johnson, the late Governor of South Carolina, complained to James Oglethorpe, so John recounted, "that having the public prayer was a great inconvenience to him. He said he could not bear to stay in the same room when so many people were in it, and that he could not stay out of it while they were there, for fear of catching cold. After some dispute the matter was compromised that the prayers in the morning (during which Mr. Johnson was in bed) should be read in the cabin, and the afternoon prayers between decks (the quarter deck being too cold); for the fore hatchway was the best place we could find there, though indeed it was very dirty and very noisy, and so small it would not hold above a quarter of our congregation, and so low none of them could stand upright. . . ."

As the days passed, Mr. Johnson "grew more and more impatient of the contrary winds; and at last, on Monday, December 1, despairing of their ever being fair while he stayed in the ship, he left it and took boat for Portsmouth in order to return to London." To which notation John added this very human postscript: "In the afternoon we held public prayer in the great cabin, one of the many blessings consequent of his leaving us."

Another indication of the passengers' unsympathetic attitude toward the parson's missionary zeal was the treatment John received at the hands of William Horton, Esq., a well-to-do gentleman and a close friend of James Oglethorpe. Before the *Simmonds* sailed, the Georgia founder ordered the Hortons' maid ashore, an act for which John justly got all the blame, since he had accused her of being "a known drunkard . . . suspected of theft and unchastity." Unfortunately for John, the Hortons had the cabin directly above his and, to get even with John, William kept him awake at night by dancing boisterously and untiringly over his head.

But William Horton and young Mr. Johnson inflicted only delicate pricks compared to the wounds John was to receive at the unscrupulous hands of Beata Hawkins and Ann Welch. From Sunday, November 9, when he first saw Beata and described her as "a gay, young woman who casually heard me speaking to another on the nature of Christianity . . . and appeared to be much surprised and affected," Beata caused John the greatest discomfiture. It is almost unbelievable that a man in his early thirties, a Fellow of Oxford's Lincoln College, or any other college, for that matter, could display such naïvete; such unguarded, reckless susceptibility to the wiles of women of Beata's and Ann's stripe. It is true he had never before known any like them, unless he had fleetingly met their like during his prison visits at Oxford. They were from a different world than the one he had inhabited. He had associated with only the most genteel and cultured young women, chief among them his own sisters; Betty Kirkham and her sister Damaris; the daughters of Colonel

40

and Mrs. Granville of Gloucester, Mary Granville Pendarves, the youthful widow of Mr. Charles Pendarves, who later became the Mrs. Delaney of *The Life and Letters of Mrs. Delaney*, and her younger sister Anne.

As the Reverend Mr. Curnock remarked in the Introduction of the *Journal of John Wesley:* "They [the Kirkham and Granville "girls"] fostered refinement, thoughtfulness, and religious aspiration. . . ."

It is quite safe to say Beata and Ann did not foster in John any of these admirable qualities, but they did excite in him a peculiar sort of fascination, curiosity, horror, patience, and a hungry yearning to win them for Christ. This was especially true in the case of Beata. In the long-persistent struggle for her soul, John sought her out continuously on the *Simmonds* and later in Georgia.

The struggle began when Beata joined him as he read an hour a day Mr. Law's treatise on *Christian Perfection* to Mrs. Lawley, who was dangerously ill and wished to be instructed to receive the Lord's Supper. With unmistakable enthusiasm, John noted in the Journal on November 28:

"Mrs. Hawkins, the gay young woman mentioned before, was at Mrs. Lawley's cabin when I read Mr. Law, as she afterwards was several times. She was always attentive and often much amazed."

Then, on Sunday, the thirtieth, just two days later, he wrote: "It pleased God to visit her [Beata] with sickness. I then began to hope he would perfect His work in her." Then again, on December 10, the very day the *Simmonds* and *London Merchant* and the *Hawk*, the man-of-war that had joined them for the voyage, finally got "a moderate sail"—as Francis Moore, one of the passengers, who also kept a journal, judged it— "and stood out to sea," John spoke to Beata "closely on the head of religion." She listened with great attention, answered all the questions John asked, and then said with many tears, "My mother died when I was but ten years old. Some of her last words were, 'Child, fear God; and though you lose me, you shall never want a friend.' I have now found a friend when I most wanted one."

John evidently accepted this touching little speech at face value, for during the following days he was extremely busy reading the Bible and other religious tomes to her and her husband Thomas, to Ann, and to others of the group. Soon Ann, "big with child, in a high fever, and almost wasted with a violent cough, earnestly desired to receive the Holy Communion before she died." John complied, and, according to his ecstatic report, "At the hour of receiving it, she began to recover and in a few days was entirely out of danger."

The skeptics on the ship could have argued that she recovered because, at the height of her illness, James Oglethorpe had moved her into his own cabin, which was more comfortable and more protected from the weather. Benjamin Ingham, however, agreed with John.

"When he [Oglethorpe] gave his cabin to Mrs. Welch," Benjamin wrote, "he slept for several nights in a hammock until another cabin could be made ready for him. Also, he constantly supplied her with the best things in the ship. Yet, notwithstanding, the doctor gave her up; everybody thought she would die; Mr. Oglethorpe continued to hope. She had a desire to receive the Lord's Supper before she died; and Lo! from the moment she received it, she began to recover."

As soon as this crisis passed, John again became involved with Beata. She had had a quarrel with Mrs. Francis Moore and Mrs. Lawley, which moved John to set himself up as a peacemaker. As a result, both Mrs. Moore and Mrs. Lawley became so infuriated with him that they vowed nevermore to attend prayers. But this painful state of affairs was compensated for by Beata's announcement that she would like to receive Holy Communion. Elated, John conferred with "several" on the matter, among them Bishop Nitshmann, Delamotte, John Brownfield, his brother Charles, Benjamin Ingham, and even with his late tormentor, William Horton. All of them heard the news with outspoken skepticism.

Nevertheless, after more talk with Beata, John declared he could "no longer doubt of her sincere desire to be not only almost but altogether a Christian" and so, the next Sunday, administered to her the Lord's Supper.

A series of storms that now blew up diverted John somewhat from Beata's spiritual well-being. The first began in the evening.

"It rose higher and higher," he recorded. "About nine the sea broke over us from stem to stern; burst through the windows of the state cabin (Mr. Oglethorpe's cabin where three or four of us were sitting with a sick woman). About eleven I lay down in the great cabin and in a short time fell asleep, though very uncertain whether I should awake alive, and much ashamed of my unwillingness to die. Oh how pure in heart must he be who would rejoices to appear before God at a moment's warning!"

Toward dawn the winds and sea died down and there was a vast calm. But on Friday, the twenty-third, a second storm began. By morning it was so fierce, the captain was compelled to let the ship drive. John noted the situation in his Diary with vivid terseness:

"10 . . . We drove

"11 . . . Prayed, Storm greater; afraid!

"12. Prayed with Ingham. Sat with Charles and company.

"1 Washed all over and under. . . ."

He explained the washing experience in more detail in the Journal:

"About one in the afternoon almost as soon as I had stepped out of the great cabin door, the sea did not break as usual, but came with a full, smooth tide over the side of the ship. I was vaulted over with water in a moment, and so stunned that I scarce expected to lift up my head again till the sea should give up her dead. But, thanks be to God, I received no hurt at all. About midnight the storm ceased."

But John could not believe the calm meant the end of the siege. By now he had suffered through so much that he was completely pessimistic about what the night might bring. "While the calm continued," he confessed, "I endeavoured to prepare myself for another storm."

And he was right to do so, for at noon the next day the third one broke:

"At four it was more violent than any we had had before. Now, indeed, we could say, 'The waves of the sea were mighty, and raged horribly. They rose up to the heavens above, and clave down to hell beneath.' The winds roared round about us and—what I never heard before—whistled as distinctly as if it had been a human voice. The ship not only rocked to and fro with the utmost violence, but shook and jarred with so unequal, grating a motion, that one could not but with great difficulty keep one's hold on anything, nor stand a moment without it. Every ten minutes came a shock against the stern or side of the ship, which one would think should dash the planks in a thousand pieces. In the height of the storm a child, privately baptized before, was brought to be publicly received into the Church. It put me in mind of Jeremiah's buying the field when the Chaldeans were on the point of destroying Jerusalem, and seemed a pledge of the mercy God designed to show us, even in the land of the living."

We need only read Benjamin Ingham's account of that gale to see that John did not exaggerate its thrust. As Benjamin commented at the beginning, he "observed it well"; then continued:

"I never saw anything hitherto so solemn and majestic. The sea sparkled and smoked as if it had been on fire. The air darted forth like lightning; and the wind blew so fierce that you could scarcely look it in the face and draw your breath.

The waves did not swell so high as at other times, being pressed down by the impetuosity of the blast; neither did the ship roll much; but it quivered, jarred and shook. About half an hour past seven, a great sea broke in upon us, which split the main sail, carried away the companion, filled between decks and rushed into the great cabin. This made most of the people tremble."

So savage was this storm that the reaction of the Moravians to it made an especially profound and lasting impression on John. Their sweet serenity and amazing faith increased the admiration that their behavior had already inspired in him.

It was about seven o'clock in the evening, while the elements were still raging, that he went to the Moravians to see how they were conducting themselves under such terrifying circumstances. As he explained in his Journal:

"I had long before observed the great seriousness of their behaviour. Of their humility they had given a continual proof, by performing those servile offices for the other passengers which none of the English would undertake; for which they desired and would receive no pay, saying, 'it was good for their proud hearts' and 'their loving Saviour had done more for them.' And every day had given them occasion of showing meekness which no injury could move. If they were pushed, struck, or thrown down, they rose again and went away; but no complaint was found in their mouth. There was now an opportunity of trying whether they were delivered from the spirit of fear, as well as from that of pride, anger, and revenge. In the midst of the psalm wherewith their service began . . . the sea broke over, split the mainsail in pieces, covered the ship, and poured in between the decks, as if the great deep had already swallowed us up. A terrible screaming began among the English. The Germans looked up, and without intermission calmly sang on. I asked one of them afterwards, 'Was you not afraid?' He answered,

45

'I thank God, no.' I asked, 'But were not your women and children afraid?' He replied mildly, 'No, our women and children are not afraid to die.'

"From them, I went to their crying, trembling neighbours, and found myself enabled to speak with them in boldness and to point out to them the difference in the hour of trial between him that feareth God and him that feareth Him not. At twelve the wind fell. This was the most glorious day which I have hitherto seen."

And so, beset with storms from without and storms from within, John and his fellow passengers finally arrived, on Wednesday, February 4, 1736, off the green shores of Georgia.

THREE

After lying off the banks of Georgia all night, the *Simmonds* and *London Merchant* crossed over the bar "with the first of the flood" in the late afternoon of February 5 to anchor in the wide mouth of the Savannah River, close by two islands—Tybee, the largest and most easterly, and Peeper, an uninhabited area "only a few miles in extent." Tybee itself could boast only a handful of workmen whom James Oglethorpe, before departing for England, had ordered there to build a lighthouse.

The brilliant green of the trees and the eye-smarting, rose-red ball of the sun were a welcome surprise to the new settlers, judging by the enthusiastic lines in John's Journal:

"The pines, palms and cedars running in rows along the shore made an exceedingly beautiful prospect, especially to us who did not expect to see the bloom of spring in the depth of winter. The clearness of the sky, the setting sun, the smoothness of the water conspired to recommend this new world and prevent our regretting the loss of our native country."

At eight o'clock the next morning, John, Benjamin, Charles Wesley, Delamotte, and David Nitschmann went ashore on Peeper Island with James Oglethorpe. They made their way through what John described as "moorish land" to a slightly elevated piece of ground where they knelt down to give thanks to God for bringing them safely to this new land and to "beg the continuance of His fatherly protection."

Their whole beings must have brimmed over with gratitude. In spite of having been on shipboard for just short of four wearying months under the most crowded conditions and in the most wretched, typhoonlike weather, they had survived unscathed. One passenger, in a letter from Savannah on February 14, rejoiced:

"Though we had a long, stormy passage across the Atlantic, yet we arrived without the loss of a soul out of any of our ships."

Evidently this happy gentleman did not count the eight-month-old girl who died on October 28 before the ships set sail from Cowes. After all, as Francis Moore penned in his Journal, "she was dangerously ill when she came on board."

After the prayers on Peeper Island, James Oglethorpe took a small boat and went up to the settlement of Savannah. John, however, stayed on Peeper and found a little cleared space in the midst of a jungle of myrtle, bay, and cedar, where he and the others from the ship, when they joined him, could have prayers sheltered from the wind and the too-hot spears of the unaccustomed Southern sun. It must have been during the prayers, that the settlers heard James Oglethorpe welcomed to Savannah, for Francis Moore related that the head of the Colony "was received by the freeholders under-arms with the salute of 21 cannons which we heard plainly, being about ten miles distance."

The feel of solid ground so delighted John that he even

dined on the island and then walked with Beata, who "as he conversed was seriously affected." When at last he did return to the *Simmonds*, he suffered a painful shock. All the members of the crew and practically all the passengers who had remained on board were riotously drunk. Some . . . sutlers had come on board with provisions to sell to the passengers and had smuggled on the rum.

Rum in the early eighteenth century was the bane of the English poor; it and gin had ruined countless numbers of men and women, frequently hurrying their footsteps into debtors' prisons. James Oglethorpe, as early as the first summer of the new Colony, had urged the Trustees to ban rum from within its borders.

On August 11, 1733, according to Rev. George White's *Historical Collections of Georgia*, the Trustees "Read a letter from Mr. Oglethorpe with an account of the death of several persons in Georgia, which he imputed to the drinking of rum (and) resolved that the drinking of rum in Georgia be absolutely prohibited and that all which shall be brought there be staved."

To wean the colonists further from drinking rum, so the *Colonial Records* of Georgia set forth, "the Trustees endeavoured to supply the stores with strong beer from England, molasses for brewing beer, and with madeira wines."

But these moves were not sufficient to prevent the swilling of this destructive beverage not only by the Georgia settlers but also by the neighboring Indians, causing such "havoc" among them that fights and even killings frequently resulted.

So, on June 24, 1735, the Trustees responded to the situation with "a decree that no rum, brandy, whisky, or strong water" should be brought into Georgia. James Oglethorpe had brought the decree with him, for in a letter to the Georgia magistrates dated October 10, 1735, the Trustees wrote:

"Oglethorpe will bring with him three acts: an act prohibiting the use of Negroes in Georgia, which was confirmed by the King in Council, also another act prohibiting the use of rum in Georgia and an act for maintaining the Peace with the Indians, which regulates the trade with them. . . ."

Yet, here on the *Simmonds*, the crew and passengers were reeling about the decks as drunk as ever they had been in London. It was up to John to act. James Oglethorpe had commissioned him and John Brownfield to take care of the settlers in his absence. John did not hesitate. "Staved rum," he noted briefly.

Gossiping Francis Moore did not describe the scene. He skipped over the incident completely to announce the return from Savannah that evening of the Colony's founder, bringing "strong beer and small beer," which surely could not have arrived at a more opportune moment, "and fresh beef, fresh pork, venison, wild turkeys, soft bread [the word "soft" is to distinguish it from biscuit], turnips, and garden greens."

James Oglethorpe also brought an experienced midwife, one Mrs. Stanley, who had contacted him in Savannah because she said she had "heard several women on board were near their time." How right she was! Just two days later Ann gave birth to a girl, but not before her behavior and that of her friends (Beata and Mrs. Lawley) had scandalized John. He took up considerable space in his Journal bemoaning their conduct.

"Mond 9- Mrs. Welch was safely brought to bed by Mrs. Stanley. On this occasion I received a fresh proof how little extraordinary providences avail those who are not moved by the ordinary means He hath ordained to devote their whole souls to His service. Many burials and some deaths I have been present at, but I never knew a soul converted by the sight of either. This is the second time I have been witness— there being only a door between us—of one of the deepest distresses life affords. The groans of the sick persons had very short intermissions. And how were they filled by the assistants? With strong cries to God? With counselling her that was encompassed with sorrows of death to trust in Him?

With exhortations to each other to fear Him who is able to inflict sharper pains than these? No; but with laughter and jesting, at no time convenient, but at this least of all. Verily, if they hear not Moses and the Prophets, even the thunder of His power they will not understand."

Besides the midwife, James Oglethorpe brought back to the *Simmonds* Herr August Gottlieb Spangenberg, the leader of the first group of Moravians to arrive in Georgia. He was a scholarly man and a historian of note; he had been a professor of theology at the University of Halle; besides, he was an excellent administrator. His jolly looks, however, denied his considerable business abilities. He had a full, fat-jawed, cherubic face, with thin, curly wisps of hair turning up over his white stock.

He and John took a walk on shore and fell immediately into the most intimate conversation. Herr Spangenberg asked John, "My brother, have you the witness within yourself? Does the spirit of God bear witness with your spirit—that you are a child of God?"

John, as he recorded in his Journal, "was surprised and did not know what to answer."

Herr Spangenberg noticed his hesitation and asked, "Do you know Jesus Christ?"

John again paused; then replied, "I know he is the Saviour of the World."

"True," replied the German leader, "but do you know He has saved you?"

John said, "I hope He has died to save me."

Herr Spangenberg persisted, "Do you know yourself?"

John answered that he did, but later he added in his Journal, "I fear they were vain words."

Then John talked about Beata and asked how he should behave toward her.

"My dear brother," Herr Spangenberg said, "I believe our friend Kempis advises well, *'Omnes bonas mulieres devita, easque Deo commenda!'* "

51

(John translated the Latin freely to mean, "Be not familiar with any woman, but in general commend all good women to God," but the Reverend Mr. Curnock protests that what Kempis' statement actually meant was: "All good women avoid, and commend them to God.")

"Not that I would advise you to give her up quite," the Moravian elaborated, "but to converse much may be dangerous either to her or you. It may be best to speak to her seldom, and in a few words, and earnestly pray to God to do the rest."

That John did not take the Moravian leader's advice to heart is clearly indicated by his Diary's cryptic notation of the very next day: "With Mrs. Hawkins too long, therefore did nothing."

After that session, the arrival of more visitors prevented John from speaking to Beata for some days. The visitors were a party of Indians, including Tomochichi, the chief of a small Yamacraw tribe that occupied the land nearest Savannah; his nephew Toonahowi; his wife Scenauki; an unnamed brave; a half-breed, Mary Musgrove; two other women, and three children. They had sent word the day before of their coming and had delivered a side of venison.

On hearing they had arrived, John and Charles Wesley put on their surplices and John picked up his Greek Testament. Then the two of them, accompanied by Benjamin and Delamotte, went to the great cabin. As they entered, the Indians rose and Scenauki offered her hand, which took John back apace, for he had heard that the Indians allowed no man other than their husbands to speak to or touch their women even though they were "ill or in danger of death." Evidently John shot a quick, alarmed glance at Tomochichi, for immediately the chief said a few words that Mary Musgrove translated: "Mico Tomochichi says it is permissible to shake his wife's hand for you have come as friends."

John had heard of Mary Musgrove from James Oglethorpe. It was she who, on his first landing three years be-

52

fore, had led the Georgia founder to Tomochichi and urged the chief to allow the white man to settle on land the Indians claimed as their own. Since that day she had helped keep the Indians friendly.

Mary was the daughter, so the romantics claimed, of an Indian princess and an Englishman from South Carolina who traded among the red men. From her mother's people she had inherited wide cheekbones and wiry, straight black hair that she wore in two long plaits down her back. A jaunty eagle feather, held at the hairline by a band of bright beads, shot up from the center of her forehead. Her dress consisted only of an osnaburg shift and a red stroud petticoat. In spite of her native costume, Benjamin described her in his Journal as a "well civilized woman."

Her late husband, John Musgrove, had accompanied Tomochichi, Scenauki, Toonahowi, and a few other influential Indians when James Oglethorpe had taken them back to England with him to help awaken interest in the new Colony. John Musgrove had gone as an interpreter but, wrote the Earl of Egmont, a member of the Board of Trustees, in his diary, he "was frequently too drunk to interpret."

Mary now had a trading post and hog crawl about three miles from Savannah at a prettily wooded, slightly elevated spot known as the Cowpen.

Having been assured of the propriety of shaking Scenauki's hand, John recovered his composure, stepped forward, and took her bony fingers in his. Charles Wesley, Benjamin, and Delamotte followed his example.

Then all of them—except Tomochichi, who began to speak—sat in a semicircle on the cabin floor. Tomochichi was old—in his nineties—but he was well preserved and carried himself with ease and grace. If his face had not been streaked with red paint and his hair had not been black, straight, shiny, and cut short—except for one tuft that hung like a pony's tail above his left ear—he could have passed for an Englishman, for his features were not noticeably Indian

53

and he was wearing British-tailored clothes that had been purchased for him by the Trustees during his London visit.

Adelaide L. Fries, in her history, *Moravians in Georgia*, quotes Herr Spangenberg as having said of Tomochichi: "He is a grave, wise man, resembling one of the old Philosophers, though with him it is natural, not acquired. Were he among a hundred Indians, all clothed alike, one would point him out and say, 'That is the king.'"

"I am glad you are come," Tomochichi began. "When I was in England I desired that some would speak the Great Word to me and my nation; then we desired to hear it. But since that time we have been all put into confusion. The French have built a fort with one hundred men in one place and a fort with one hundred men in it in another. And the Spaniards are preparing for war."

He spoke, so John wrote in his Journal, "with great earnestness, and much action both of his hands and head, and yet with the utmost gentleness and softness both of tone and manner."

"The English traders, too, put us into confusion," the chief continued, "and have set our people against hearing the Great Word, for they speak with a double tongue; some say one thing of it and some another. Yet, I am glad you are come. I will go out and speak to the wise men of the nation and I hope they will hear. But we would not be made Christians as the Spaniards make Christians; we would be taught before we are baptized."

Tomochichi then fell silent and John sprang to his feet. His small figure was dwarfed by towering Tomochichi, but John seemed unaware of the disparity. "There is but one, He that sitteth in heaven, who is able to teach man wisdom," John said deliberately, with Mary Musgrove translating. "Though we are come so far, we know not whether He will please to teach you by us or no. If He teaches you, you will learn wisdom; but we can do nothing."

Scenauki now stood. She had brought two presents, a jar

of milk and one of honey, to remind them, she explained, that the Indians were but children and that the English should be as sweet as honey to them.

Again there was handshaking all around; then the would-be missionaries withdrew to their cabins, to talk and pray. Judging from John's comments in his Journal, he and his companions were astounded at the Indians' "utmost gentleness and softness, both of tone and manner," and dreadfully disappointed at Tomochichi's suggested postponement of their mission to his people.

In a few days James Oglethorpe, with fifty single male passengers of the *Simmonds* and *London Merchant*, departed in a scout boat and sloop hired for the purpose for Frederica, approximately one hundred miles by water to the south, to prepare some sort of shelter for the remaining men, women, and children. The Georgia founder had expected the ships to carry all the passengers to the new site and "house" them while their homes were being built; but the captains refused, on the grounds that they had no pilot and were unfamiliar with these waters. This necessitated erecting temporary huts and hiring enough small, flat-bottomed boats, called periaguas, to transfer the new settlers thither. Benjamin and a hymn-singing German, Herr von Hermsdorf, were among the vanguard of men.

Soon after their departure, John and Charles Wesley went up the Savannah River to pay their first visit, as John noted, "to the Heathen." They rose at three thirty from a "cold bed" and set out at five thirty in a boat with sails. The wind, however, was so high and contrary that they were unable to use the sails and had to row the ten miles to Savannah. Here they stopped briefly, evidently for a guide, then proceeded on up the river for approximately three miles to Mary Musgrove's Cowpen. After a short visit, they invited her to accompany them as interpreter to the Indian village, New Yamacraw, just a stone's throw away, to see Tomochichi and Scenauki. This day, unfortunately, neither Tomochichi nor Scenauki was at home so John, reading his Greek Testament "to solace him," and Charles returned to Savannah. Here they met Bailiff Thomas Causton for the first time. In a *List of Early Settlers of Georgia*, Thomas is described simply as "age 40; calico printer; embarked 6 Nov. 1732 [the first Georgia embarkation]; arrived 1 Feb. 1732–3 [sic]; lot 24 in Savannah. At first appointed 3rd bailiff, then 2nd, and lastly 1st bailiff in 1734. He was also Public Store Keeper. . . ." This last notation meant he was in charge of doling out allotments of food, clothing, oil, beer, tools, and other necessities to all the inhabitants who came to Georgia on the charity of the Trustees, which included practically everyone.

Another, more biased, source, *A True and Historical Narrative* of Georgia—written by a surgeon, Dr. Patrick Tailfer, and other disgruntled Scotsmen who deserted the Colony in 1740 for South Carolina—pictured Causton in this unattractive fashion: "A dictator under the title of bailiff and store keeper left by Mr. Oglethorpe 1734 [the date on which Mr. Oglethorpe departed for his first visit back to England] whose will and pleasure were the only laws in Georgia. He would often threaten juries and especially when their verdicts did not agree with him. He was infatuated with himself, being before that a man of no substance or character, having come over with Mr. Oglethorpe with the first forty and left England upon account of something committed by him concerning His Majesty's duties. However he was fit enough for a great many purposes, being a person naturally proud, covetous, cunning and deceitful, and would bring his designs about by all possible ways and means.

"As his power increased, so did his pride, haughtiness and cruelty, insomuch that he caused eight free-holders with an officer to attend at the door of the court every day it sat, with their guns and bayonets, and they were commanded by his orders, to rest their firelocks as soon as he appeared, which made people in some manner afraid to speak their minds, or juries to act as their consciences directed them.

"He was seldom or never uncovered on the bench, and threatened people with the stocks, whipping-post and log-house, and many times put these threatenings into execution so that the Georgia stocks, whipping-post and log-house were famous in Carolina."

While his wife Martha, his son Jacky, and his wife's niece Sophy were still in London, Thomas wrote Martha a letter that shows him in a more human light than does *A True and Historical Narrative*. His heart, he said, was "immovably fixed on niece Sophy" and on "my dear Jacky." Then, man-like, he instructed Martha to bring any furniture she wanted, but as for himself, he needed "thread or cotton stockings, some good checquered linnen of a dark blue and strong linnen for waist coat and trousers."

John offered no opinion of Thomas after their first meeting other than to say he had had a "good time": but in two letters written six months apart he did express great admiration for the Magistracy, which is most significant in light of the bitterness he felt about this body toward the close of his Georgia stay.

In a letter in November, 1736, to James Vernon, one of the most active Georgia Trustees, John wrote:

"The good I have found here has indeed been beyond my expectations; the contrary behaviour of many was no more than I looked for; being convinced several years before I left England that in every city or country under heaven the majority of the people are not the wisest or best part. But we have an advantage here, which is not frequent in other places —that is a Magistracy not only regular in their own conduct, but desirous and watchful to suppress as far as in them lies whatever is openly ill in the conduct of others."

Then, on March 4, 1737, in a letter to the Georgia Trustees, he declared:

"I can't but acknowledge the readiness of the Magistrates here, Mr. Causton in particular, in assisting me, so far as pertains to their office, both to repress vice and immorality and to promote the glory of God by establishing peace and mutual goodwill among men. Many ill practices seem to lose ground daily and a general face of decency and order prevails beyond what I have seen anywhere else in America. . . ."

Not only did John fail, after this first visit to Savannah, to give an opinion of Thomas, but he also failed to give a description of the town. Instead of being highly curious and outspoken about this three-year-old, philanthropic, experimental settlement—especially since his own father, Samuel, had once been thrown into prison for his debts—John, judging from his Journal and Diary, was completely indifferent to Savannah's physical aspects.

Fortunately, Francis Moore also paid a visit to Savannah at practically the same hour and put down in considerable detail its main features. He was impressed by the far-spread view from the Strand. First, there was the Savannah River, a thousand feet across, according to his estimate; then Hutchinson Island, which split the river in two; and, finally, across the northern branch, the dim, green shores of Carolina. Eastward, one could see the river—very wide now, having been rejoined by the northern branch—rolling toward the Atlantic until many little wooded islands near its mouth blocked its further view; and westward, another view of the river with Tomochichi's Indian village in the distance on its southern bank.

The first forty houses of Savannah were built of unplaned, feather-edged boards, the floors of "rough deals" and the roofs shingled. They were all the same size, even the one in which James Oglethorpe lived, just 24 feet wide and 16 feet deep. However, a great many larger and more handsome houses had been built since—Francis estimated between a hundred and a hundred and fifty—and the boards of these were planed and painted.

All of them sat on lots 50 feet wide and 90 feet deep, facing streets and backing on narrow alleys. The people had fenced their lots with split pales and a few had what Francis termed "palisades of turned wood" before their doors, though "the generality had been wise enough not to throw away their money."

The streets were exceedingly wide—even for that time— with large squares interspersed every few blocks. The only public buildings were the Public Store on the west side of Johnson Square; the courthouse-church, and, on the river bank, a guardhouse, enclosed with palisades a foot thick and mounted with "nineteen or twenty cannons." Here an around-the-clock guard, made up of citizens of Savannah, kept watch.

In addition to the town lot assigned to each free male (that is, a male who was not an indentured servant), each received a 5-acre garden plot near the town and a 45-acre farm farther out. Those who had cleared their 5-acre lots, according to Francis, "made a very good profit . . . by green roots and corn. Several have improved the cattle they had at first and have now five or six tame cows; others, who to save trouble of feeding them let them go in the wood, can scarcely find them."

While John and Charles were having a "good time" with Thomas Causton, taking a look at the town, Herr Spangenberg joined them and they walked in the Trustees Garden. The Trustees had visions of Georgia bringing great wealth to England through the production of silk and, to a lesser degree, of wine and drugs, and so had ordered, as one of their very first acts, a public nursery to be planted with mulberry trees—on the leaves of which the silk worms feed—grapevine slips, rare medical shrubs, and many other plants. It was a 10-acre area on the east side of the town, stretching from above Bay Lane to the river, and dropping from the flat, high ground of the Bluff to the low, marshy ground at its base.

It was laid out with crosswalks planted with orange trees. The first ones had been killed the winter before by an unusual snowstorm. Their replacements, however, were now leafing out, and in the squares between the walks grew the vast supply of mulberry trees for all who wanted them.

59

"Besides the mulberry trees," wrote Francis, "there are in some of the quarters in the coldest part of The Garden all kinds of fruit trees, unusual in England, such as apples, pears, etc.

"In another quarter are olives, figs, vines, pomegranate and such fruits that are natural to the warmest parts of Europe. At the bottom of the hill, well sheltered from the north wind and in the warmest part of The Garden, there was a collection of West India plants and trees, some coffee, some coca-beans, cotton, Palma-christi, and several West Indian physical plants, some sent by Mr. Eveleigh, a public-spirited merchant at Charleston, and some by Dr. Houston, from the Spanish West Indies, where he was sent at the expense of a collection raised by that curious physician, Sir Hans Sloan. . . ."

As the Wesleys and Herr Spangenberg and the First Bailiff paced The Garden paths, they were joined by the Reverend Samuel Quincy, whose place John was to fill. John gave no hint in either the Journal or Diary that this was an awkward meeting, in spite of the fact that the Reverend Mr. Quincy had been rather callously and abruptly dismissed by the Trustees. Some versions have it that he was let go because he performed the marriage ceremony for an Englishman, Joseph Fitzwalter (at the time, he was in charge of the Trustees Garden) and an Indian, even though Tomochichi gave the bride away and the settlers considered it a "pretty affair." However, according to an entry in Lord Egmont's Diary on October 14, 1736, when Mr. Quincy appeared before the Georgia Trustees to know the charges against him, "they said the abandoning the colony to go to New England for six months together and leaving a wheel wright to read public prayers, comfort the dying and bury the dead was a behaviour the Trustees could not excuse."

But the moment that could have been the most momentous in John's long day still lay ahead. After accompanying August Spangenberg to the House of the Moravians to sing

German hymns, he went to the Caustons' home on Duke Street, facing Johnson Square, where Sophy Hopkey lived. Alas, she had retired early and so, unconscious of how close he had come to beginning the first page of his one great romance, he slept peacefully for three hours before taking a boat for the mouth of the Savannah River and his hard pallet on the *Simmonds*.

He still did not comment specifically on the little, raw settlement of Savannah, but he did put down in his Diary a rather puzzling line about this day—his thirteenth in the New World: "Beware America, be not as England."

On the days following, John went again to the Cowpen— this time to select a piece of ground on which to build a schoolhouse for Indian children; thence to Savannah to visit the Germans and view the ordination of Anton Seifart as bishop of the Moravians ("a far-seeing, humble-minded man," John described him); then back to the *Simmonds* to get instructions on several matters from James Oglethorpe, who had returned from his visit to Frederica and was setting out again with the main contingent of settlers. Most vital was John's plan to do everything in his power to strengthen Beata in her newly proclaimed faith before she departed.

Beginning on Monday, March 1, he left no stone unturned. That afternoon he and Beata conversed and she was "deeply melancholy and . . . would not speak." He confessed his disappointment in his Diary. "In despair! Got no good!" Part of the devotional hour that evening with the two Charleses was spent in prayers for "this unhappy woman." Next John saw her husband, Thomas, and prayed for her with him, and at nine he devoted still another hour in prayer and meditation for her. "O Jesu!" he exclaimed; then cried out an exclamation in Greek, followed by the groan, "the cross." Still he persisted. He talked about her with busy James Oglethorpe. The Georgia leader could not "guess her trouble" and, considering the grave problems under which he was laboring, could not have cared very much.

61

The next morning John was at it again. The very first line in his Diary reads: "Sung; prayed for Mrs. Hawkins." All morning long he talked with her and prayed for her in the company of "devoted friends." In the afternoon he once more discussed her with James Oglethorpe and August Spangenberg. The latter had come to the ship to bid the Georgia founder and others farewell, as he was leaving the next morning for Pennsylvania to join a large Moravian settlement there. Again John discoursed with Beata. She was, so he wrote, "in a fever, mild but utterly unconsolable."

Then came the last hours in which he might have the opportunity to loose her completely from the Devil's bindings. She would be living in that difficult-to-get-to settlement on the southern frontier; he would be in Savannah. He rose at three thirty to pray for her; at five he sang, prayed, and fasted, and at six he spoke with her and felt cheered; she appeared "sad, but mild."

At seven she and the other passengers got into the fleet of periaguas that had finally been assembled to take them to Frederica. As they sat in the bobbing, open boats, ready to cast off, John stood by the *Simmonds'* rail, head bowed, and prayed for everyone, and at the last moment Beata "softened." It was the one and only word John chose for his Diary.

FOUR

So John had been in Georgia a full month, most of it spent on the deck of the *Simmonds* or on the shore of Peeper Island, when he stood in the pulpit of the little clapboard courthouse-church in Savannah that first Sunday in March and read those reassuring verses of Luke.

Finishing them, he drew in a long breath; hesitated a suspenseful moment; then quietly announced his text for the morning: First Corinthians, 13:3: "And though I bestow all my goods to feed the poor, and though I give my body to be burned, and have not love, it profiteth me nothing."

The congregation was motionless, expectant. John had already shocked them with the rules he had read, rules as new to them as was the little parson himself. What next? their wary eyes questioned.

Meeting those eyes directly, John plunged into the sermon's introduction: "There is good reason to fear that it will hereafter be said of most of you who are here present that this

Scripture, as well as those you have heard before, profited you nothing."

It was not an especially diplomatic opening, but then, John had never been one to beat around the bush. Today, at the start of his ministry, he evidently saw no reason to soften his words.

"Some perhaps are not serious enough to attend it," he continued bluntly. "Some who do attend will not believe it; some who do believe it will yet think it a hard saying and so forget it as soon as they can; and of those few who receive it gladly for a time, some, having no root of humility or self-denial when persecution ariseth because of the word, will, rather than suffer for it, fall away. . . ."

Methodically, then, he outlined the body of his message. Though contrary to the custom of the Church of England, he had spoken extemporaneously several times aboard the *Simmonds;* today he followed a carefully prepared text.

"It concerns all of us to the highest degree," he went on, "to know: first, the full sense of these words, 'And though I bestow all my goods to feed the poor, and though I give my body to be burned'; and second, the true meaning of the word, love, and third, in what sense it can be said, 'That without love all this profit us nothing.'

"As to the measure of His love, our Lord hath clearly told us, 'Thou shalt love the Lord thy God with all thy heart.' Not that we are to love or delight in none but Him. For He hath commanded us not only to love our neighbor, that is, all men, as ourselves—to desire and pursue their happiness as sincerely and steadily as our own—but also to love many of His creatures in the strictest sense; to delight in them, to enjoy them. . . ."

John's words could be heard easily in the back row of the church and beyond. His voice was powerful and far-carrying. When writing about a sermon he gave in June, 1745, near Chapel-en-le-Frith, he recounted: "The poor miller near whose pond we stood endeavoured to drown my voice by letting out

64

the water, which fell with a great noise. But it was labor lost; for my strength was so increased that I was heard to the very skirts of the congregation."

But besides his voice being audible to great numbers, it must have been exceedingly pleasant, for why else would he have asked in his *Address to the Clergy* (1756): "In our public ministrations would not one wish for a strong, clear, musical voice and a good delivery, both with regard to pronunciation and action?"

He also stressed the importance of the voice in a penny tract entitled *Directions Concerning Pronunciation and Gesture*, which he first published in 1749. In the first section, headed, "How we may Speak so as to be heard without Difficulty and with Pleasure," he urged speakers to begin the study of elocution early, before they formed bad habits, and reminded them that their first business was to make themselves "heard and understood with ease." To accomplish this they should not speak "too loudly or too softly" or "too rapidly or too slowly," or in a "thick, cluttering manner," or "with a tone" such as "womanish," "squeaking," "singing," "canting," "swelling," "theatrical," "whining," "odd," "whimiscal." He further advised them to talk in public "just as you do in common conversation," with "a natural, easy and graceful variation of the voice, suitable to the nature and importance of the sentiments to be delivered" and he warned against straining the voice: The words should "flow like a gliding stream, not as a rapid torrent."

In the final section of the tract he discussed gestures, which he called "the silent language of face and hands." He believed the face, which "gives the greatest sense of life to action," was the most important. There should be nothing unpleasant in it and it should mirror the speaker's emotions. The eyes should meet candidly the eyes of all the listeners, "with an air of affection and regard. . . ." He was opposed to twisting the mouth askew or biting and wetting the lips.

The body, hands, and arms also came in for serious attention. The movement of the body should not be incessant, but natural and graceful, according to circumstances. The head should be kept "modestly and decently upright," its mobility adjusted to that of the body. There should be no clapping of the hands or pounding on the pulpit. The speaker should "seldom stretch" his arms "sideways more than half a foot" from the "trunk of the body" and the left hand should not be used as frequently as the right. Furthermore, the hands and eyes "should always act in concert."

Considering all these dos and don'ts, is it any wonder that the distinguished aristocrat, Horace Walpole—about whom Dr. Doughty said, "the bleakness of [his] spiritual world chills one to the bone"—wrote many years later to John Chute: ". . . Wesley is a lean, elderly man, fresh-colored, his hair smoothly combed, but with a soupcon of curl at the ends. Wondrous clean, but as evidently an actor as Garrick."

Whether Wesley was acting or not, the writer John Nelson credited him with magnetic power: "As soon as he got up on the stand," Mr. Nelson wrote, "he stroked back his hair and turned his face toward where I stood and, I thought, fixed such an awful dread upon me, before I heard him speak, that it made my heart beat like the pendulum of a clock; and when he did speak I thought his whole discourse was aimed at me. . . . He spoke to no one but me, and I durst not look up, for I imagined all the people were looking at me."

Another testimony to John's magnetism was made by Sarah Clay, a Londoner, in a letter to John that she described as a "fresh and frank confession":

"In the year 1739 I went one Sunday morning to Islington Church. There was a great stir among the people. I was very inquisitive to know the cause and gave great attention. At last I heard them say, 'One of the Wesleys is to preach.' When you went up into the pulpit I fixt my eyes on you and thought you were more than man. Your text I have forgot; but you spoke so plain to the rich and great that it delighted me. I went home and told my mother, I had heard a man in Islington Church that I would go ten miles to hear again."

So doubtlessly, with considerable charm, John, on this March Sunday, continued to expound on his subject—love. "Love suffereth long or is long suffering," he explained. "If thou love thy neighbor for God's sake, thou will bear long with his infirmities. If he wants wisdom, thou will pity him and not despise him. If he be in error, thou will mildly endeavour to recover him, without any sharpness or reproach. If he be overtaken in a fault, thou will labor to restore him in the spirit of meekness; and if haply that cannot be done soon, thou will have patience with him if God, peradventure, may bring him at length to the knowledge of love of the truth. In all provocation, either from the weakness or malice of men, thou will show thyself a pattern of gentleness and meekness; and be they [weakness or malice of men] ever so repeated, will not be overcome of evil; but overcome evil with good. Let no man deceive you with vain words; he who is not thus long suffering, hath not love."

It is difficult to comprehend why these beautiful sentiments on patience and "long-suffering" love did not re-echo in his heart and stay his hand one year and five months later.

Finally, after many more observations on love, John reached his peroration:

"And if you love your neighbor as yourself, you will not be able to despise anyone any more than to hate him. As the wax melteth before the fire, so does pride melt away before love. All haughtiness, whether of heart, speech or behavior, vanishes away where love prevails. It bringeth down the high looks of him who boasted in his strength, and maketh him as a little child; diffident of himself, willing to hear, glad to learn, easily convinced, easily persuaded. And whosoever is otherwise minded, let him give up all vain hope; he is puffed up, and so hath not love. . . ."

The service over, John contemplated it with pleasure. He expressed in his Journal his amazement and joy at "the number of people crowding into the church, the deep attention with which they received the word and the seriousness that afterwards sat on all their faces."

Did one face in particular stand out from that sea of faces? Did he notice especially a pair of young, questioning, thoughtful, awestruck eyes?

FIVE

John finally met Sophy Hopkey six days later, on Saturday, March 13, 1736, at nine o'clock in the morning. Apparently Thomas Causton introduced him, for John met her at the Caustons' in the company of her dearest friend, Elizabeth Fawsett, who had recently lost her widowed father. Whether John realized at the time he had met the young woman who would completely captivate his heart and dominate his thoughts he did not say; but, when writing of the meeting two years later, he did underscore the date as one of the momentous days of his life.

Despite John's constant references to Sophy in his Journal and Diaries, there is very little to be found about her in the writings of contemporaneous authors or newspapers. The Reverend Mr. Henry Moore, in his biography of John, could not recall her name ("Mr. Wesley told me her name, but I cannot recollect it," he wrote); nevertheless, he described her as a "lady, who had improved understanding and elegant person and manner" and "even consulted the General [James

Oglethorpe is meant, in spite of his having had no military title during John's stay in Georgia] what dress be most agreeable to Mr. Wesley and therefore came always dressed in white."

A later biographer, taking his cue from the Reverend Mr. Moore, declared, "Miss Hopkey was a young lady of good sense and elegant in person and manner."

Then, too, John Telford, who edited *The Letters of the Rev. John Wesley, M.A.*, wrote in his foreword to John's letter to Sophy on February 6, 1737: "The young lady was beautiful, refined and intelligent."

Even Robert Southey, England's poet laureate, in his volume, *The Life of Wesley and Progress of Methodism*, described her as "a woman of fine person, polished manners and cultivated mind."

Considering that her uncle-in-law, Thomas Causton, had been a calico printer in London and that he and all his family, including Sophy herself, had come over on the charity of the Trustees, it is difficult to give credence to all these laudatory comments. "Improved understanding," "intelligent," and "beautiful," perhaps; but to say she was "elegant in person" is, under the circumstances, going a bit far. As to her always wearing white, it sounds charming; but, as far as we have been able to uncover, John himself never once mentioned such a habit in his Journal, Diaries, existing letters, or other writings. Besides, how exceedingly impractical and almost impossible in the crude, trash-strewn, impoverished, frequently muddy, frequently dusty, one-public-well frontier town of Savannah!

(In evaluating the statements of John's early biographers —and there were a rash of them—one has to keep in mind the vitally important point that none of them was familiar with John's own account of his relationship with Sophy as he related it in the Georgia Diary. For if, as they claimed, they had access to the Diary immediately after John's death, it meant little to them, since they were unable to read it. As we know, it was not until the early part of this century that Mr. Curnock finally broke the code in which the Diary was written and published it, word for word, in Volume One of *John Wesley's Journal.*)

In spite of what John wrote about Sophy later, she appears to have been just a simple, sweet-tempered, impressionable, easily swayed eighteen-year-old.

One fact we do know about her is that she was unofficially engaged to a reckless young blade, Thomas Mellichamp, who was at this time serving a term in the Charles-Town jail for counterfeiting and had threatened in a letter that if she dared marry anyone else, he would kill both her and her husband.

A considerable amount of ink was poured out on foolscap by various Savannahians about this counterfeiting scandal that involved not only Tommy, but his father, William; his brother, Lawrence; and a friend, Richard Turner.

One W. Augustine, writing on July 13, 1735, lamented: "Have had sad doings here with counterfeiting money supposed 'twas uttered by Ould Mellichamp; and myself lame with bite of a dog in my leg."

It was the First Bailiff, however, in a fairly literate letter to James Oglethorpe on July 25, who went into the details: "Carolina money counterfeited," he announced bluntly; then went on to say that William and Lawrence, his son, were guilty, "being detected at Wineyaw and were fled. We had information that Richard Turner and Thomas Mellichamp, another son, were likewise guilty and had rolling pins for that purpose."

Recorder Christie, in a later letter, on July 31, announced further news: "We hear Thomas Mellichamp is taken in Carolina in one Underwood's barn together with one Morgan of Charles-Town who was lately here with Cyder and Rum. They were taken with several counterfeit orders and bills on

71

them together with all their utensils and engraving tools and are now in Irons in the Charles-Town gaol in order to be tryed."

Thomas Causton made the news official in another report to James Oglethorpe on September 18: "Thomas Mellichamp, who was indicted for forgery and fled hence, is taken in the act and all his implements with him. . . ."

There is no evidence to show that John was familiar with Thomas' crime or with his engagement to Sophy on the Saturday morning he met her; but Savannah was a very small, gossipy town where news, especially of a scandalous nature, blew as constantly and swiftly as the sea breezes. Then, too, we do know from an entry in John's Journal that he went quite promptly to call on Sarah Mellichamp, Thomas' mother, and it is only being realistic to assume he discussed with her the relationship of her son and Sophy. After all, Sophy was one of his parishioners.

But whether or not he was aware of Sophy's "understanding" with Tommy, he administered the Eucharist to her and her friend Elizabeth Fawcett the very day after their meeting. They were "affected," he wrote in his Diary. Indeed, Elizabeth was "much affected."

For a few days after this entry in the Diary, John and Sophy apparently made no progress in getting to know each other better. These first weeks of March, John and Delamotte were living with the Moravians while they waited for Samuel Quincy to move out of the parsonage. Though they had no privacy, they felt perfectly at home there, having become intimately acquainted with most of the brethren while on the *Simmonds*. They prayed and sang daily with Anton Seifart, the new bishop, and with David Nitschmann, John Toltschig, and the other intimates of the House.

John was drawn particularly to a young member of the sect, John Reigner, the minute he learned that Reigner was interested in medicine, for Wesley himself was deeply concerned in all matters pertaining to health, his own as well as other people's. He frequently fasted for both his body's and soul's sake and he was constantly trying new diets. He had begun these experiments while a student at Christ Church College. About that time a Dr. Cheyne had published *A Book of Health and Long Life*, urging his readers to avoid everything salty or highly seasoned; also pork, fish, and stall-fed cattle; and to subsist every twenty-four hours on two pints of water and one of wine, with only eight ounces of animal food and twelve of vegetable. John was greatly impressed by this diet. For a while he even considered following the doctor's advice precisely, but finally compromised on a regime of little food of any kind and quantities of water.

Off and on, in his spare time, he was working on a book of household remedies that he planned to publish someday under the title, *Mr. Wesley's Primitive Physix*. He was compiling cures for "Chopt Hands," "The Colic," "Rash-Fever," "Corns," "Old Age," "Hard Breasts," "Shingles," "Canine Appetite," and many other ailments.

Young Reigner had come to Georgia from Vevey, Switzerland, to which his father had fled to practice his profession, physic, when the family was run out of France by religious persecution. Though the son had considered following his father's profession, he had a greater yearning for the New World and so had worked his passage to Philadelphia as a deckhand. Then, hearing of the Moravians in Georgia and deciding their beliefs and communal existence were the answer to his restless spirit, he had walked all the way from Philadelphia to Savannah and moved in with them.

These early spring weeks he was deeply concerned with the case of an elderly Moravian weaver, Henry Roscher, who, already ill, had come over on the *Simmonds*. Since reaching Savannah, he had grown steadily weaker with what was supposed to be consumption. Reigner, however, was fairly sure that something besides consumption was eating away the man's life and he interested John in the case. Both men believed new diagnosis and treatment were necessary; but when

73

they broached the matter to Bishop Nitschmann, he was supremely unconcerned.

Smiling sweetly, he said, "Yes, he will soon be well; he is ready for the Bridegroom."

Several weeks later, when Roscher did join the "Bridegroom," Reigner performed an autopsy, in which John assisted. They discovered the poor man had a large hematoma in the left wall of the abdomen.

But the two Johns did not wait for Herr Roscher's death to start the study of anatomy. Practically from the very first day of their meeting, they began to read Drake's *Anatomy* together.

Samuel Quincy finally left Georgia in the middle of March and John and Delamotte moved into the parsonage, which stood alone on the edge of the East Common, with a wide, treeless space between it and the nearest houses on Drayton Street. Close by was the Public Garden and beyond that the jungle-thick woods of pines, magnolias, swamp maples, sycamores, myrtles, water oaks, and palmettos, many of them matted with moss, smilax, honeysuckle, and jasmine vines.

Samuel had recently added to the parsonage so it could accommodate Indians and other visitors to Savannah, making it the largest house in the town. It had, so John noted, "many conveniences" and a "good garden." Nevertheless, it was sparsely furnished. There was not even one bed, and John and Delamotte slept on pads laid on the bare floor in opposite corners of the bedroom.

John, besides being meticulously neat in his person, was also neat about his surroundings and so began immediately "to sort" his own books and the mountains of other books in the parsonage. These had been sent to Georgia by the Trustees and other Englishmen concerned with the religious and educational life of the settlers. Many of them had arrived three years before on the first ship, *Ann*, and were badly mildewed from the warm, damp sea air of the Georgia coast.

When John finished sorting them, he counted and listed them.

There were forty-nine Bibles, sixty-six Testaments, one hundred and sixteen Common Prayer Books, seventy Psalters, three hundred and twelve Catechisms, sixty copies of *Duty of Man*, sixty-two copies of the *Christian Monitor— Containing an Earnest Exhortation to a Holy Life* and *An Answer to all the Excuses and Pretences which men ordinarily make for their not coming to the Holy Communion*, fifty-six copies of Bishop Gibson's *Family Devotion*, fifty copies of *Christians Instructed*, twelve copies of *Guide to Christian Families*, and three copies of Nelson's *The Practice of True Devotion*.

In addition to these religious volumes, there were books for use in the instruction of children in school: one hundred primers, seventy spelling books, and one hundred Horn-Books.

Other ships after the *Ann* had also brought books. The English at home were determined that their unfortunate brothers in the wilderness of the New World should not lack reading matter to improve their minds and, especially, their morals. More Bibles, Common Prayer Books, Psalters and Catechisms flooded in, as did generous numbers of Mr. Law's *Serious Call to a Devout and Holy Life;* Bishop of Man's *On the Lord's Supper; The ABC with the Catechism;* Richard Allestree's *Whole Duty of Man; Sacred and Moral Poems by a Cambridge Gentleman; Principles and Duties of Christianity;* Harriett Leonard's *The Great Importance of a Religious Life Considered;* and Dr. Thomas Gouge's *Christian Directions how to walk with God all the day long.*

One Londoner, sobered by the thought that rum and brandy had brought a great many of the colonists to the state of penury that precipitated their egress to Georgia, had given two hundred copies of *A Friendly Admonition to The Drinkers of Brandy and other distilled spirituous Liquors*. There were also German grammars, Josephus' *Works*, and Plato's

75

Works. The last had been purchased by the hard-pressed Trustees themselves.

But there was much more for John to do than getting the books in order and the rectory cleaned and straightened up. He must write long letters to his friends back in England and to his brother Samuel, and above all to his mother, Susannah. In the letter to her, he finally wrote of Savannah:

"We are likely to stay here some months," he said. "The place is pleasant beyond imagination; and by all that I can learn exceedingly healthful—even in Summer, for those who are not intemperate. It has pleased God that I have not had a moment's illness of any kind since I set my foot upon the continent; nor did I know any one of my 700 parishioners who is sick at this time. Many of them, indeed, I believe very angry already, for a gentleman no longer ago than last night made a ball; but the public prayers happening to begin about the same time, the church was full, and the ballroom so empty that the entertainment could not go forward. . . ."

He ended the epistle with the plea: "Pray for us and especially for, dear Mother, your dutiful and affectionate son, John Wesley."

A garden had to be planted immediately, the season being already far advanced; a school had to be organized for the children (John believed Delamotte would make a satisfactory teacher); and more religious instruction had to be given to the young people of the parish.

It was this intense desire to disseminate Christian knowledge to the young members of his flock that opened the door quickly to a close association with Sophy. Under the date, Thursday, the eighteenth of March, he wrote: "Walked with Miss Sophy and Miss Fosset, conversing. . . ."

What a picture springs to the mind: John's short, erect figure in surplice and cassock, the Prayer Book spread open in his outstretched, slender hands as he walks energetically in spite of his soft-soled black pumps sinking at every step into the sandy ground of the garden paths.

76

And mockingbirds, cardinals, thrushes, larks, and blue jays singing madly and darting from one tree limb to another as swiftly as tossed shells; dew spangling the spread fans of the low-lying palmettos, yellowed by winter; clumps of wire grass and dark green splashes of smilax growing wild in the uncleared spaces; and the rays of the sun, which had not yet scaled the solid walls of trees to the right of the garden, brushing the blue sky with a pinkish-golden light.

Then on Tuesday, the twenty-third, after the six-o'clock morning exposition, he invited Sophy and Elizabeth "to go home" with him, where they again walked in the garden and conversed. And the next day he invited them again . . . and the next . . . and the next. Then he invited them to remain for a breakfast of sassafras tea, cheese, and cold biscuit. This proved so very pleasant that soon the walks in the garden, followed by breakfast, became a regular part of his days.

Judging entirely from his own words, it was John who sought Sophy's company from the very beginning of their acquaintance. Nowhere is there a hint in the Journal or Diaries that she ever forced her attentions upon him, then or later. Those allegations that she did evidently stemmed from the wishful thinking of John's biographers, friends, and church historians; or possibly—though it seems hardly probable—from his private papers that have long since been destroyed, or from personal conversations.

Dr. Thomas Coke—John's contemporary, a preacher, and an enthusiast of the Methodist movement as well as a famous historian—and the Reverend Mr. Moore present Sophy in this bold, conniving light in their co-authored biography. After claiming in their preface, "All his [Wesley's] private papers were open to our inspection for several years" and "He himself informed us of many important passages in his life, which he never inserted in his Journals and are known to a few but ourselves," they declared: ". . . There is a silence observed in Mr. Wesley's Journal in respect to some parts of this event [the love affair] which it is possible has caused even friendly readers to hesitate concerning the propriety of his conduct; or at least concerning the propriety which they might be led to expect from so great a character.

"General Oglethorpe was what is called an excellent judge of human nature. He was also a man of courage and enterprise. He had enlarged views of what might be done with proper instruments on the wide continent of America. He had heard much of Mr. Wesley before he engaged him as a missionary, having been intimate with his eldest brother. But he saw during the voyage that the half was not told him. He saw here a man of great ability, a man superior to everything that usually captivates human nature. He saw a man, as he thought, fit for his purpose. But Mr. Wesley's religion or, as he termed it, his enthusiasm, the General lamented as standing in the way. On their arrival therefore in Georgia, he resolved to try if that obstacle was not to be surmounted.

"Mr. Causton . . . had a young lady in his house of an improved understanding, and elegant [in] person and manners. The General thought he had found in her a proper bait for this soaring religionist. And as some of the greatest men that are recorded, even in the oracles of God, have fallen by this snare, he had some ground to hope for success. . . .

"The young lady mentioned above was introduced to him as a person who had severely felt the anguish of a wounded spirit and now was a sincere inquirer after the way of eternal life. After some time he [John] observed she took every possible opportunity of being in his company. . . ."

Some other early biographers, chief among them Robert Southey and B. L. Tyerman, follow closely in the thought-steps of Coke and Moore. In fact, Tyerman's discussion of who pursued whom is so similar to that of his predecessors, it would be repetitious to quote him; but Poet Laureate Southey strikes a few new notes. Calling her erroneously Sophia Causton, as Dr. Coke and others had done, he declares she "had fixed her eyes upon Wesley; and it is said that Mr. Oglethorpe wished to bring about a marriage between them, thinking it the likeliest means of reclaiming him from those eccentricities which stood in the way of his usefulness. She was a woman of fine person, polished manners and cultivated mind, and was easily led to bear her part in a design which was to cure an excellent man of his extravagances and give her a good husband. Accordingly she was introduced to him as one suffering under a wounded spirit and inquiring after the way of eternal life. Nor was it enough to place herself thus in a more particular manner under his spiritual guidance; she became his pupil also, like another Heloise. . . ."

The Reverend Mr. Curnock, however, does not go along with these apologists for John's capitulation to Sophy's charms. In a footnote on the page of *The John Wesley Journal* that tells of John's and Sophy's second meeting, this lifelong Wesley scholar writes: "Miss Sophy was not more than eighteen years old. Her home had no protective influence, except the presence of her aunt. She was harassed by a masterful and, as the event proved, unprincipled lover. With few exceptions, the people among whom she lived . . . were not helpful to a young girl. For the first time she now fell under the influence of a very intense form of religion. Her minister was unmarried, thirty-three years of age, an ascetic, a gentleman, a scholar, a singularly attractive and susceptible personality. At first there was no thought on either side of love. Wesley, for the time being, until he could become a missionary, was pastor and tutor. The Diary shows that all his friends were treated as pupils. He used for them the letter which in his Oxford Diaries stands for pupils. His conception of duty was that, without ceasing, he must pray and care for those he taught. Obviously there was danger in the relationship. And the danger was all the greater because the tutor curate, in spite of all his striving, had not yet succeeded in destroying his human nature."

Though the morning sessions in the garden, followed by breakfast, became an important part of John's day, it was in measurement of time a small part. His days were extremely long and full, his chores divided into hours and even minutes. They usually began at five o'clock in the morning and ended at ten in the evening. First, he shaved, bathed, and dressed; then prayed with Delamotte; sang hymns with the Moravians; read prayers and preached in the courthouse-church; strolled and breakfasted with Sophy and Elizabeth; wrote letters; prayed; studied the Bible; filled in his Diary; worked in the garden (he planted Seward beans, for one thing); visited his parishioners; and read, read, read. When a book engrossed him, he read it several times a day.

Naturally, the routine was sometimes varied with other activities. He married John Brownfield to a young woman named Polly; he continued the study of anatomy with John Reigner; he prayed for Beata and James Oglethorpe and he practiced the flute, which he enjoyed. Indeed, he found life so much to his liking that he replied to a letter from Charles in Frederica with a glowing one about his own situation, except for a last-minute reservation written in Greek alluding to the unease he was already experiencing in his relations with Sophy. The letter began:

"Dear Brother,

"How different are the ways wherein we are led! Yet, I hope toward the same end.

"I have hitherto no opposition at all. All is smooth and fair and promising. We cannot see any clouds gathering. But the calm cannot last; storms must come hither, too; and let them come, when we are ready to meet them."

Next he urged Charles to act as a guardian angel to his "friend . . ." (the Reverend Mr. Moore asserts this part of the letter refers to Sophy, who he says went to Frederica with the passengers of the *Simmonds* and *London Merchant;* but this was not so; she was still in Savannah. John is, of course, writing of Beata). "Watch over her; keep her as much as possible. Write to me, how I ought to write to her.

"If Mr. Ingham were here, I would try to see you. But omit no opportunity of writing."

At the close of the letter were the lines in Greek. (In their early months in Georgia, John and Charles frequently put the most secret parts of their correspondence to each other in Greek or Latin for fear of prying eyes; later, they used Byrom's shorthand, in which Charles excelled.) Editor Telford made these lines public in his edition of *The Letters of the Rev. John Wesley* in 1931. Translated, they read:

"I stand in jeopardy every hour. Two or three are women, younger, refined, God fearing. Pray that I know none of them after the flesh."

SIX

While John was congratulating himself on such pleasant, rewarding days in Savannah, Charles Wesley and Benjamin Ingham were floundering miserably as the spiritual
leaders of the new settlers at Frederica.

This most southern English outpost was stationed on the
west side of St. Simons Island, where a branch of the Altamaha River took a shallow bite out of the flat, sandy, heav-
ily wooded land just a few miles before it emptied into Jekyl
Sound. James Oglethorpe had chosen this site because it was
strategically located to stop the Spaniards in Florida if they
tried to invade Georgia and recover it for the Spanish Crown.
Since there had once been Spanish missions along this coast,
he expected (in spite of the Treaty of Utrecht, which in his
opinion ceded the territory between the Savannah and St.
John's Rivers to the English and their Indian allies) that
Spain might someday attempt to take it back.

Benjamin had reached Frederica on Sunday, February 22,
only five days after James Oglethorpe had arrived there with

the first group of males from the *Simmonds* and *London Merchant* and other laborers from Savannah to lay out the streets for the town and to build palmetto bowers as temporary housing for the new colonists.

As Benjamin set foot on the narrow, oyster-shell-encrusted shore at the foot of the low bluff on which Frederica was rising, he heard gunfire in the nearby woods and excitedly demanded of the Georgia founder, who was at the landing preparing to return to the ships at the mouth of the Savannah, "Sir, do you consider Sunday a proper day for sporting?"

Though the hunters were openly engaged in their "sporting" without Oglethorpe's having uttered a reprimanding word, he, so Benjamin reported in his Journal, "immediately put a stop to it; then returned to Savannah, having already put people in the method of proceeding."

Naturally, the settlers did not take kindly to Benjamin's interference. It was an outrageous come-off when men couldn't shoot on Sunday, especially in view of the fact that on weekdays Mr. Oglethorpe worked them twelve and fourteen hours. How were they supposed to get the game that roamed so plentifully in the woods? Or bring down the innumerable birds that filled the air? God knows that the dried beef they had been fed for months was beginning to turn their stomachs. Who gave this young upstart the right to stick his long nose into their affairs?

Benjamin was perfectly aware of their displeasure, for he recounted it with considerable bitterness: "My chief business was daily to visit the people, to take care of those that were sick and to supply them with the best things we had. For a few days at the first, I had everybody's good word; but when they found I watched narrowly over them and reproved them sharply for their faults, immediately the scene changed. Instead of blessing came cursing, and my love and kindness were repaid with hatred and ill-will."

Still he was not deterred from doing his duty as he saw it. The following Sunday, after the morning service, which he conducted under the sweeping limbs of a huge live oak, he reminded them of James Oglethorpe's order and then added for good measure a few words of warning of his own.

"It is the Lord's Day," he declared, looking into their scowling, bewhiskered faces partially hidden by long hanks of uncombed hair, "and therefore ought to be spent in His services. You ought not to be a-shooting or walking up and down in the woods; and I will take notice of all those who do."

"One man asnwered that there were new laws in America!" Benjamin recounted. "This man, as well as several others, went out; but he, I think, was two days before he could find his way back again. I reproved most of them afterwards, in a friendly manner, laying before them the heinousness of the sin, and the dreadful consequences that would necessarily follow. One or two took my advice well; but the rest were hardened and, instead of reforming, raised heavy complaints and accusations to the gentleman that was left in commission, that I had made a black list; and that I intended to ruin them. . . ."

Nine days later, on the heels of the second visit of the Georgia leader and the arrival of the remaining passengers of the *Simmonds* and *London Merchant*, Charles Wesley arrived. A noisy, bustling, disorderly scene met his eyes. Three large tents, with the British flag whipping briskly above them in the breeze from the Atlantic, stood several feet back from the rim of the river. James Oglethorpe had pitched them the day before: one for himself; one for his good friends, Mr. and Mrs. William Horton; and one for those women and children whose bowers were not yet ready.

A street, twenty-five yards wide, named Broad, stretched from the Water Gate on the west to the Port Gate on the east. Alongside this street, at the rear of the lots, the first dozen huts, fashioned Indian style of palmetto fans and ridge poles, were in the building stage. Also almost completed was a large Storehouse to hold the food and other goods, and, right on the edge of the arc cut by the Altamaha, a handful of workmen were mixing dried grass (later they would use crushed oyster shells), water, and sand to form thick walls of tabby for a fort.

The first moment Benjamin could draw Charles's attention from the activities along the waterfront, he poured into his ears the incident of the Sunday shooting and his protest to the Georgia leader.

"I rejoice, sir, in your vindication of the Lord's Day," Charles commended him; then added, "However, I must say that this specimen of the ignorance and unhappy temper of the people with whom we are to labor is not promising."

In this apprehensive frame of mind, Charles probably appeared more immature than his twenty-eight years and unsure of himself. There was a strong family resemblance between him and John; but his face was broader, his cheeks much fuller, and his eyes larger. Whereas John's features were finely chiseled and in perfect proportion to his small stature, with lines of refinement and intelligence stamped upon them, Charles's were less distinguished, more benign.

When the drums rolled at seven o'clock for the evening service at the entrance to the unfinished fort, Charles was ready. He felt he must begin prayers this very first day; the more ignorant and unteachable his parishioners, the more rigorous the religious discipline must be.

The next morning he held another service. He rose before dawn from the hard floor of the periagua in which he had traveled to Frederica, no accommodations having yet been made for him in the town, and read "short prayers," as he recorded, "to a few at the fire before Oglethorpe's tent in a hard shower of rain."

So far, so good; but toward noon, not even one full day after landing, the maelstrom that was to continue during Charles's entire stay and beyond, broke. At that hour he found "an opportunity of talking at the tent door with Mrs. Welch" and, learning that she and Beata had had a falling out, fell into the same yawning pit in which John had found himself on the *Simmonds*—acting the role of peacemaker between two angry women. In his gentlest manner he assured Ann that Beata "bore her no ill will."

To this she answered vehemently, "You must not tell me that. Mrs. Hawkins is a very subtle woman. I understand her perfectly. There is a great man in the case, therefore I can not speak, only that she is exceedingly jealous of me." As "company" joined them at that point, she said no more.

"A great man," Charles surely repeated to himself in dismay, hurrying from the tent door. A great man! Could she possibly mean James Oglethorpe? No, no! But if she did not mean James Oglethorpe, who could she mean? He was the only man at Frederica who could by the widest stretch of the imagination be described as "great."

Scenes on the *Simmonds*, which had meant nothing to him at the time, must have flashed across his mind in a sinister light. Ann Welch, pale and faint, lying in James Oglethorpe's cabin with the Georgia leader leaning solicitously above her, inquiring after her comfort and health while Beata sat nearby narrowly eying them both. Had he been blind all those months on shipboard? But even if what Ann had insinuated was true, why was Beata jealous of her? Could she, too, be intimately involved with Oglethorpe?

What was he, as her pastor, supposed to do about her? And about Beata Hawkins? Oh, blessed Saviour, why should he, so incapable of dealing with such matters and so inexperienced, be inflicted with two such vixens? If he could only talk to Mr. Oglethorpe about them! But how could he, if Mr. Oglethorpe was entangled with them in some dark fashion?

He did, however, go to see the head of the Colony that evening on another matter and received still another blow. As he reported in his Journal, "In the evening I heard the first harsh notes from Mr. Oglethorpe when I asked for something for a poor woman." And the next day, when Charles approached him on a matter "that deserved still greater encouragement," he received even "a rougher answer."

Naturally he was dumfounded by James Oglethorpe's behavior. As he said himself, "I knew not how to account for his increasing coldness."

Ann, too, waxed "all storm and tempest," Charles mourned. "The meek, the teachable Mrs. Welch that was in the ship was now so wilful, so untractable, so fierce that I could not bear to stay near her."

In spite of these aggravations, when Sunday came he read prayers and preached out of doors to about twenty people, among them his baffling, inscrutable, unnerving chief. Yet he preached with such a boldness and singleness of intention that he returned to the palmetto hut of a Mr. Reed, one of the constables of Frederica, that he now belatedly occupied and made a note of it.

For a few days Charles spoke neither to Beata nor to Ann. He explained his silence frankly. "The reason I have not talked to you lately," he told Ann, "was my despair of doing you any good. You are a changed woman from the one I knew on the ship."

"Yes, I am changed," she readily admitted.

When Charles asked her why, she said she could not tell him. Charles persisted, but she still refused. Was it possible —just possible—he finally ventured, that Beata Hawkins was in love with Mr. Oglethorpe and resented the attention the Georgia leader paid to Ann?

"Yes," Ann agreed.

Alas, alas, Charles's worst suspicions appeared to be verified. How disgraceful the situation was! He was revolted.

On Thursday, March 18, James Oglethorpe set out to hunt the buffalo, so he announced; but in truth to survey the waterways and islands that lay between his southern outpost and the St. John's River, the boundary between the English and the Spaniards.

Charles did not describe his going. He was evidently in his palmetto hut, suffering in body, mind, and spirit. James Oglethorpe despised him—for what, only God knew; Beata Hawkins despised him and refused to speak to him, and Ann Welch despised him and spoke to him only when she had something scandalous to say about Beata. In despair he confided to the pages of his Journal, "I would not spend six days more in the same manner for all Georgia."

The following Sunday there was another shooting incident. In spite of the Georgia founder's order that there was to be no "sporting" on the Lord's Day, Dr. Hawkins, Beata's husband, hunting in the woods close by Frederica, fired off a gun in the middle of Charles's sermon and then flew into a wild rage when a constable, Samuel Davison, took him into custody.

"What do you mean, arresting me?" the surgeon shouted angrily. "Don't you know I'm not to be locked up as a common fellow?"

The constable, uncertain about what to do, went to confer with Herr von Hermsdorf, the German whom James Oglethorpe had commissioned a captain and left in charge of Frederica during his absence.

"Get two sentinels and take the surgeon to the guard-house," the captain ordered.

A highly wrought-up Charles recounted in his Journal the events that followed: "Hereupon Mrs. Hawkins fired a gun and then ran hither like a madwoman, crying she had shot and would be confined, too. The constable and Hermsdorf persuaded her to go away. She cursed and swore in the utmost transport of passion, threatening to kill the first man that should come near her.

"In the afternoon while I was talking in the street with poor Catherine [Beata's maid, who was accustomed to being flogged by Beata], her mistress came up to us and fell upon me with the utmost bitterness and scurrility; said she would blow me up and my brother; that I was the cause of her hus-

88

band's confinement, but she would be revenged and expose my damned hypocrisy, my prayers four times a day by beat of drum, and abundance more, which I cannot write and thought no woman, though taken from Drury Lane, could have spoken. I only said I pitied her, but defied all she or the devil could do; for she could not hurt me. I was strangely preserved from passion, and at parting told her I hoped she would soon come to a better mind."

While Charles was praying that evening, he was interrupted by the arrival of a letter from the incarcerated surgeon:

"Mr. Wesley,

"Being by your priestly order confined, the care of the sick is no longer incumbent on me. As you have been busy in intermeddling with my affairs I request, sir, the following patients may have proper assistance . . . and no neglect laid to your injured friend,

"Thomas Hawkins.

"P.S. I dispute they have the right of confining a surgeon, and especially for a day in confinement." [Mrs. Lawley was expecting any hour.]

After writing the surgeon a note denying he had anything to do with his arrest and saying a short prayer, Charles visited all the patients Dr. Hawkins had listed.

The next day, while Charles was arguing with James Welch "not to concern himself in the disturbance," he heard Beata cry out, "Murder!" and, as he frankly admitted, "walked away." Apparently his nerves could stand no more for the time being.

The cause of the "murder" outcry was Beata's appearance at the guardhouse with bottles of rum, beer, or wine for Thomas and the refusal of John Haydon, another constable, to allow her to deliver them. The details Charles heard when he returned "out of the woods." He recounted them in graphic detail: ". . . he [John Haydon] had civilly told

Mrs. Hawkins that his orders were not to suffer her to come within the camp, but he would carry those bottles for her. She replied she would come, and upon his holding open his arms to hinder her, broke one of the bottles on his head.

"He caught her in his arms, she striking him continually and crying out, 'Murder.' Hawkins, at the same time, ran out and struck him. He closed and threw him down, set his foot upon him, and said if he resisted he would run his bayonet into him. Mark Hird, the other constable, was meantime engaged in keeping off Mrs. Hawkins, who broke the other bottle on his head. Welch coming up to her assistance, Davison, the constable, desired him to keep off the camp. Nevertheless he ran upon him, took the gun out of his hand, and struck him with all his might on his sides and face till Haydon interposed and parted them. Welch then ran and gave the Doctor a bayonet, which was immediately taken from him. Mrs. Hawkins cried out continually against the parsons and swore revenge against my brother and me."

That evening Charles moved his pallet from the ground to the top of his sea chest, for a cold that had been plaguing him for several days was worse and he could not speak above a whisper. After staying in bed for two days, he was able to get up and pray for his enemies, the chief one, in his opinion, being James Oglethorpe.

Wondering whether to "interpose for the prisoners," he consulted the Bible, which he referred to as the "Oracle," and read in Jeremiah, 44:16, 17, this message: "As for the word that thou hast spoken to us in the name of the Lord, we will not hearken unto thee. But we will certainly do whatsoever thing goeth forth out of our own mouth. . . ." Influenced, one suspects, by his own inclination, Charles interpreted the words to mean he should not meddle with his incarcerated parishioners.

But he did call on another parishioner, Catherine Perkins, and heard her unequivocally accuse Beata of going to bed with James Oglethorpe. Charles had been afraid of this appalling possibility ever since Ann had told him that Beata was involved with a "great man," but now to hear it in an emphatic, bald statement sickened him to the core of his being. Beata, a common whore? No, he could not accept it. He would go at once and see Ann. Perhaps she would say that Catherine Perkins did not know what she was talking about and that was not what she had meant by her own insinuations. Let this be the way of it!

But a few minutes after he entered the Welches' palmetto bower, this hope was dashed. Ann not only verified Catherine Perkins' accusation, but announced that she, too, was sleeping with the Georgia leader and had been for many months. She had been his mistress, she said, even in London.

Though she displayed no shame at her conduct, she was wildly frightened at what James Oglethorpe would say and do if he found out she had revealed their cohabitation and so pleaded with Charles not to breathe a word of it to him. Moved by her plight, Charles foolishly promised. Then he went to his hut and confided to the pages of his Journal: "Horror of horrors! Never did I feel such access of pity."

Two days later, while he and Benjamin were praying for Ann and reading the Psalms, Charles was notified that his chief had returned from his trip to the south and wanted to see him. When he, accompanied by Benjamin, reached James Oglethorpe's tent, he found practically the whole population of Frederica milling around outside and Beata, Thomas, and the constable inside. After a brief hearing, the Georgia leader reprimanded the officers who had performed the arrest and dismissed the prisoners. As Beata swaggered out, she cut her angry eyes at Charles and snapped that she had more to say against him, but she would save it for another time.

With the departure of the Hawkinses, the Colony's leader looked over at Charles and said brusquely, "Mr. Wesley, I am convinced and glad that you had no hand in all this." He then pointedly began to read the dispatches that had accumulated during his absence. After a few hesitant moments, Charles blurted out, "Mr. Oglethorpe, I have something of importance to impart to you when you are at leisure."

The Georgia founder did not even lift his bushy brows, much less his eyes. In Charles's words, "He took no notice, but read his letters." Charles was utterly astonished, as was Benjamin.

When the second drum beat for prayers the next morning, Charles, who had had chills and fever all night and felt "much weakened," longed to stay in bed and let Benjamin conduct the service; but, considering the attacks made against him by Beata, he decided it would not do to give in to this temptation. As he got up, he remembered those "animating" words in John 12–26: "If any man serve me, let him follow me; . . . him will my Father honour," and was strengthened. He needed all the strength he could get that morning, for an hour later—it was just seven thirty—he was again summoned to appear before James Oglethorpe.

Abruptly, with no preliminaries, Charles's chief accused him of mutiny and sedition. He charged that Charles had stirred up the people to desert the Colony to such a point that they had had a meeting the night before and resolved to depart. Already this morning they had sent the founder a message, asking leave to go.

"A representative has informed against them," James Oglethorpe declared, "and has said that you, Mr. Wesley, were the spring of it all. He said the leaders were those men who constantly came to prayers, therefore you must have instigated them. I would not scruple, Mr. Wesley, shooting half a dozen of them at once; but out of kindness I spoke first to you."

With a small show of dignity, Charles answered, "Sir, I desire you would have no regard for my brother, my friends or the love you had for me if anything of this charge can be proved against me. I assure you I know nothing of their meetings or their designs. Of those you have mentioned, not one comes constantly to prayers or sacrament. I never incited anyone to leave the Colony. I desire to answer my accuser face to face."

The Georgia founder said that Richard Lawley was the accuser and that he would bring him if Charles waited.

"Sir, I'm not surprised that Mr. Lawley is my accuser," Charles answered, his voice harsh with suppressed fury. "This Mr. Lawley is a man who has declared that he knows no reason for keeping fair with any man, but a design to get all he can from him. He knows, however, there was nothing to be got by the poor parson and so he turns on me. . . ."

Charles must have known that his chief was impatient to get this matter disposed of so he could move on to the countless other matters that pressured him; nevertheless, he determined this time to have out his say. "Aren't you assured, sir, that there are enough men in Frederica who would say or swear anything against any man if he were in disgrace? Why, sir, if you yourself were removed from here by Parliament or if you succeeded ill, aren't you assured that the whole stream of people would be turned against you? This is the old cry—'Away with the Christians to the Lions.' For days now Dr. Hawkins and his wife have been scandalizing my brother and me, vowing vengeance against us both, and threatening me just yesterday, even in your presence, Mr. Oglethorpe."

All the pent-up frustration that Charles had been harboring for days pushed to the surface: "What redress or satisfaction do you consider is due to my character, sir? What good can I do in my present parish if I'm cut off by calumnies from ever seeing one half of it? . . . What ——"

Suddenly it must have dawned upon Charles to whom he was talking so vehemently, for he abruptly broke off his diatribe to assure the Georgia leader that he had made it his business "to promote peace among all" and he would continue to make it his business.

"I felt no disturbance while speaking," Charles wrote, commenting on the interview, "but lifted up my heart to God, and found Him present with me." And thus feeling God's presence, he reported, "While Mr. Oglethorpe was fetching Lawley, I thought of our Lord's words: 'And ye shall be brought before governors and kings for my sake. . . . But when they deliver you up, take no thought how or what ye shall speak: for it shall be given you in that same hour what ye shall speak."

Charles at this point joined Benjamin, who was waiting anxiously outside the Georgia leader's tent, and asked him to pray for him; then, walking back and forth "musing on the event," he opened the Bible on Acts 15: 31–3: "Which when they had read, they rejoiced for the consolation. And Judas and Silas, being prophets also themselves, exhorted the brethren with many words, and confirmed them. And after they had tarried there a space, they were let go in peace . . ."

When James Oglethorpe returned with Richard Lawley, he observed that his tent was too public a place to talk, so Charles offered to take them to his "usual walk in the woods." On the way, out of Richard's hearing, Charles managed to say to the Georgia leader, "Sir, if you will show only the least disinclination to find me guilty, you shall see what a turn it will give to the accusation." James Oglethorpe took the hint. Immediately Richard, "who appeared full of guilt and fear," dropped the charges or, as Charles recorded it, "shrunk it" to Charles's forcing the people to prayers.

"The people themselves will acquit me of that," Charles retorted.

At this point, seeing the argument was getting nowhere, James Oglethorpe tried to reconcile matters. He instructed Richard to tell the petitioners he would not so much as ask who they were if they were but peaceful in the future. "I hope they will be so," he concluded, "and Mr. Wesley here hopes so, too."

"Yes, sir," answered Richard meekly. "I really believe it of Mr. Wesley. [I] had always a very great respect for him."

At this fast about-face, Charles could not resist turning to his chief and whispering, "Did I not tell you it would be so?"

James Oglethorpe did not reply to Charles directly; instead, he smiled wryly at Richard and, his voice tinged with sarcasm, said, "Yes, you had always a very great respect for Mr. Wesley. You told me he was a stirrer-up of sedition and at the bottom of all this disturbance." And with that he dismissed him.

Charles strolled back to the settlement with his chief, ending up, to his embarrassment, at the Hawkins' house, a two-story, red-brick building that had recently been completed. But Charles wasn't the only one taken aback. Beata came out "aghast," so Charles reported, "to see me with him." Hurriedly Charles bade James Oglethorpe good day and headed for his own hut.

When he recounted to Benjamin how he had been "delivered out of the mouth of the lion," Benjamin was not impressed. "I'm afraid this is just the beginning of our sorrows," he predicted.

The events of the next few days appeared to bear out Benjamin's doleful forecast. Early the next morning James Oglethorpe once again sent for Charles, this time to tell him in tones high with rage that Mrs. Lawley had had a miscarriage because she had been "denied access to the doctor for bleeding." And it was all the parson's fault, he stormed, because he had had the doctor locked up so he could not attend to his patients.

Before Charles could deny the accusation, the Georgia leader rushed on: "The other day when I chose to overlook the part you played in having the doctor locked up, I did not know that Mrs. Lawley's life had been endangered and that she was to suffer a miscarriage. This, naturally, puts an en-

95

tirely new light on the matter. It makes your action, Mr. Wesley, inexcuseable and I would be a tyrant if I passed by such intolerable injuries."

"I know nothing of the matter, sir," Charles finally was able to say, meaning that he was not responsible for the miscarriage, "and it is hard that it should be imputed to me. From the first Hermsdorf told the doctor he might visit whom of his patients he pleased; but the doctor would not visit any. I hadn't the least hand in the whole business as Hermsdorf has declared."

Still furious, Oglethorpe shot back quickly, "Hermsdorf himself assured me what he did, he did by your advice."

"You must have mistaken his imperfect English," Charles argued, "for many have heard him say the contradictory of this. Yet, I must be charged with all the mischief."

Apparently the Colony's chief heaved a great sigh of weariness and cleared his voice of anger, for his next remark is plaintive, puzzled, even pitiful: "How is it, Mr. Wesley, that there is no love, no meekness, no true religion among the people, but just formal prayers?"

"As to that, sir," Charles replied ruefully, "I can answer for them that they have no more of the form of godliness than the power. I have seldom seen above six at the public service."

"But what would an unbeliever say to your raising these disorders?" James Oglethorpe persisted.

Charles answered with apparent calmness, "Why if I had raised them, sir, he might say there was nothing in religion, but what would that signify to those who had experienced it? They would know better."

After a moment, the Georgia founder, letting up his attack on Charles, became quite confidential. He told him the settlers "were full of dread and confusion; that it was easier to govern a thousand men than sixty; for in so small a number, every one's passion was considerable; that he durst not leave them [again] before they were settled."

Then Charles asked him with some sarcasm, "Would you have me forbear conferring at all with my parishioners?"

James Oglethorpe did not answer; it appeared that he did not even hear the question.

After a long, embarrassing pause, Charles stumbled on: "Sir, I want you to know the reason I did not interpose for or against the Doctor was his having at the beginning charged me with his confinement. I talked less with my parishioners these last five days than I have done in any one afternoon before. I shunned appearing in public, lest my silence should be deciphered into advice. But one argument of my innocence I can give, which will convince even you of it. I know my life is in your hands; and you know that were you to frown upon me and give the least intimation that it would be agreeable to you, the generality of this wretched people would say or swear anything."

Surely shaking his handsome head in sad perplexity, the Colony's founder admitted this was the case, not only with the generality, but with them all.

"Must I not therefore be mad if I would in such a situation provoke you by disturbing the public peace?" Charles prodded. "Innocence I know is not the least protection; but my sure trust is in God."

In spite of this frank discussion, Charles, during the next few days, felt that the situation in Frederica worsened instead of improved, chiefly because Ann grew more and more like Beata, asserting boldly that she would "no longer be priest ridden," jesting at prayers, and talking in the same loose, scandalous fashion as her sometime bosom companion. Heartsick, Charles decided to send Benjamin to Savannah to urge John to come and help him.

The day that Benjamin left—Sunday, March 28—was filled with unhappiness. Charles described the events quite simply, yet movingly, in his Journal:

". . . After prayers, poor Mr. Davison stood behind to take his leave of Mr. Ingham. He burst into tears and said,

'One good man is leaving us already; I foresee nothing but desolation. Must my poor children be brought up like these savages?' We endeavoured to comfort him by showing him his calling. At ten o'clock Mr. Ingham preached an alarming sermon on the day of judgment. . . .

"While Mr. Ingham waited for the boat, I took a turn with Mr. Horton. He fully convinced me of Mrs. Hawkins' true character: ungrateful in the highest degree, a common prostitute, a complete hypocrite. He told me her husband and she had begged him upon their knees to intercede with Oglethorpe not to turn them out of the ship, which would be their utter ruin. This he accordingly did; though Oglethorpe at first assured him he had rather give them 100 pounds than take them. . . .

"I hasted to the waterside where I found Mr. Ingham just put off. O! happy, happy friend! He has gone; he has broke loose; he has escaped; but woe is me that I am still constrained to dwell in Meshech. I languished to bear him company, followed him with my eye till out of sight and then sunk into deepr dejection of spirit than I had known before."

The week following, Charles's misfortunes continued. Knowing he was to live with James Oglethorpe, he had brought nothing with him from England except his clothes and books, so on Monday morning he went to his chief's tent and asked a servant—perhaps Mrs. Francis Moore, James Oglethorpe's housekeeper—for a teakettle. No, she said, he could not have one; Mr. Oglethorpe had given orders that no one should have any of his things.

"That order surely did not extend to me," protested Charles.

"Yes, sir," she said, "you were excepted by name."

This refusal so galled Charles that he scorched a page of the Journal with the line: "Thanks be to God that it is not yet made a capital offense to give me a morsel of bread."

In less than twenty-four hours he was again rebuffed. Having slept until now on the ground or on his sea chest and hearing that some boards were to be disposed of, he attempted to get a few, but they were given to practically everyone but him. Again with his pen dipped in gall he wrote: "The minister of Frederica only must be treated as an enemy to society, as an unjust person and be destitute of an habitation. . . . I begin now to be abused and slighted. I could not be more trampled upon was I a fallen minister of state. . . . The people have found out I am in disgrace. My few well wishers are afraid to speak to me. Others desired I would not take it ill if they seemed not to know me when we should meet. The servant who used to wash my linen sent it back unwashed."

The next day, the Colony's founder treated Charles to more puzzling abuse. It followed the accidental death of a scout-boatman. A cannon, which was fired at the new home-site of William Horton so James Oglethorpe might know where it lay in relation to the settlement, exploded and blew off half the boatman's head. Unfortunately, he lived in shrieking agony until, right in the middle of the morning service, he reached the landing at Frederica. Charles rushed out and found the man senseless and dying.

Though ill with fever, Charles the following evening "was led out to bury" the boatman. Seeing him lying so still and peaceful in the black, narrow yawn in the sandy ground, Charles "envied him his quiet grave"; then secured for himself the old bedstead of the dead man. But once more James Oglethorpe cruelly rebuffed him. He gave away the bedstead from under him and refused to spare him one of the carpenters "to mend" him another. It was a crowning insult.

SEVEN

When Benjamin arrived in Savannah, John noted simply in his Journal: "Mr. Ingham, coming from Frederica, brought me letters, pressing me to go hither." In his Diary, however, John said that they talked first of Savannah and then of Frederica. From the lines that he penned at the foot of the page it is clear that he understood the seriousness of the situation in that southern outpost:

"P. [Prayer]. Mr. Ingham came.

"Talk of! Oh God! meditation; the cross."

The next day John and Delamotte began to fast. In Mr. Curnock's opinion, this action grew out of John's great distress at Benjamin's news. The editor argues in a footnote in *The Journal of John Wesley:*

"This obviously was the beginning of a great fast, undertaken not capriciously or by way of mere experiment, but for some special purpose. The three members of 'our Company' shared it. Its special feature was not abstinence from food and drink for prolonged periods, but the living exclusively on one kind of food, and the simplest—dry bread. It began in, but not with, Lent, and does not seem to have had more than an accidental connexion with the great church fast which was being religiously kept when this inner and quite extraordinary fast commenced. A probable suggestion is that this fast, in its beginning, was connected with the trouble in Frederica—a veritable case, Wesley might believe, of devil possession. Only by prayer and fasting could they hope to cast out these devils that threatened to destroy Charles, Oglethorpe, and a number of persons upon whom they had bestowed so much pastoral care on board the Simmonds."

John, though, offered no explanation. He simply stated: "The next day Mr. Delamotte and I began to try whether life might not as well be sustained by one sort as by a variety of food. We chose to make the experiment with bread; and were never more vigorous and healthy than while we tasted nothing else. 'Blessed are the pure in heart'; who, whether they eat or drink, or whatever they do, have no end therein but to please God! . . ."

John resolved to go at once to his brother and Delamotte resolved to go with him. Benjamin would carry on their duties while they were gone. They were not able, however, to leave for five days. For three of these, exceedingly high winds and heavy rains swept Savannah from the southwest, locking all boats to shore. Hour after hour, the winds and rains tormented the whisk-broom tops of the tall pines; tore off the wide-leafed limbs of magnolias; snatched long, gray swags of Spanish moss out of the live oaks and cypresses and sent them spiraling along the streets; scooped up the loose white sand and hurled it beneath the doors and through the paper panes of those windows without shutters; and beat down the new corn and wheat and kidney beans. Only the low-growing carrots, cabbages, lettuce, cucumbers, radishes, canteloupes, watermelon, gourds, and herbs escaped the storm's fury.

John spent the time of waiting in prayer, meditation, and fasting. The first day that he began the fast of bread and water, he practically abandoned his usual schedule. He did get up at his customary before-dawn hour; but instead of holding the regular early-morning service and walking and breakfasting with Sophy and Elizabeth, he ate his breakfast of dry bread alone, talked with Benjamin about Frederica, visited with Thomas Causton, and, in spite of the wind and rain, walked in the garden, reading his Greek Testament and praying for Charles.

It was ten o'clock before he put in his appearance at the courthouse-church for the prayer service and found Sophy and Elizabeth still waiting for him. Perhaps there were others; but they are the only two he mentioned in his Diary. "After the exposition" he had a "conversation" with them, probably telling them of the situation in Frederica and of his decision to go there.

At three o'clock he ate his second meal of the day—bread —and prayed with Benjamin. Then in the drenched garden, he again prayed and sang. He also spent the five-o'clock hour in praying, singing, and meditation. At six he offered the fast-day prayer with Delamotte and Benjamin and then walked with Benjamin "conversing." In the Diary he used only the word, "conversing"; but assuredly he could have written "questioning, questioning, questioning." Perhaps Benjamin had overlooked some incident or conversation that could throw a little light into the darkness of Frederica. Then John spent some time again in the garden with his Greek Testament in preparation for more prayer and more exposition. Finally he ended the long, long day singing with the Moravians.

The next morning, the wind blowing harder and still from the wrong direction, he grew more anxious about Charles. Picturing him from the details Benjamin had given him—ill with a heavy cold, lying upon the wet ground, his fever-racked mind seething with the puzzling, antagonistic, un-Christian behavior of James Oglethorpe and other parishioners—John was so sure his brother was dying that he could not even pray for him, but spent the hours upon his knees, addressing supplications to God, first, on behalf of James Oglethorpe and second, on behalf of Beata. Then he reversed the order. He was so deeply troubled, however, that he could not attain the peace he needed to commune freely with his Maker and so, after several frustrating attempts, he forced himself into a variety of other activities. He read Greek with Delamotte; he expounded the Scriptures twice; he revised the proofs of a volume of poems that his brother Samuel had written and that Samuel's publisher, Charles Rivington of London, had sent to him; he compiled a catalogue of German hymns; he read his own Journal to Benjamin, and he paid pastoral calls.

The next day he grew more anxious and more restless. Using all his will power to quiet his wildly harassed spirit, he prayed determinedly, again and again, for the Georgia leader, for Beata, and for himself; he finished reading Echard and began two new volumes: *Solid Virtue* and *The Light of the World*.

The third morning dawned fair, with the wind down, but the periagua on which he and Delamotte had taken passage refused—for a reason John did not consider valid—to set out, and he was outdone. "Yet, they will not go!" he cried impatiently in his Diary. A hundred miles to the south his brother more than likely was drawing his last breath and here he was, helplessly caught by indifferent, lazy, rum-sodden boatmen.

Two days later, in spite of the boat still not being ready and no hour set for departure, John and Delamotte went aboard. By their very presence John hoped they might bestir the coxswain and rowers into action. All the action he got, however, was a return of the lowering clouds that sent thunder crashing, lightning blazing, and sheets of rain descending about his head, followed by swarms of black flies that were prevalent this time of year when the wind was offshore.

For twenty-four interminable hours, John and Delamotte

waited on shipboard, both praying for Beata and James Oglethorpe; meditating; conversing; and reading *The Light of the World*. How John must have wished for wings to fly across the acres of swamp, marsh, pine barren, winding rivers, creeks, and gaping inlets that separated him from Charles.

At long last the anchor was hoisted and the lines cast off.

The trip was uneventful until the second night when the periagua anchored in about fifteen feet of water, a little off-shore from Skidoway Island. It was hoped the distance from land would save them from the black flies; but the maneuver failed. The flies attacked by the hundreds, the thousands, the millions. John wrapped himself up from head to foot in his long, heavy cloak and lay down on the quarterdeck.

"Between one and two," so he wrote in his Journal, "I waked under water, being so fast asleep that I did not find where I was till my mouth was full of it. Having left my cloak, I know not how, upon deck, I swam round to the other side of the periagua, where a boat was tied, and climbed up by the rope without any hurt more than wetting my clothes. Thou art the God of whom cometh salvation; Thou art the Lord by whom we escape death."

It took five days to make the trip. Often the wind was against them and they were unable to use their sails, and frequently the many open inlets they crossed were choppy with waves. John fortunately had brought plenty to read. Besides *The Light of the World*, he had his Greek Testament, Thomas à Kempis, prayer books, and his Bible. He whiled away many hours, singing alternately with Delamotte verses of the hymns they had learned from the Moravians, and he prayed. Mostly, as he had done in Savannah, he prayed for Beata and the Georgia founder; but once he prayed for Benjamin and once for all the parishioners of Savannah and Frederica. If he prayed for "Miss Sophy," he did not mention it.

They finally reached Frederica late on the afternoon of April 10 and, though Charles had been waked by Mr. Reed, whose palmetto hut he occupied, with the news that his brother and Delamotte were nearing the landing, he was not there to meet them. James Oglethorpe, however, "came on board" and, in John's words, greeted him "with the utmost love." It was apparent that the Colony's founder felt no animosity toward him; whatever it was that Charles had done to alienate his chief did not involve John. For the hundredth time John must have wondered what in God's name was Charles's crime.

While Delamotte was transferring his and John's chests to the Storehouse, where they were to stay while in Frederica, John hurried to Charles's palmetto bower. "I found my brother exceedingly weak," John recorded, "having for some time been ill of the flux. But he mended from the hour he saw me."

Indeed, Charles was so weak, John had to help him into the woods where they went to talk so as not to be heard, for, as Charles wrote in his Journal, "there was no talking among a people of spies and ruffians; nor even in the woods unless in an unknown tongue." (The Reverend Mr. Moore says in a footnote to this quotation in his *John Wesley* that the brothers conversed in Latin.)

The next morning—Sunday, April 11—at the misty dawn hour of five, John again joined Charles and then John, as he wrote in his Diary, "heard Charles's diary!!!!"

Despite Benjamin's having told John at length of the goings-on in Frederica, Charles's account, judging from those four exclamation points, came as a terrific shock.

He had to lay aside the Diary at eight to read prayers and expound. Afterward he talked with Ann Welch, noting briefly that she was "serious, open." Later he discussed her with Charles. At eleven, Charles had strength enough to consecrate at the Sacrament; but John had to perform the rest of

105

the service. He preached in the Storehouse, just a few feet away from the pallet on which he had spent the night.

Innumerable romantic statements recount that John preached to the Indians under a live oak on St. Simons, but there are no facts to substantiate this story. (The live oak of this legend blew down in a big wind in August, 1954, and from its generous trunk many beautiful, highly polished crosses have been carved. One hangs in the Georgia Room of the Wesleyan College Library in Macon, Georgia.)

Actually, neither John, Charles, Francis Moore, Benjamin Ingham, nor any other colonists of the period ever mentioned John preaching under any tree to any Indians. John, at this stage of his ministry, did not believe in holding religious services out of doors; it was only years later, when the Episcopal churches of England were closed to him, that he came around to preaching in the open. And he certainly never delivered a sermon, or even any part of a sermon, to Indians in Georgia. We shall see as his story proceeds that John was not permitted to preach to the Indians; nor did he ever find, as he himself said later, any Indians "who had the least desire of being instructed." Apparently he did not take seriously the invitation Tomochichi had extended to him on the *Simmonds*.

As to the allegation that Charles preached under the now fallen oak, that could well be for, before the Storehouse was finished, he did hold services out of doors, though never once did he mention having an Indian among his listeners.

John had a large congregation on that first Sunday of his stay on St. Simons. As the news had spread that the despised Charles was too ill to occupy the pulpit, many who had been staying away put in their appearance.

The next morning James Oglethorpe took John and Charles to breakfast with Beata. "The modest Mrs. Hawkins," Charles called her. What a bitter pill this must have been for Charles, who was now confident he was eating with a prostitute. Just the day before, he had written in his Journal: "I was fully persuaded of the truth of Mrs. Welch's information against Mr. Oglethorpe, Mrs. Hawkins, and herself."

However, John, with his trusting nature, could not yet bring himself to believe the worst of Beata. His Diary of the next six days is the deadliest give-away to his simplicity—truly, the simplicity of a child where women in general were concerned—and to his total blindness in dealing with Beata in particular. He wanted to see no wrong in her and so, for an incredibly long period, he saw none.

Daily, almost hourly, he hurried in his energetic, purposeful fashion from Beata to Ann, from Ann to Beata, and from them both to James Oglethorpe, talking, talking, talking. . . . There was no end to his patience. On the fifth day of his visit, he reported exultantly: "Mrs. Hawkins and Oglethorpe seem innocent! Amen!"

They seemed innocent because the Georgia leader said so. John had marched into the founder's tent that day and told him directly what the settlers were saying about him and Beata. He wanted to accuse him also of sleeping with Ann, but since Charles had given Ann his word that he would not reveal to James Oglethorpe what she had revealed to him of their intimacy, John felt bound to hold his tongue.

"Thank you, Mr. Wesley," James Oglethorpe answered, unruffled. "I consider your coming to me an act of friendship. I always prefer to be accused to my face rather than to be talked about behind my back." Then he added casually, "Naturally, Mr. Wesley, I don't regard the accusations as seriously as you do. It is not such things as these that hurt my character; they would pass for gallantries and rather commend me to the world——"

"O, my dear sir," John interrupted, shocked, "how terribly mistaken you are! Such a scandal as this could destroy the Colony."

A slight smile, with a touch of condescension and amusement must have touched James Oglethorpe's full lips as he replied, "I very much doubt it, Mr. Wesley, but since you

107

are so troubled about it and since I hold you in the highest esteem and would like you to hold me in equal esteem, I will tell you there is no truth in this story."

Encouraged by Oglethorpe's apparent openness and friendliness, John persuaded Charles to overlook past rebuffs and go once more to request the items he so sorely needed. Having made the requests, Charles got up to go; but his chief called him back.

"I hear, Mr. Wesley," he began in icy tones, "you have spread several reports about me and Mrs. Hawkins. There is a great difference, you know, between telling such things to another and telling them to me. In you, who told them to your brother, it is a scandal; in him, who repeated them to me, it is friendship."

Charles was so taken aback, he could not find voice to answer.

James Oglethorpe, seeing that Charles was not going to reply, went on: "My religion, unlike the Pharisees, does not consist in long prayers, but in forgiving injuries as I, Mr. Wesley, forgive you this injury."

At this Charles did find his voice. "First, Mr. Oglethorpe, I want to say that since you suppose me guilty of spreading scandal about you, it is the greatest possible kindness that you forgive me. But I deny the whole charge. I have neither raised this report nor spread it, but wherever I heard it, I checked it immediately. Some who themselves spoke it in my hearing have, I suppose, gone to you and fathered their words upon me. As for my telling the stories to John instead of to you, I did that simply because he was in your favour and I was not."

James Oglethorpe replied indifferently, "All right, Mr. Wesley, we will let by-gones be by-gones. I promise I'll be the same toward you as I used to be."

The last day of John's stay in Frederica, he again sought out James Oglethorpe, still hoping to get to the heart of this loathsome, intricate web. But the Colony's leader was in no mood for further talk. Having discovered that John was a much better secretary than Charles, he pressed him into many hours of letter writing. Eight, nine, ten o'clock . . . he was still writing for him. Then none other than Beata showed up. ". . . she very angry, sad," reported John.

Finally at noon he was free of his secretarial duties and immediately plunged into his search for the truth. He talked with practically everyone he thought might help him solve the mystery. He was like a little frustrated terrier with a leather-covered doll clamped between his teeth, shaking it, beating it against sharp surfaces, determined to get at the stuffing inside. When night came, he was still at it.

Charles, too, was busy. He went again to see Ann. His once cheerful, cherubic face appeared long and pale and his voice was accusing: "Mrs. Welch, you have deeply injured me," he said. "I never built upon Mr. Oglethorpe's friendship; for I have no worldly expectations. But you have turned my best friend into an enemy for life. . . . Why should you even invent falsehoods to hurt me and say to Mrs. Hawkins, and to Mr. Oglethorpe that I raised the report about them! Did I deserve this at your hands? Was this gratitude?"

"Lo, very far from it," Ann confessed. "I know not what I meant. I was mad. I was out of my senses. . . ."

After many more protestations, Charles broke in curtly, ". . . Answer me, sincerely. Are you not in love with Mr. Oglethorpe? And did you not invent all these falsehoods to gain credit with my brother and thereby employ him to throw out Mrs. Hawkins and so make room for yourself?"

"You say the very thing," Ann wailed. " 'Tis so."

Charles left then, but an hour later he was back. He had made up his mind to tell Ann that he intended to set James Oglethorpe right "as she, in justice to him, ought to have done."

"I have been almost distracted at the thought of my treatment of you," she answered. "That I should have incensed

Mr. Oglethorpe to such a devilish outrage! That I should be the devil's instrument in crushing you, in destroying the innocent! The devil surely was in me. I raised Mr. Oglethorpe's suspicion of you. I complained of you being . . . troublesome to me. . . ."

Charles could hardly believe his ears. "How did I provoke you to do it?" he cried out in bewilderment. "Did you receive aught but good from me?"

"No. But Mrs. Hawkins was continually instigating me to it, saying we must supplant these parsons and then we shall have Mr. Oglethorpe to ourselves. . . . You accuse Charles Wesley to him, and I will accuse the other. . . ."

At last he had unearthed the reason for James Oglethorpe's contempt. If the Georgia founder belived that he, his secretary and spiritual adviser, had made improper advances to Ann Welch, no wonder he despised him. He, a servant of God, lusting after a married woman!

When Charles repeated this conversation to his brother, John was, in Charles's words, "utterly confused." And still "utterly confused" and confounded, he, with Delamotte, set out for Savannah the next day.

EIGHT

At ten thirty in the morning of the day John and Delamotte were to arrive back in Savannah, they were still many watery miles from their destination. On an unfamiliar shore they had a meal of oysters; then set out in a "hard rain." After three rough hours, they reached Thunderbolt, a village on the Wilmington River, where they disembarked and took a short cut through the dense woods and swamps to Savannah, a distance of approximately five miles.

That evening at seven forty-five John had prayers and expounded. At eight thirty he went to the House of the Moravians for more prayers and expounding and singing (he did so love to sing!), and there he fell sound asleep in the midst of the service. With what sympathy and gentle amusement the Brethren must have eyed him! This little bundle of enthusiasm and energy deep in sleep. Naturally they did not disturb him; however, at nine thirty he waked, hurried back to the parsonage for "conversation and prayer and singing with Benjamin and Delamotte."

111

He was overjoyed to be back in Savannah. "Oh, blessed place," he caroled in his Journal, "where having but one end in view, dissembling and fraud are not; but each of us can pour out his heart without fear into his brother's bosom."

He also said as much and more to James Oglethorpe when he wrote him the next day:

"Savannah was never so dear to me as now. I believe, knowing by whom I send this I may write as well as speak frankly, I found so little, either of the form or power of religion at Frederica, that I am sincerely glad I am removed from it. Surely never was any place, no not London itself, freer from one vice, I mean hypocrisy.

"*O curve in terrie animae, et coelastium manes*! [O groveling souls, bent to the earth, and void of heavenly good!]

"Jesus Master have mercy upon them! There is none of those who did run well whom I pity more than Mrs. Hawkins; her treating me in such a manner would indeed have little affected me had my own interests only been concerned. I have been used to be betrayed, scorned and insulted by those I had most laboured to serve. Yet when I reflect on her condition my heart bleeds for her—Yet with Thee nothing is impossible!"

John then boldly pointed an accusing finger at the Georgia founder himself. "With regard to one who ought to be dearer to me than her, I cannot but say that the more I think of it the more convinced I am that no one, without a virtual renouncing of the faith, can abstain from the public as well as the private worship of God. All the prayers usually read morning and evening, at Frederica and here, put together, do not last seven minutes. These cannot be termed long prayers: no Christian assembly ever used shorter: neither have they any repetitions in them at all. If I did not speak thus plainly to you,which I fear no one else in England or America will do, I should by no means be worthy to call myself, Sir,

"Yours, etc. John Wesley"

In the letter John wrote to Charles the same day he did not

1. The Stairs going up.
2. Mr. Oglethorpe's Tent.
3. The Crane & Bell.
4. The Tabernacle & Court-House.
5. The publick Mill.
6. The House for Strangers.
7. The publick Oven.
8. The draw Well.

To the Honble the Trustees for establishi.

This View of the Town of Savanah is h

VUE de Savanah dan

Map of Savannah, Georgia, as it appeared in 1734, just prior to Wesley's first voyage.

Colony of Georgia in America.
dedicated by their Honours
Obliged and most Obedient Servant,
Georgie.   Peter Gordon

9. The Lott for the Church.
10. The publick Stores.
11. The Fort.
12. The Parsonage House.
13. The Pallisadoes.
14. The Guard House and
    Battery of Cannon.
15. Hutchinsons Island.

*John Wesley as a Fellow of
Lincoln College, Oxford.*

*John and Charles
Wesley contemplat-
ing their morning
devotions.*

*(Courtesy Abingdon
Press)*

rejoice over his return to Savannah. Why make his brother feel any worse about that beastly place, Frederica, than he already felt? He concentrated on Beata, though he had already written Charles one letter about her from the boat. He said in part:

"I still extremely pity poor Mrs. Hawkins; but what can I do more till God show me who it is that continually exasperates her against me? Then I may perhaps be of some service to her."

These two urgent letters and other papers out of the way, he had a long conversation with Sophy and Martha Causton; then a second one with Sophy alone, and from that hour on his Diary is sprinkled with such notations as "Miss Sophy open and much affected," "Miss Sophy, who is open, came in the early morning," and the especially joyous one to the effect that one Sunday after Holy Communion he had "an impressive conversation with Miss Sophy alone, her friend being with Mrs. Musgrove."

Did John realize the significance of that last happy notation? Did he understand that being with "Miss Sophy alone" stirred his heart to such an extent that he was moved to the point of recording it? Was he aware that he was drifting into a relationship that would submerge him in a torrential whirlpool of passion? It is very doubtful, for, like a celibate priest, he had dedicated his life to God.

As we remember, in his letter to Dr. Burton, accepting the call to Georgia, he had expressed his aspiration to attain that state "wherein they neither marry nor are given in marriage" and in the early days of his ministry in Savannah he implored Charles to pray that he would not "know after the flesh" the young women he had met there.

If he did suspect danger ahead in his almost daily association with Sophy, he did nothing at this juncture to circumvent it. In fact, he moved back into the same hour-by-hour routine as if he had never been away. Once again he resumed his old schedule of two daily church services; Bible reading,

113

prayer, and meditation; the instruction of Sophy and Elizabeth in the Scriptures; pastoral calls (because of the midday heat, he visited between twelve and three o'clock, when he was confident of finding his parishioners at home taking their siestas); the study of German with the Moravians; the translation of German hymns; and the catechizing of the boys in Delamotte's school.

The school now had between thirty and forty boys, who presumably had their classes in the courthouse-church. There is no record in John's Journal and Diaries of his taking a hand in their education other than to catechize all of them on Saturday afternoons and on Sundays before the evening service and to lecture a selected few after the Second Lesson on Sunday; but an appealing story of a week John spent with them is related by B. L. Tyerman and other biographers.

"A part of the boys in Delamotte's school wore stockings and shoes, and the others not," the Reverend Mr. Tyerman recounts. "The former ridiculed the latter. Delamotte tried to put a stop to this uncourteous banter but told Wesley he had failed. Wesley replied, 'I think I can cure it. If you will take charge of my school [John must have been referring to the lessons he gave Sophy and Elizabeth and other young people] next week I will take charge of yours and will try.'

"The exchange was made and on Monday morning Wesley came into the schoolroom barefoot. The children seemed surprised but, without any reference to past jeerings, Wesley kept them at their work. Before the week was ended, the shoeless ones began to gather courage; and some of the others, seeing their minister and master come without shoes and stockings, began to copy his example, and thus the evil was effectually cured."

Still, in spite of John's full routine, he was not satisfied with the progress he was making. He felt he should do more to deepen and enrich his own life and the lives of his parishioners. So, with the help of John Toltschig and the Moravian bishop, Anton Seifart, he drew up a list of people to form what he described as "a sort of little society and to meet once or twice a week, in order to reprove, instruct, and exhort one another," and also an "inner circle" to meet on Sunday afternoons.

John was delighted with the organization. It reminded him of the group he had led in Oxford. This regular coming together to study and to strengthen one another's faith was a continuation, he liked to think, of that original conception of several years before.

(Later he was to divide the origin of Methodism into three distinct periods. "The first rise of Methodism was in Nov., 1729, when four of us met together at Oxford," he wrote; "the second was in Savannah, in April 1736, when twenty or thirty persons met at my house; the last was on this day, May 1, [1738] when forty or fifty of us agreed to meet together every Wednesday evening, in order to [have] free conversation, begun [beginning] and end [ending] with singing and prayer.")

The membership of the Savannah Society was largely German, leading the Reverend Mr. Curnock to point out in a footnote in *The Journal of John Wesley* that "the plan was a Moravian graft upon the Oxford Methodist stock." Among the English minority were Sophy, Elizabeth, James Burnside; two sisters, Becky and Margaret Bovey, who lived on Duke Street—one door from Drayton, in sight of the parsonage—and a young Hollander, William Appee.

The presence of the Bovey sisters, without a male in their household, was a mysterious phenomenon in the Colony that has never been explained. According to the terms drawn up by the Trustees for the settling of Georgia, only men could be allotted houses and land. To every fifty acres of land there had to be at least one freeholder for the protection of the Colony and the cultivation of the crops. In case the head of the family died, the house and fifty acres reverted to the Trustees to be reallotted. Yet here were those unattached women living

115

in the house that had been originally signed to one Thomas Pratt, who had forfeited it the year before by picking up his few worldly goods and, without even so much as by-your-leave, departing from Savannah.

The Hollander, William Appee, who had come over on the *London Merchant*, was a frail-looking young man. According to an unsubstantiated story that circulated about Savannah, William had offered to go to Frederica with the new settlers, but the Georgia founder had refused to take him. Using as an excuse the dandified way the young man was dressed—buckskin weskit, coat and breeches—James Oglethorpe said, "With all due respect to you, Mr. Appee, I don't believe you comprehend sufficiently the hardships that lie ahead."

For some hours William had nursed his wounded feelings; then, flinging aside his wig and fine clothes, he had dressed in a plain, polka-dotted shirt, dark gray serge coat and leathern breeches and again presented himself to the Colony's leader. This time James Oglethorpe told him the truth. Though the dandified dress on the Georgia coast, without the proper occasion, had been distasteful to him, he had a more serious reason for turning Appee down. "Frankly, sir," he said, "you do not impress me as strong enough to stand up under the rains and winds and cold that everyone going to Frederica must endure. Nevertheless, I tend you my thanks."

William had been in Savannah only a little over two months, but he was already in love with the younger Bovey sister, Becky.

James Burnside, another member of the Society, had arrived in Georgia in December, 1733, apparently with the expectation of being a schoolteacher, for on September 15, 1735, he wrote the Trustees: "As you have by license empowered me to instruct the youth of this province in writing and accounts . . . ," but somehow he switched to keeping the accounts for the Store and doing other odd bookkeeping jobs.

116

Not all John's parishioners were as pious and diligent in good works as these members of the newly formed organization. Some, indeed, bucked out of the traces completely. Surprisingly, two of these were Henry Parker, the Second Bailiff, and his wife Anne. Their antagonism began at the baptismal font over their newborn daughter. John was determined to dip the infant three times in water as the Rubric directed in the First Edw. VI Prayer-book, while the Parkers were just as determined their infant should be sprinkled.

"Neither Mr. Parker or I will consent to its being dipped," insisted Anne.

"If you certify that your child is weak, it will suffice to pour water upon it," replied John, following that provision of the Rubric.

"Nay, the child is not weak," declared Anne, "but I am resolved it shall not be dipped."

At this, John, with his little quick steps, marched out of the church.

Though he was doing only what his careful conscience dictated, this act did not endear him to the great majority of his flock. As Robert Southey mourns in his biography of John: "All might have continued well, could he but have remembered the advice of Dr. Burton to consider his parishioners as babes in their progress and therefore to feed them with milk. Instead of this, he drenched them with the physic of an intolerant discipline."

Wesley's contemporary biographer, John Hampson, also criticizes him frankly and objectively for this narrow outlook: "[The] Colonists have general been remarked as an obstinate and ungovernable people, but perhaps the fault was not wholly in the Georgians. The Americans were not to be managed, but by a delicate and skilful hand. His father [John's] had . . . observed to him, that in order to do good to mankind, 'a particular talent is necessary, great prudence as well as fervor.' Mr. Wesley's conduct (to say the least of it) was, on many occasions, capricious and fanciful; in some instances, absolute and despotic. He gave great offence by insisting upon baptizing their children by immersion, which, though provided in the rubric, was not at all necessary, and which no clergyman did but himself. . . ."

No one grieved more in later years over the "intolerant discipline" of his Georgia days than John himself. About twelve years after the termination of his pastorate in Savannah, he inserted in his Journal "a beautiful letter," written to him in September, 1749, by John Martin Bolzius, his Salzburger friend, to which he added this abject comment: "What a truly Christian piety and simplicity breathe in these lines! And, yet, this very man, when I was in Savannah did I refuse to admit to the Lord's table because he was not baptized; that is not baptized by a minister who had been especially ordained. Can any one carry high church zeal higher than this? How well have I since been beaten with my own staff."

Alas, in 1736, John's spirit had not yet been "regenerated by that power from on high," and instead of learning from the resentful attitude of the Parkers to loosen the tight ecclesiastical reins with which he drove his flock and himself, he pulled them even tighter. The following Sunday he announced that from that day forth he would follow the laws of the Church of England even more strictly and, beginning the next Sunday, he would divide the public service according to the original appointment of the Church, still observed in a few places in the British Isles. The morning service would be at five o'clock, the communion and sermon at eleven, and the evening service at three.

There was also one other innovation on this Sunday, May 9. John began that day to hold services in the new courthouse-church, "a large and convenient place," as he described it, between Duke and St. Julian Streets, facing Percival Square. It was fashioned of wood, as the old building had been, with a variety of benches, one of which was decidedly more elegant than the others and slightly elevated. In front of this bench and below it was a plain table of "equal use" for sacred and civil purposes. (Shortly after 1736 a colonnade or cloister, encompassing the front and both sides of the building, was added to help dispel the heat. "Otherwise," one anonymous writer explained, "the heat was so strong upon the house 'twas hardly to be bourne.")

Following these changes, John was stricken with a boil on his leg that grew angry and inflamed with what Dr. Tailfer diagnosed as St. Anthony's fire. John was compelled to give up his pastoral duties and take to his pallet.

The boil had not yet subsided when Charles, completely recovered in body, if not in mind, arrived in Savannah in his role of Secretary of Indian Affairs to meet with a convention of traders concerning the issue of licenses permitting them to trade with the tribes within the boundaries of Georgia. Charles could not hide his pleasure at being there. "I'm overjoyed at my deliverance out of the furnace of Frederica," he declared; then, somewhat ruefully he added, "And not a little ashamed of myself for being so."

He had much personal news to tell John and Delamotte about Frederica, but the hour being late, as he noted in his Journal, they "each retired to his respective corner of the room where, without the help of a bed, we slept soundly until the morning." Then, probably referring frequently to his Journal, he related the happenings that had befallen him since John's and Delamotte's departure.

On the day before Easter, April 24, at ten in the morning, he told John, he had been sent for by James Oglethorpe. "Mr. Wesley, you know what has passed between us," the Georgia founder began without any preliminaries, holding in his outstretched hand some sheets of foolscap. "I took some pains to satisfy your brother about his reports concerning me, but in vain. He here renews his suspicions in writing. I did desire to convince him, because I had an esteem for him. . . . I could clear up all, but it matters not. You will soon see the reasons for my actions."

Then, dramatically tossing the letter aside, the founder announced: "I am now going to my death. You will see me no more." He picked up a ring from his desk and offered it to Charles. "Take this ring and carry it to Mr. Vernon. If there is a friend to be depended upon, he is one. His interest is next to Sir Robert's [Sir Robert Walpole, who was also one of the Georgia Trustees]. Whatever you ask within his power he will do for you, your brother and your family. These letters show that the Spaniards have long been seducing our allies and intend to cut us off at a blow. I fall by my friends: Gascoigne, who has not yet come with the Man-of-War [during the voyage across the Atlantic, the *Hawk* had been separated in a storm from the *Simmonds* and *London Merchant*] and the Carolina people who have not yet sent their promised succours. But death to me is nothing. I will pursue all my designs and to Him I recommend them and you."

He then handed Charles the ring, which was set with a large diamond. Charles accepted it, but with no words of appreciation. Speaking as dramatically as his chief, Charles said, so he reported without a blush: "If, as I believe, these are my last words to you, hear what you will quickly know to be true as soon as you are entered upon the separate state. This ring I shall never make any use of for myself. I have no worldly hopes. I have renounced the world. Life is bitterness to me. I come hither to lay it down.

"You have been deceived as well as I. I protest my innocence of the crimes I am charged with, and take myself to be now at liberty to tell you what I thought never to have uttered.

"Mrs. Welch excited in me the first suspicion of you after we were come here. She afterwards told you her own words as if they had been mine . . . as likewise that she had falsely accused me to you of making love to her. She was put upon it by Mrs. Hawkins, saying, 'Let us supplant these parsons, and we shall have General [this title the Reverend Elijah Hoole, who interpreted Charles's journal, put mistakenly into Beata's mouth, for as we have already noted the Georgia founder had no title at this time] Oglethorpe to ourselves.' "

When Charles had finished "this relation," his chief seemed entirely changed and "full of his old love and confidence" in him. Indeed his warm attitude gave Charles sufficient assurance for him to ask, "Are you satisfied?" To which Oglethorpe replied, "Yes, entirely."

At this, Charles exclaimed, "Why then, sir, I desire nothing more upon earth; and care not how soon I follow you."

This declaration turned out to be a needless piece of heroics on Charles's part, for just a few days after James Oglethorpe left for the south, he was safely back. Charles was at the landing to meet him and gratefully blessed God "for still holding his soul in life." That evening they took a walk together and Charles returned the ring, declaring, "Sir, I need not, indeed I cannot tell you how joyfully and thankfully I return this!"

The next day, still in his mellow mood, James Oglethorpe begged Charles to ask him for whatever he could think of that he wanted, and even went so far as to promise to have a house built for him immediately, all of which so softened Charles that he was convinced of his chief's innocence. In fact, he was so convinced and overjoyed, he took it upon himself to convince Francis Moore of it. Francis, however, would accept none of this and, to back his opinion, showed Charles a list of the officers to be announced for Frederica. And who should be appointed First Bailiff but Charles's anathema, Dr. Hawkins?

Once more Charles was plunged into a morass of doubts, as were John and Delamotte and Benjamin when they heard this news; but they need not have been freshly troubled if they had only known that in the minutes of the common council of the Trustees as far back as September 26, 1735, was this item of business:

"Read a deed appointing Thomas Hawkins, Samuel Perkins and Edward Addison, bailiffs, Francis Moore, recorder, and William Allen, tything men of Town of Frederica."

So Charles was the bearer of much information of deep concern to John, but what concerned him most was what was going to happen to the poor people of Frederica in Charles's absence. After considerable discussion, it was decided that John and Benjamin should take turns in serving them. John would take the first turn.

NINE

Just a few hours before John, still in pain from the St. Anthony's fire, set out for Frederica, he mentioned in his Diary: "At six Mrs. Causton and Miss Sophy came." It was his first written reference to Sophy since he had fallen ill and been confined to the parsonage. Not only had she not visited him, apparently, during that time, but even when she did come to say good-by, she was chaperoned by her aunt.

He gave no intimation of his feelings on leaving her; but on reaching Frederica his very first move was a visit to James Oglethorpe to talk to him about Sophy and Elizabeth. He discussed a plan he had conceived of having the two girls come to Frederica when his presence was next required there so their Bible lessons need not be interrupted.

This attended to, he began a long day of pastoral duties, ending in the evening with another visit with the Georgia founder. He read him his Journal; not all of it, to be sure, but the lengthy sections concerning the Frederica machinations. Then, at one o'clock in the morning, he talked of Beata and

123

Ann; at two of Frederica and Savannah; and at three of
"Oglethorpe's life and company he affected." Finally, at four
o'clock, John slept. As he had been up since five thirty of the
preceding morning, he had had a day of twenty-three and a
half hours.

And so the days continued, as long and crowded as days
could be. To illustrate with just one more: On Wednesday,
May 26, three days after his arrival, he waked early and
prayed for Frederica. Then he conversed with Ann; with
William Appee, who was visiting in that southern outpost;
with James Oglethorpe—this time about Mrs. Lawley—and
with all the other members of the Frederica parish whom he
could corner. And when he wasn't conversing, he was singing and conducting services of prayer and exposition. The
Diary entries, except for the one next to the last, sound all too
familiar. The unusual one reads: "Q. Is she in love?" Of
whom was John thinking? Beata? Ann? Elizabeth? Of
Sophy? More and more frequently as his interest in her deep-
ened, he must have wondered whether Sophy was still in love
with Tommy Mellichamp.

It was on Beata, however, that he now concentrated his
pastoral efforts. In spite of all she had said and done, he still
hoped to save her soul. He visited her again and again and
read her passages from Gother's *Sinners Complaint to God*
until she furiously rebelled and refused to hear it.

"In fact, Mr. Wesley, I don't intend to listen any longer to
any subject dealing with religion," she declared emphatically.

John was shocked. "Why, Mrs. Hawkins, if I can't talk to
you about religion, I will talk to you about nothing else."

That gave her a perfect opening to retort saucily, "That
suits me," which made John realize he should not have
spoken with such finality. He should have known she had too
much spirit to be threatened. He decided to try reason. "Suppose, ma'm, you were going to a country where everyone

spoke Latin and understood no other language and neither would converse with any that did not understand it; and suppose one was sent here a short time on purpose to teach it to you; suppose that person, pleased with your company, should spend his time trifling with you and teaching you nothing of what he came for, would that be well done?

"Yet, this is our case. You are going to a country where everyone speaks the love of God. The citizens of heaven understand no other language. They converse with none who do not understand it. Indeed, none such are admitted there."

Doubtless Beata gazed fixedly at him, her gay face brimming with amused wonder.

Still he went ahead: "Mrs. Hawkins, I am sent from God to teach you this. A few days are allotted to us for that purpose. Would it then be well done in me, because I was pleased with your company, to spend this short time in trifling and teaching you nothing of what I came for?"

Answering his own rhetorical question, he exclaimed, "God forbid! I will rather not to converse with you at all. Of the two extremes, this is the best."

Beata must have caroled wickedly, "Do you solemnly promise, Mr. Wesley?" for, indignant, he left the room.

Yet he returned again and again, trying by every wile he could think of to win her for his Master. Even when she was the one who threw down the gauntlet, he came back. Once she screamed, "I utterly renounce your friendship!" and he quietly accepted it with a dignified, "Be it so"; but after a restless night, during which not only his spirit troubled him but also the fleas of his moss pallet, he was in the throes of composition for four full hours, struggling to write a letter that would soften her as none of his spoken words had done.

Still he made no progress. Not with her; nor with Dr. Hawkins; nor with Ann Welch. He even made a new enemy, William Horton, who had never been overly fond of him since the maid episode on the *Simmonds* but had nevertheless treated him politely since their arrival in Georgia. Now, however, he displayed such coldness that John inquired the reason for it.

"Do you really want to know, Parson?" William questioned.

"Yes, Mr. Horton, I'm truly desirous of knowing."

"Well, Parson, to be perfectly frank with you, I like nothing you do. All your sermons are satires upon particular persons, therefore I will never hear you more; and all the people are of my mind, for we won't hear ourselves abused.

"Besides, they say they are Protestants. But as for you, they cannot tell what religion you are of. They never heard of such religion before. They do not know what to make of it." The longer William talked, the angrier he became. "And then your private behaviour—all the quarrels that have been here since you came have been 'long of you. Indeed, there is neither man nor woman in the town who minds a word you say. And so you may preach all you wish, but nobody will come to hear you."

Realizing that William was too furious to listen to his side of the matter, John said stiffly, "I thank you, sir, for your openness," and walked away.

The visit to Frederica, however, was not all loss. Besides paving the way for Sophy to come to Frederica on his next tour, John succeeded in getting under way, on the acre lot set aside for religious purposes, the house that James Oglethorpe had promised Charles. Almost daily he spent many hours there, rounding up the laborers, encouraging them to work steadily, and even taking a hand himself in the actual carpentry. The house, like the parsonage in Savannah, was to serve two purposes. It would be a home for the Wesleys and Benjamin and Delamotte when they were on St. Simons and also a meeting place for small religious groups.

The latter was the more urgent in John's opinion and so, just as soon as the building was habitable, he announced plans for the formation of an intimate company, similar to

126

the one in Savannah. It was to meet on Sunday afternoons and in the evenings after the public service "to spend some time in singing, reading and conversation." He felt that Frederica, especially, needed a closely associated band of earnest Christians. He already suspected that Charles would not return to this "furnace" in the role of minister and he feared that Benjamin and he would be able to come only periodically. If he could create a social force—a spiritual, united, consecrated "Company"—then a successful religious life might be cultivated.

The first meeting of the Society was attended only by Delamotte and one convert, Mark Hird, the young constable. Undaunted by this inauspicious beginning, the indefatigable John led them in prayer, singing, and conversation for an hour. To the next meeting, one more came; to the next, three more. They began the study of Law's *Christian Perfection*.

Ten days later John left Frederica and returned to Savannah. On the very first day back he saw Sophy at the Caustons'; then became enthusiastically involved with the many Indians who had come to Savannah to meet James Oglethorpe. The Indians were everywhere; at night they took over the parsonage completely, forcing its occupants to sleep in the garden until they found refuge with the Germans.

Of all the representatives of the various tribes milling about the town, John was most impressed with the Choctaws. He felt they were the "least polished, that is, the least corrupt," and, as he was not yet disillusioned by the "savages" and their desire for salvation, he decided that he would like to begin immediately his missionary work among them. But when he broached the matter, the Georgia founder objected because, John noted in his Journal, "of the danger of being intercepted or killed by the French there, but much more, the inexpediency of leaving Savannah destitute of a minister."

Henry Moore, in his biography, insists James Oglethorpe's objection was part of his plot to keep John in Savannah in order to give him the necessary time to fall in love with and marry Sophy, but Mr. Curnock considers Oglethorpe's decision simply a smart diplomatic move. In a footnote in *The John Wesley Journal*, Dr. Curnock says ". . . whatever may have been Oglethorpe's antecedent convictions with reference to the desirability of such a mission, his present conviction was clear and decisive, namely, that Wesley had a peculiar fitness for work among the colonists. . . . In John Wesley Oglethorpe had discovered, providentially as he believed, a man of extraordinary capacity and aptitude for affairs. The Indian mission might be important, even from a political point of view, but not in comparison with the new colony."

As was John's custom when "anything of consequence" confronted him, he took the matter up that very evening with the Moravians, and heard it was their opinion, too, that he should not yet go among the Indians.

From John's writings it does not appear that he felt particularly thwarted. He began the study of a new language, Spanish (he already knew French, German, Greek, Latin and, of course, English); and, it now being July and exceedingly hot and humid, he indulged himself in his favorite sport—swimming—in the Savannah River. He reported himself as "lively" and "in the water with Charles and Delamotte" one morning at four o'clock. That is the beginning and end of John's account of that before-dawn dip; but Charles added some scalp-tingling details in his Journal.

"We chose this hour for bathing," he wrote, "both for the coolness and because the alligators were not stirring so soon. We heard them, indeed, snoring all around us; and one very early riser swam by within a few yards of us. On Friday morning we had hardly left our usual place of swimming when we saw an alligator in possession of it. Once afterwards Mr. Delamotte was in great danger, for an alligator rose just behind him, and pursued him to the land whither he narrowly escaped."

John also methodically went on with his many clerical duties and pastoral calls. One of these was a hurried evening visit to the Bovey sisters. He had heard Becky was not well; but on reaching the house he found she had "only prickly heat, a sort of rash" very common in Savannah in summer. Still, the call was not wasted. Becky and the older sister, Margaret, and he fell into a serious conversation during which he asked, "Do you not think you are too young to trouble yourselves with religion?" and received the more-than-acceptable reply, "If it will be reasonable ten years hence to be religious, it is so now. I am not deferring for one moment."

In a few days he called again and discovered James Burnside there. James was courting Margaret, though John did not suspect it at the time. Just four days later John went back, "determined now to speak more closely," but "prudence" induced him to put it off as company was again present—company probably consisting of William Appee, who was now acknowledged as Becky's fiancé; Margaret's suitor, James; and Sophy and Elizabeth, who were dear friends of the Boveys.

Very shortly after that afternoon, just as the Bovey sisters finished tea, Margaret, seeing Becky's color change, asked if she was ill. Receiving no answer and fortunately catching a glimpse of Dr. Tailfer strolling by, she called urgently to him to come in.

"Sir, my sister is not well," she explained.

He looked earnestly at her, felt her pulse, and replied, "Well, madam, your sister is dying!" However, he thought it not impossible bleeding might help. She bled about an ounce, leaned back and died.

The minute John heard this news, he hurried to the house and, so he wrote, ". . . begged they would not lay her out immediately, there being a possibility, at least, she might only be in a swoon; of which, indeed, there was some slight hope, she not only being as warm as ever, but having a fresh

129

colour in her cheeks, and a few drops of blood starting out upon bending her arm; but there was no pulse and no breath; so that, having waited some hours, we found her 'spirit was indeed returned to God that gave it.' "

John must have spent most of the night at the Bovey home, doing all he could to comfort Margaret, for Charles Wesley wrote in his Journal, "I was waked by the news my brother brought us of Miss Bovey's sudden death."

Only once before had Charles mentioned the Boveys in his Journal and then rather offhandedly. About three weeks before he had noted: "Walking in the Trustees Garden, I met the Miss Boveys, whom I had never been in company with. I found some inclination to join them; but it was a very short-lived curiosity." Now, on learning of Becky's death, his mind winged to William Appee and he wrote these lines: "Mr. Appee was just set out for Charlestown [Charles differed from most of the colonists in spelling Charles-Town as one word] on his way to Holland, intending to return, when he had settled his affairs, and marry her. 'But death has quicker wings than love.' The following evening I saw her in her coffin and soon after in her grave."

John, too, saw her in her coffin and in her grave and, affectionate and sensitive as he assuredly was, he wrote with warmth: "I never saw so beautiful a corpse in my life. Poor comfort to its late inhabitant! I was greatly surprised at her sister. There was, in all her behaviour, such an inexpressible mixture of tenderness and resignation. The first time I spoke to her, she said, 'All my afflictions are nothing to this. I have lost not only a sister, but a friend. But this is the will of God. I rely on Him; and doubt not but He will support me under it.' "

Greatly saddened by the death of this young woman, John instinctively turned more and more to Sophy for companionship and solace. The very next day, after five-o'clock prayers, he "conversed seriously" with her and her name appears more and more frequently in his Diary in the days following. He visited her at the Caustons' and saw her often at the Bovey home. Once he mentioned he went to "Miss Bovey's" and there met Sophy and began the reading of Young's *Last Day;* another time he wrote: "The evening at Miss Bovey's with Mr. B. Burnside [John meant James Burnside; he was careless about names] and Miss Sophy present."

And so until July 21 the days and evenings passed with not too much happening on the surface of John's and Sophy's lives, though inwardly their feelings were undergoing the most heart-shaking change. On that day it was decided Charles would return to England and that John, after accompanying him to Charles-Town, would go to Frederica where Sophy and Elizabeth would be waiting for him. In fact, he saw the two girls off for that southern outpost before he and Charles departed for Charles-Town.

No ill will on either the part of Charles or James Oglethorpe influenced Charles's decision. He was simply unsuited to the shocks, vulgarity, and conniving of Frederica. The Georgia founder even gave him words of advice, some of them quite personal, on the eve of his leave-taking.

"After prayers he took me aside," Charles wrote in his Journal, "and said, 'I would desire you not to let the Trustees know your resolution of resigning. There are many hungry fellows ready to catch at the office; and in my absence I cannot put in one of my own choosing. The best I can hope for is an honest Presbyterian, as many of the Trustees are such. Perhaps they may send me a bad man; and how far such a one may influence the traders, and obstruct the reception of the gospel among the heathen, you know. I shall be in England before you leave it. Then you may put in a deputy or resign. . . .

" 'On many accounts I should recommend to you marriage rather than celibacy. You are of a social temper, and would find in a married state the difficulties of working out your

131

salvation exceedingly lessened, and your help as much increased.' ''

And so, with this farewell message of concern from James Oglethorpe, Charles abandoned Georgia and John to their fates.

TEN

After seeing Charles off, John moved at a gait even faster than his usual one to reach Frederica. He spent only one day in Savannah, giving the excuse that he found James Oglethorpe gone. Then, for once, he left behind Delamotte and also Benjamin, now living and teaching very diligently at his Indian school at Irene. He took with him Jemmy Billinghurst, a servant-boy in his teens, and cut across land to Thunderbolt where his boat, which he had sent the long way by water, awaited him.

While walking to Thunderbolt, he was caught in such a heavy downpour that his clothes were as wet as if he had been swimming. This led him to boast, as he was wont to do on occasions dealing with his usual excellent health: "I cannot but observe that vulgar error concerning the hurtfulness of rains and dews of America. I have been thoroughly wet with these rains more than once, yet without any harm at all. And I have lain many nights in the open air, and received all the dews that fell; and so, I believe might any one, if his constitution was not impaired by the softness of a genteel education."

Martha Causton showed up at the Thunderbolt landing, presumably with last-minute messages to be delivered to Sophy.

John embarked at four o'clock in the afternoon and "sang" his "way to Skidoway," a two-hour sail. This Diary note suggests great excitement and happiness; but on the other hand he could have just been practicing the hymns he had translated from German composers and the ones he had composed that he was now having published by the printer, Lewis Timothy, in Charles-Town. Four words in the schedule of one of his days in the Carolina port, "On business in town," suggest that he had gone to see Mr. Timothy while there.

Singing all four days of his trip, except for one when he was depressed by stormy weather that delayed him several hours, he reached Frederica in the evening and went directly to see James Oglethorpe, who had arrived from Savannah the day before. John's purpose was to give him letters from South Carolina and to talk of Sophy. But talking of her was not enough. Leaving the leader of the Colony, he hurried to the palmetto hut at the rear of the Thomas Hird lot where she and Elizabeth were staying and, finding her there, "conversed." What genuine delight rings out from the Diary's next line: "She quite right!"

There was no mention of Elizabeth in John's account of that evening. She could have been left in Savannah as far as John seemed to care. However, she was in Frederica, indisposed.

The next day at noon John returned to the Hirds'. This time he found not only Sophy there, but James Oglethorpe. Shortly, though, the "governor" had to go home for dinner, giving John the opportunity to read to Sophy his *Collection of Psalms and Hymns.*

The following day was Sunday, a very busy day of church

meetings; yet John found the time to take Sophy to the myrtle walk in the woods, which he and Charles so loved, and there read her part of his Journal covering the trip to Charles-Town. It is easy to imagine him, Sophy close by his side, the Journal in his slim hands, pacing in step up and down the sandy path. How pungent the green-gold myrtle must have smelled in the August heat; how soft and fitful the breeze from the close-by sea. Did Sophy, in her quiet, gentle way, fix her eyes upon him as he read? They were large, expressive, warm eyes, for, as their affair progressed, John more than once mentioned them staring at him attentively. And did wayward strands of her hair blow now and then across her sun-warmed cheeks?

John was unable to finish all of the account that day; he had to stop for the afternoon Society meeting; but the next morning, quite early, he completed it.

Then, suddenly, after the ten-o'clock morning service, he became ill. From what cause, he did not say; but this could not have been the time (if there ever was such a time, which seems preposterous) that Dr. Coke and Henry Moore and Poet-laureate Southey declared Sophy nursed John day and night in order to work her way into his affections.

". . . the General called upon him," Messrs. Coke and Moore write, and invited him to dine, adding, " 'Mr. Wesley, there are some here who have a wrong idea of your abstemiousness. They think that you hold the eating of animal food and drinking wine to be unlawful. I beg that you will convince them of the contrary.' John resolved to do so. At table he took little of both, but a fever was the consequence, which confined him for five days.

"Now the time to try if indeed, 'His heart was made of penetrable stuff.' Notwithstanding an extreme reluctance on his part (who would hardly suffer even Mr. Delamotte to do anything for him) she [Sophy] attended him night and day. . . .

135

"Those who have known Mr. Wesley will forestall our judgment here; they well know what impression all this was likely to make. He was indeed, as our great poet observes

. . . Of a confident, loving nature
That thinks men honest, if they seem but so.

"How then must this appearance of strong affection from a woman of sense and elegance, nay, and, as it should seem of piety too, affect him! Especially considering (it is his own account) that he had never before familiarly conversed with any woman, excepting near relations. We hardly need to add that upon his recovery, he entertained his pupil with more than ordinary complacency."

Poet Laureate Southey echoes the words of these authors: ". . . When in consequence of his having taken meat and wine one day at the General's express desire . . . he was seized with a fever, and confined to his bed, she attended him night and day with incessant and sincere solicitude. Wesley's manner of life had hitherto estranged him from women, and he felt these attentions as it was designed that he should feel them."

The claims of Dr. Coke and Mr. Moore that John "had never before familiarly conversed with any woman, excepting near relations," and of the Poet Laureate Southey that his subject had been "hitherto estranged from women" are clearly negated by the facts. John always enjoyed the company of women; as has been noted earlier, he had while at Oxford several female friends, chief among them Betty Kirkham and the young widow, Mary Granville Pendarves. Indeed, his attachment to Betty was so warm, he carried on a long, tender correspondence with her in which he called her Varanese and himself, Cyrus. And the same was true in the case of Mrs. Pendarves—his pet name for her was Aspasia.

This illness of John's could not have been the occasion of which these gentlemen write not only because the "General" had left Frederica the evening before John took to his bed, but also because John did not once hint that Sophy came to see him, though he mentioned the names of other women who did.

Apparently appalled by the illness, he listed his hour-by-hour symptoms and reactions:

"10 At home; shocks; headache; sung; slept.

"11 Hot fit; sung; meditation; slept.

"12 Hot fit; wrote diary; began to walk; sweat.

" 1 Sweat; slept; cool . . ."

On Tuesday he spent an hour or two with a *System of Theology* and *British Theology* and then the fever returned. "A little cold," he jotted down, "a little hot, sweat, headache, sweat." Then Thomas Hawkins came and his patient must have grasped the opportunity to prescribe spiritual medicine for him, for John recorded the surgeon was "serious and open." By three in the afternoon he had recovered sufficiently to hold a Society meeting, and afterward to pay calls on Beata and Mrs. Lawley. Then Grace Hird, the wife of Thomas, and a Mrs. Robinson came and fed him bread and butter, which strengthened him sufficiently to read prayers and expound and to hold another Society meeting.

He began his Wednesday schedule as usual; but at nine thirty he had a hard chill that lasted until two in the afternoon. In the evening he "took a vomit."

Thursday, at last, Sophy came. Instead of nursing and feeding him, she listened while he read a letter he had written to "Morgan" (the father of the late William Morgan, his beloved Oxford friend) and a letter Morgan had written in return.

Friday, in spite of still feeling rather wobbly from the bout of chills and fever, he put in a full and happy day until late in the afternoon. He saw Sophy at least twice; he first "conversed" with her and then sang, read Law, and sang again with her and Mark Hird. But then Beata, who had definitely been shoved into the wings of his daily routine and of his

137

thoughts (he mentioned seeing her only once since his return), walked back onto the stage.

Between five and six o'clock John called at Dr. Hawkins' for "the decoction of the bark" the surgeon had prescribed for him. Thomas was not at home, but Beata urged him to come in and sit down. He complied and she sat beside him. Instead of talking lightly in this cozy proximity, John began to upbraid her for her husband's behavior regarding an old letter Charles Wesley had written to him, which John had lost and the surgeon, of all people, had recovered.

"Being ill-treated by those from whom I expected it has given me little concern," John began. "But it has grieved me to find Mr. Hawkins joining with them, whom I used to look upon as my friend."

"How has he treated you ill?" Beata asked innocently.

"By exposing my brother's paper, which as a friend he should have shown to me only."

"All the women in the town are uneasy and affronted at the two Greek words there," she answered heatedly. "They think them a general reflection on them all. Pray tell me, who do they mean?"

John answered her with amazing diplomacy, considering his usual lack of tact: "First, what my brother says is not said by me, neither am I accountable for it; second, this was writ . . . when all things were dark; third, I take him to mean by those words only two persons, you and Mrs. Welch."

Beata's reaction was quick and violent. John described it vividly: "She started up, said I was 'a villain, a scoundrel, a pitiful rascal,' with several other titles of the same kind. In the midst of her speaking Mr. Hawkins came in. She told him I said, 'that dog my brother meant her by those d———d words'; upon which he immediately joined her, bestowed much of the same sort of eloquence both upon him [Charles] and me, only intermixed with more oaths and impressions. I was much grieved, and indeed could not refrain from tears. I

138

know not whether they interpreted this as fear; but they rose in their language, and told me they would uncase [unfrock] us both. I replied, 'The sooner the better, and that I would go to Mr. Oglethorpe just now.' "

And go he did, to give him a "plain relation" of all that had been said. James Oglethorpe must have been exceedingly weary, having just returned that afternoon from the long, punishing trip to Fort St. George, for he put off until after prayers the summoning of the Hawkinses to give their side of the story.

After a long hearing, during which the Georgia founder was "obliged to check more than once" the Hawkinses for their "warm" and vulgar language, he announced that Charles had been guilty of an indiscretion in writing the letter but this was not imputable to John, who was in no way accountable for what his brother said and, furthermore, the Hawkinses had done very ill in abusing John in a fashion "no way justifiable or excusable."

John was so carried away with the favorable outcome of the dispute, he decided to take on his old, outspoken enemy, William Horton; but as he admitted ruefully, "It was labor in vain. He had heard stories which he could not repeat and was consequently immoveable as a rock."

And, John could have added, as venomous as the bite of a rattlesnake. "Mr. Wesley, you are always prying into other people's concerns, in order to set them together by the ears," he spat out. "You have betrayed everyone who trusted you; you have revealed the confessions of dying men. You have belied every one who you have conversed with, myself in particular, to whom you are determined to do all the mischief you can."

"What motive do you think I had to proceed thus?" John asked when he could get in a word.

"I believe you take pure delight in doing mischief. I believe in the morning when you say your prayers, you resolve against it; but by the time you have been abroad two hours, all your resolutions are vanished, and you can't be easy until you're at it again."

Tears must have sprung once more to John's eyes at such cruel words; but he was to hear more before he could escape the scene. While he was still facing William, Ann came up and, in front of a fast-gathering crowd, demanded to know with a curse what he meant by calling her an adulteress. She proceeded to "regale" him "with such a mixture of scurrility and profaneness" as he had never heard before.

John felt desperate. He decided that his only recourse with these people was "to look upon" them as "dead," neither to speak to them further or to speak about them. Yet no sooner had he come to this resolution than Beata sent him a note requesting him to come to her to talk "upon an affair of importance."

He hesitated; then asked the maid Catherine, who had brought the note, "Do you know what your mistress wants of me?"

"No, sir," she answered.

Shaking his head in resignation, he said, "If a parishioner desires my company, I must go; but be sure, stay you within."

When John arrived, Beata said curtly, "Sir, sit down."

John sat on the side of the bed where he had sat the day before, that apparently being the only piece of furniture in the room, and Beata came and stood in front of him, her hands behind her. "Sir, you have wronged me," she announced with no preliminaries. "And I will shoot you through the head this moment with a brace of balls."

John's description of what happened then needs no elaboration:

"I caught hold of the hand with which she presented the pistol," he reported, "and at the same time of her other hand, in which she had a pair of scissors. On which she threw herself upon me, and forced me down upon the bed, crying out all the while, 'Villain, dog, let go my hands,' and swearing

140

bitterly with many imprecations both on herself and me, that she would either have my hair or my heart's blood. I was very unwilling either to cry out, which must publish to all the world what, for her sake, I desired should be more private; or to attempt rising by force, which could not have been done without hurting her. Just then the maid came in, whom she ordered to reach a knife, swearing she would be the death of her if she did not. The woman stood trembling, not knowing what to do. Her [Beata's] two boys [servants] came in next, whom she bid to hold my hands, and I desired to take hold of their mistress. But they did not dare to do either. Then came in Mr. Davison the constable, and Mr. Reed, who, on my desire, were going to take her by the arms when Mr. Hawkins came in, asked what that scoundrel did in his house, and commanded them at their peril not to touch his wife. Upon this encouragement she struggled again to get her hands loose; but not being able, seized on my cassock with her teeth and tore both the sleeves of it to pieces, and then fixed upon my arm, four men (for Mr. Robinson and Ward were now come) standing by, and not daring to hinder her. I then spoke to Mr. Hawkins, who seeing the company increase, took her round the waist and lifted her up. I went to Mr. Oglethorpe and gave him a simple narration of what had happened. He sent for them both and for Mr. Horton. She defended all, saying he had not done her justice for the wrong she had received, and therefore she had done herself justice. After a long hearing, her husband and she, promising better behaviour for the future, were dismissed."

(Some Wesley biographers, among them B. L. Tyerman, insist that Beata also snipped off half of John's hair. "The wicked woman cut off from one side of his head the whole of those long locks of auburn hair, which he had been accustomed to keep in the most perfect order," writes the Reverend Mr. Tyerman. "After this he preached at Savannah with his hair long on one side and short on the other, those sitting on the side which had been cut observing, 'What a cropped head

141

of hair the young parson has.' " However, from John's own account, the mutilation was impossible; John never let go of Beata's hands.)

Though the Hawkinses promised to better their behavior toward John, he had reason to believe, after just two days, that they were up to their old tricks of vilifying him. Thereupon he sent James Oglethorpe the following letter:

"Aug. 23
"Sir,

I choose to write rather than speak, that I may not say too much. I find it utterly impossible anything should be kept secret unless both parties are resolved upon it. What fell out yesterday is already known to every family in Frederica; but to many it has been represented in such a light that 'tis easy to know whence the representation comes. Now, Sir, what can I do more? Though I have given my reputation to God, I must not absolutely neglect it. The treatment I have met with was not barely an assault; you know one part of it was felony. I can't see what I can do but desire an open hearing in the face of all my countrymen of this place. If you (to whom I can gladly entrust my life and my all in this land) are excepted against as partial, let a jury be impanelled, and upon a full inquiry determine what such breaches of the law deserve.
"I am, Sir,
"Your obliged and obedient Servant."

The letter alarmed the Georgia leader. The Colony could ill afford to have a public trial such as John was demanding. There were already too many dissensions, dissatisfactions, fights. A trial would split the province even more widely apart and, besides, it would consume valuable time that neither he nor the people could spare.

He was expecting a Spanish delegation toward the end of the month and he needed all his energy and wits to prepare for it. The Spaniards, he knew, were coming to make new demands on England; he felt reasonably sure they would seek to have the English withdraw from their outposts in the South. His colonists, and especially John, whom he counted on to take down the minutes of the meetings, must be in a peaceful, co-operative mood.

He sent for John and explained the critical situation, then said, "Of course, Mr. Wesley, if you insist on it, I will hold a court, but to speak frankly I think it will be much better to terminate matters in a more friendly manner."

"Sir, I have no desire of doing any hurt to either Mr. Hawkins or Mrs. Hawkins," John answered, "but I feel I must secure myself against future insults and put a stop to misrepresentations of what is past."

Apparently James Oglethorpe considered that John had a good point, for he declared, "I will talk to them on those heads and will let you know their answer."

Georgia's chief devoted practically the entire day to bringing about a peaceful settlement. He sent for the Hawkinses; he sent for John; then in the evening he sent for the three of them together. "For above an hour," so John recorded in his Journal, "was he labouring to reconcile us." John insisted he had "obliged them [the Hawkinses] beyond all reconciliation," and Beata and the doctor were just as adamant. At last, however, an agreement was reached stipulating that the Hawkinses would never again speak to the parson and that John, likewise, would never speak to them.

The pact came as a relief to John. He had done all in his power to free Beata of her shackles of sin; now he need struggle no further; the issue had been taken out of his hands. He poured out his gratitude in his Journal: "Blessed be God who hath at length given me a full discharge, in the sight of men and angels, from all intercourse with one, 'whose heart is snares and knots and her hands as bands.' "

This crisis past, John resumed his habit of seeing Sophy two, three, and four times daily. On some occasions he went to her and on others she came to him. Apparently he was

143

living in the "meeting house" that he had helped build during his last Frederica visit. The Diary glows with such jottings as "read with Miss Sophy" (every morning after prayers he read to her Heylin's *Tracts*); "writing an account when Miss Sophy came"; and with a brief report of a walk he took with Sophy and Elizabeth to Constable Reed's five-acre lot in the country where he helped build an arbor, a job at which he had excelled when he was an Oxford student; and of another walk with Sophy alone to the land of another parishioner, a Mr. Colwell, where he had, as he noted enthusiastically, "a good time" though he "met a rainstorm and returned home very wet."

The many hours he spent with Sophy did not lead to neglect of the other settlers who needed him. He went quite often to read Hickes' *Prayers and Psalms for the Afflicted* to Mrs. Mary Patterson, a Scotch Presbyterian who was dangerously ill. One morning while he was reading, none other than Beata walked in and sat down quietly in a corner. He ignored her as if she were a piece of kindling; in fact, he commented rather smugly that he did not exchange one word with her "good or bad."

The time came, however, when he decided he must return to Savannah; there was nothing urgent to keep him in Frederica, the Spanish delegation having come and gone. He had been away almost a month and felt that was a long time to absent himself from his parishioners with only Benjamin, preoccupied as he was with his Indian school, to look after their spiritual needs. But how he must have hated to leave Sophy!

The day of his departure—a Thursday in early September —he spent practically every moment with her. He conducted the early-morning service as usual, she sitting at his feet; until eight o'clock he conversed with her and read Hickes' *Matins*; then, with her by his side, he went to the landing so as to be on hand whenever the boat should pull up anchor. Presumably, since he didn't mention her being present, he did leave her briefly in order to bid James Oglethorpe good-by, noting happily that he was "at one with him." After that he rejoined Sophy and, as the boat did not leave until noon, he read to her Worthington *On Resignation*, sitting, perhaps, under one of the great live oaks on the river bank; then dined with her, probably on bread and butter and raisins.

When the boat pulled out and finally nosed around the northern tip of the shallow crescent, blotting Sophy from sight, he tried to ease the pangs of loneliness that assailed him with another dose of *On Resignation*.

ELEVEN

Once more in Savannah, John buckled himself into an even more restrictive harness than before: so many minutes for praying (usually six minutes at the end of each waking hour, but sometimes five and sometimes seven); so many minutes for church services (he began holding the early-morning service at a quarter past five and planned to keep it at that hour through the fall and winter months); so many minutes for writing up his Journal and Diary and for writing letters (he wrote to Sophy and Mark Hird and James Oglethorpe, as well as to the members of his family and to the noted evangelist, George Whitefield, who would later come to Georgia and establish the first orphanage in the New World, and to other old friends in England); so many minutes for catechizing the children; so many minutes for studying Spanish and writing a German grammar; and so many minutes—hours, really—for visiting his parishioners. The visiting took from one until five o'clock and even then he didn't get to see the sick as often as he would have liked.

One evening, after the number of ill had increased so alarmingly that seeing patients broke into his regular routine for two consecutive days, he poured out his frustration in the pages of his Journal, with the idea, it seems, of copying it in a letter to Mr. Whitefield or to old friends at Oxford.

"Not even that [the regular four hours and extra time] is enough to see them all (as I would do) daily," he mourned. "So that even in town (not to mention Frederica and all the smaller settlements) there are about five hundred sheep that are (almost) without a shepherd. He that is unjust must be unjust still. Here is none to search out and lay hold on the *Mollia tempora fandi* [Pleasant times for talking] and persuade him to save his soul alive. He that is a babe in Christ may be so still; here is none to attend the workings of grace upon his spirit, to feed him by degrees with food convenient for him, and gently lead him until he can follow the Lamb wherever He goeth. Does any crr from the right way? Here is none to recall him. He may go on to seek death in the error of his life. Is any wavering? Here is none to confirm him. Is any falling? There is none to lift him up. What a single man can do is not seen or felt. . . ."

Despite this wave of inadequacy that so overwhelmed him, he was happy these early fall weeks. He wrote his Journal and Diary with a steady hand; he walked long distances; he cleaned the "parlor" for company; he felled trees; and he spent much time with the Caustons. One day he saw Thomas six times; evidently he never tired of talking to them of Sophy and they never tired of listening.

He also saw Margaret Bovey frequently. He read her his *Collection of Psalms and Hymns* and also a collection of *Prayers* he had composed. He instructed her, too, in the Scriptures and other religious writings and in French. He was training her to be a deaconess, a sort of lay pastor, in the church. In the critical *True Account* of Georgia, one of the complaints lodged against John was that he "appointed deaconnesses." As the Reverend Mr. Curnock points out in a footnote in *The John Wesley Journal*, Margaret and Mark Hird and Mr. Reed in Frederica "were to the Church in Georgia what helpers, class-leaders, and leaders of bands were to the Methodism of the next decade."

That John was delighted with the progress Margaret was making is testified to in two paragraphs of a letter he wrote about her and about Becky's death to his old friend, Anne Granville:

"I am persuaded that heavy affliction will prove the greatest blessing to the survivor which she ever yet received. She is now very cheerful, as well as deeply serious. She sees the folly of placing one's happiness in any creature, and is fully determined to give her whole heart to Him from whom death cannot part her.

"I often think how different her way of life was at St. James and yet the wise, polite, gay world counts her removal thence a misfortune. I should not be at all grieved if you were fallen in the same misfortune, far removed from the pride of life, and hid in some obscure recess, where you were scarcely seen or heard of, unless by a few plain Christians and by God and His angels. . . ."

John also, according to one line in his Diary, visited with Tommy Mellichamp, who must have been incarcerated temporarily in the log-house jail in Savannah. Tommy had escaped several weeks before from the Charles-Town jail, but had been quickly tracked down in the company of a gang of "very vile characters" and, with part of his sentence for forgery still to be served, had been tried for stealing and had been convicted and again locked up. Mrs. Mellichamp had also been tried and expelled from the Colony on the grounds that she was involved in the proceedings of the gang and was guilty of conveying stolen goods. Just what John and Tommy talked about, the Diary leaves to our imagination— no doubt the main topic was Sophy.

There was another happening worthy of note during this Savannah stay, also covered laconically in the Journal. Two words describe it: "christened Parker." Could this possibly have been the Second Bailiff, who, in conjunction with his wife, Anne, had angrily refused to allow John to immerse his baby? Had he, whom Biographer Tyerman described, as "a slave to liquor," reformed? In the light of coming events, these questions are quite relevant. It does not seem likely that he would be an enemy of John's if he had repented of his sins and been christened by him.

But in spite of all these fairly exciting activities, the tug of Frederica, after just one month, grew so strong that John took up with the Moravians the question of his returning to the "poor people" there. To his great satisfaction they thought he should do so. Benjamin, summoned from Irene, agreed to supply the Savannah pulpit during John's absence.

Practically John's last act before departing was a visit to Thomas Causton to ask what "commands" he had for Sophy. The First Bailiff was not reticent in expressing his ideas.

"That girl will never be easy till she is married," he told John frankly.

"Sir, she is too much afflicted to have thought of it," John protested.

"I'll trust a woman for that," Thomas smirked. "There is no other way."

John, still naïve, still uncomprehending, said, "But there are few here who you would think fit for her."

Emphatically and pointedly, Thomas answered, "Let him be but an honest man—an honest, good man; I don't care whether he has a groat, I can give him a maintenance."

This statement made a real impression on John, as we shall see later from his own remarks; but at this time, he did not follow it up; instead, he acted as if he had not heard it. "Sir," he asked, "what directions do you give me with regard to her?"

"I give her up to you. Do what you will with her. Take her into your own hands. Promise her what you will. I will make it good." Thomas could not have expressed himself more clearly unless he had come right out and said, "Parson, you marry her."

For one of the rare times in his life, John was at a loss for words. If he found any, he never mentioned them.

Reaching Frederica, accompanied again by his "boy" Jemmy, he was in for a shock. Sadly and with a trembling hand, noticeably different from the even penmanship of the recent weeks in Savannah, he recounted in his Journal:

"Sat. 16—I met Mark Hird on the Bluff, who gave me a melancholy account of the state of things. The morning and evening prayers, which were read for a while after my leaving the place, had been long discontinued, and from that time everything grew worse and worse. Mr. Tackner [one of the members of the small Frederica Society] had thrown off the form as well as the power of godliness, and so had most of his neighbors who ever had pretensions to it.

"Even poor Miss Sophy was scarce a shadow of what she was when I left her. Harmless company had stole away all her strength. Most of her good resolutions were vanished away; and to complete her destruction, she was resolved to return to England. I reasoned with her much, but with no success; she could not see that she was at all changed, and continued fixed in her resolution of leaving America with the first ship that sailed. . . ."

Finally, "finding the veil was upon her heart," he argued with her no further, but tried a new approach. "Miss Sophy, you must pray very earnestly to God to direct you to do what is best," he said, not doubting for a moment that God would be on his side.

But John did not trust her to pray alone. He prayed with her and he read what he considered the most appropriate passages from the *Serious Call* and from the works of Ephrem Syrus; but, as he noted, "she got little good."

So matters continued for more than a week, when one evening, abandoning "arguments drawn from the topics of religion," which had made no impression, he "pressed her," as he frankly confessed in his Journal, "upon the head of friendship. Upon which she burst into tears and said, 'Now my resolution begins to stagger.' "

And, a few days later, while her resolution still staggered, he played on her sympathy to weaken it further. Having been snubbed by James Oglethorpe upon the founder's return from St. George, where he had been dismantling the fort and withdrawing the garrison in accordance with the agreement he had made with the Spaniards, John hurried to Sophy as fast as his short steps would take him to tell her of the incident.

"I was in the Fort with Mr. Horton when Mr. Oglethorpe came," he recounted. "He ran to Mr. Horton, kissed him and expressed much kindness, but he took no notice of me, good or bad, any more than if I had not been in the room." Then he added pitifully, "Now, Miss Sophy, you may go to England, for I can assist you no longer; my interest [influence] is gone."

His woeful tale aroused her tenderest feelings. "No, Mr. Wesley," she declared vehemently. "Now I will not stir a foot!"

John was not yet fully satisfied. "But if Mr. Oglethorpe advises you to go, he may be displeased."

"I care not," she retorted. Then, "with the utmost earnestness," she said, "Sir, you encouraged me in my greatest trials. Be not discouraged in your own. Fear nothing. If Mr. Oglethorpe will not, God will help you."

Confident that she would not again entertain the notion of returning to England, John decided then and there to overlook the Georgia leader's snub and take up with him the feasibility of Sophy's going back to Savannah. That very evening he was able to announce, "Miss Sophy, Mr. Oglethorpe thinks it best that you should return to Savannah immediately."

151

To John's amazement, Sophy "fell into a great passion of tears and said she could not bear the thought of it."

For "near an hour" John argued heatedly with her; he repeated to her Thomas Causton's assurance that he would "make good" whatever he (John) promised her, "so that she had only to make her own terms." But, even agitated as he was, he promised nothing definite. Nevertheless, he finally left her "a little more composed."

The next day, still ignoring the snub, John asked James Oglethorpe what boat Sophy should go in and he answered, "She can go in none but yours, and, indeed, there is none so proper."

At first John's heart raced with exultation. The thought of being with Sophy on a small boat for three or four days, maybe even five or six, seemed the height of happiness. He stood, tiptoe, on the mountaintop of bliss. Then, as quickly as his heart had raced with gladness, he experienced a sharp pain, a sudden catch, as if he had been running too fast. With the frightening swiftness and clarity of lightning he knew he was in love with Sophy. His physical passion was alive as any man's.

Yet we know he had planned never to marry. He considered the Church his bride. He had taken vows to be the bondslave of his Saviour, to serve Him with an undivided, unwavering, dedicated body, mind, and heart until death released him. Unintentionally and unconsciously he had allowed the relationship between him and Sophy to shift from pastor and pupil to lover and beloved. Yet he could not marry her. Not Sophy, of all people—he loved her far too much. She would crowd God to one side; he would worship her, not Christ.

It needs no flight of fancy to see him wildly pacing the floor of the little meeting house, struggling to decide his course. Should he follow the path of prudence and refuse to take her with him in the boat? Or should he follow the dictates of his whole being and trust in God to give him the

152

strength to withstand the temptation of her precious presence?

Finally he bowed to the overpowering longing to be with her. He admitted frankly that there was the gravest danger in it for him, but he argued that there were good reasons to believe he would be delivered out of the danger. One may conjecture on his agitated state as he slumped down at his writing table and drew his Journal to him; but there is no conjecture about what he wrote. Methodically, he listed the reasons for his confidence:

"(1) because it was not my choice which brought me into it;

"(2) because I still felt in myself the same desire and design to live a single life; and

"(3) because I was persuaded should my desire and design be changed, her resolution to live single would continue."

This is John's first mention of Sophy's "resolution to live single." Evidently at some past time, while discussing Tommy, she had confided to John that she never intended to marry; but since he did not intend to marry either—or, for that matter, to fall in love with her—he had not considered the statement of sufficient importance to record it. Now, however, all was different. Her determination to stay single mattered tremendously.

Having set down in black and white his three reasons, he attended in a rush to his few remaining tasks on the island. At six o'clock on the morning of his and Sophy's departure, he married Elizabeth to Welles Weston, a young man who had been a tanner in England but had given up that work to come to Georgia on the *London Merchant* and settle in Frederica; had a brief interview with James Oglethorpe, and then, at eleven thirty, helped Sophy into the small sailboat for the journey to Savannah.

It was late October and, in spite of Sophy's low spirits at

the prospect of going back to live with the Caustons, she must have taken pleasure that first afternoon in the slowly shifting scenery of what was still to her a strange, exotic land. Coastal Georgia is always beautiful; never more so than in the autumn, with the sun steeping the soft, salt-smelling air with gold and the wide, wide arc of the sky holding a steady, intense flame-blue. On the right-hand side of the Altamaha, as you steer north, grape vines spread nets of crisp yellow and crinkly brown leaves over the treetops; glistening, deep-green magnolia branches are studded with fat seed buds flecked with red as bright as blood; the aralia, nicknamed the devil's-walking-stick, brandishes huge clusters of purplish red berries, and the callicarpa winds about its slender stems thick, chunky bracelets of shiny amethyst; on the left-hand side, as far as the eye can see, stretches the flat, tawny, undulating sweep of the marsh.

The water and air are vibrant with color too. White cranes and wood ibis, with their long, skinny necks and slender legs, stand as still as picket fences amid the shallows; crows and seagulls swoop and sway above the river and the land, and now and then a crocodile rears his oar-shaped head and surveys his gently lapping world.

But John was not looking at the landscape. He was reading Bishop Patrick's *Prayers* and the first volume of Fleury's *History of the Church*. He chose the latter especially because it set before Sophy "such glorious examples of truth and patience in the suffering of these ancient worthies, who retired unto blood, striving against sin." One cannot help but wonder whether he read it more for his own benefit than for Sophy's.

After the gold gong of the sun had dropped into the marsh, a high, cold wind sprang up from the northeast. Hastily the crew beached the boat on a wooded, uninhabited island, built a fire, and prepared a supper of oysters gathered from the banks of the inlet, the tide being out. Calmly, then, as if he were at the meeting house at Frederica, John had

154

prayers. These finished, the crew hammered four stakes into the soft, moldy earth and stretched over them the boat's small sail. Beneath this inadequate strip of canvas, the little group lay down in their clothes to sleep, a blanket apiece to keep them warm. On one side of this inadequate protection lay John, Sophy, and the boy, Jemmy; on the other, the members of the crew.

The next morning the boat, its sail furled, wallowed helplessly in the deep troughs of the waves of Doboy Sound. John, astounded at Sophy's serenity, yelled above the whining of the wind, "Miss Sophy, are you not afraid to die?"

"No," she called back calmly. "I don't desire to live any longer. Oh, that God would let me go now! Then I should be at rest. In the world I expect nothing but misery."

John did not attempt to argue with her—talk was too difficult in the storm. Later, maybe, God would give him the right words to comfort her.

Tuesday evening, "the wind being contrary," they landed on the south end of St. Katherine's Island. John's account of his and Sophy's movements and conversations during part of their stay there must be given verbatim to be believed; yet it leaves much leeway for the imagination. He wrote:

"And here we were obliged to stay till Friday; so that I had time to observe her behaviour more nearly. And the more I observed, the more was I amazed. Nothing was ever improper or ill-timed. All she said and did was equally tinctured with seriousness and sweetness. She was often in pain, which she could not hide; but it never betrayed her into impatience! She gave herself up to God, owning she suffered far less than she deserved. . . .

"Wed. 27—In the afternoon we fell into a conversation on 'Lying in order to do good.' She owned she used to think there was no harm in it, and that she had herself sometimes done it to me; but added, 'she was now convinced no lying was lawful and would therefore watch against all kinds of it for the future.'

"Thursday 28—In the afternoon, after walking some time, we sat down in a little thicket by the side of a spring. . . ."

How tantalizingly brief is that reference to their walk through the near-tropical jungle of St. Katherine's Island. Surely no sooner had they set out than they were brushing and stumbling against each other as they fought their way through a dripping mass of trees, saplings, bushes, and vines. High above them the long fronds of the palms and the stiff needles of the pines ran with light, though where they walked, the leaves and the limbs of the live oaks, the sweet gums, the magnolias, the holly, and even the giant blackberry vines were so thickly thatched that no shaft of sun struck through. It was dim as dawn just before the sunrise.

They pushed past goldenrod, its feathery blossoms bowed low and drained white; past swings of Virginia creeper, party-gay with ruby-red, leafy pennants; past hummocks of small scrub oak, huckleberry, cassineberry bushes and pickerel weed; past patches of resurrection fern, coming to quick, bright-green life on the hoary trunks of the oaks after the rain; past diamond-studded webs flung by wood spiders across the more open spaces.

It was then, after walking some time, they sat down to rest "in a little thicket by the side of a spring." Was the air of the enclosure, seemingly separated from the air outside, a soft, greenish gold as if it flowed through a transom of chartreuse-stained glass, and were all sounds shut out except the soft gurgle of the spring as it watered its shallow path of coarse white sand?

John gives us no hint. He reported simply:

"Here we entered upon a close conversation on Christian holiness. The openness with which she owned her ignorance of it, and the earnest desire she showed for fresh instruction, as it much endeared her to me, so it made me hope she would one day prove an eminent pattern of it."

What a solemn topic for John to introduce in such a cozy, shut-away-from-the-world spot. That and the subject of the day before, "lying in order to do good," and all his other recorded conversations during his Georgia stay compel us to ponder how his early biographers, especially the very first one, John Hampson, after knowing him personally practically all his life, could describe him as cheerful and lively. Yet Hampson writes:

"In his countenance and demeanor, there was a cheerfulness, mingled with gravity; a sprightliness, which was the natural result of an unusual flow of spirits, and was yet accompanied with every mark of the most serene tranquility. . . .

"In social life, Mr. Wesley was lively and conversible; and of exquisite companionable talents. He had been much accustomed to society; was well acquainted with the rules of good breeding and in general perfectly attentive and polite. The abstractions of a scholar did not appear in his behavior.

"His manner, in private life, was the reverse of cynical or forbidding. It was sprightly and pleasant, to the last degree; and presented a beautiful contrast to the austere deportment of many of his preachers and people, who seem to have ranked laughter among the mortal sins. It was impossible to be long in his company without partaking his hilarity. Neither the infirmities of age, nor the approach of death, had any apparent influence on his manners. His cheerfulness continued to the last; and was as conspicuous at four score, as at one and twenty."

Perhaps "at four score" and "at one and twenty," but assuredly not in his thirties.

The day after the "close conversation on Christian holiness," though the wind continued at storm velocity, the little party started out again. "The waves dashed over the boat every moment," John wrote, "and the cold was extremely piercing. She [Sophy] showed no concern, nor made any complaint, but appeared quite cheerful and satisfied.

"It was not without some difficulty that in the afternoon we landed on St. Katherine's again. . . ."

John's next lines paint an intimate and tender scene. He began, "Observing in the night, the fire we lay by burning bright, that Miss Sophy was broad awake . . ." We can imagine him lying there beside her in the flickering shadows, "broad awake" himself, his passions agonizingly aroused.

Just how had he discovered her eyes were open? Had he stealthily turned his head toward her and stolen a look at her face? Or had he slowly, cautiously, lifted his cheek to his propped-up hand and peered over at her, his eyes searching, hovering, yearning? And how long, barely breathing, did he watch her before he spoke, his voice low so as not to wake Jemmy nearby? We will never know, for he recorded in his Journal disappointingly little besides the words they spoke.

"I asked her," he wrote, " 'Miss Sophy, how far are you engaged to Mr. Mellichamp?' "

"She answered, 'I have promised him either to marry him or to marry no one at all.'

"I said (which indeed was the expression of a sudden wish, not of any former design) 'Miss Sophy, I should think myself happy if I was to spend my life with you.' "

That was all. But many a wedding bell has pealed after a declaration much less to the point. Suppose Sophy had answered, "Oh, thank you, Mr. Wesley. I, too, would like to spend the rest of my life with you," would they not have been engaged right then and there?

But Sophy did not speak those words or any like them. "She burst into tears," John wrote, "and said, 'I am very unhappy. I won't have Tommy; for he is a bad man. And I can have none else.' Then she added, 'Sir, you don't know the danger you are in. I beg you would speak no word more on this head' and after a while, 'When others have spoken to me on the subject, I have felt an aversion to them. But I don't feel any to you. We may converse on other subjects as freely as ever.' Both my judgement and will acquiesced in what she said, and we ended our conversation with a psalm."

The next day they got off St. Katherine's Island and sailed

quite some distance; then dropped anchor at Bear Island and walked together for "near two hours." Again Sophy, as she had done first at Frederica, "expressed the strongest uneasiness and an utter aversion to living" at the Caustons'.

"I can't live in that house," she declared, weeping pitifully. "I can't bear the shocks I meet with there."

"Don't be uneasy, Miss Sophy, on that account," John reassured her. "If you don't care to be at Mr. Causton's, you are welcome to a room at our house; or, which I think would be best of all, and your aunt once proposed it, you may live in the house with the Germans."

John's "postscript" to this conversation consisted of four words: "She made little reply." How could she have made any other? Judging Sophy's remarks entirely from John's brief report, she appears to have done some thinking since the whispered interchange of the previous night and had shifted her position. Her repeated aversion to returning to the Caustons' and her many tears give the impression that she hoped to get John to renew his avowal so she could graciously accept it. If this was her intention, John certainly let her down, leaving her nothing, much less a "little" to say.

If there was any hidden meaning in her words, John was unaware of it. Almost objectively he continued the account of the trip:

"About five we took our boat again, and in the evening came to Rattonpossom, another uninhabited island about thirty miles from Savannah. Here our provisions failed; neither could we find any firewood, except one old stump of a tree, nor so much as two or three stakes to prop up our sail. Miss Sophy hung her apron on two small sticks, which kept off a little of the north wind from her head, and lay down on the ground under the canopy of heaven, with all the signs of perfect content."

When they finally reached Thunderbolt on Sunday, October 31, John and Sophy agreed he should get off, cut across country to Savannah, and meet her when she arrived at the

159

public landing. It is a mystifying decision. Did John hope to avoid gossip by appearing alone and at a different hour from Sophy? Or was he afraid to trust himself during the last agonizing miles of that intimate journey so quiveringly alive and painful with new love and unrequited passion? Whatever the reason, he abruptly dismissed those days—and nights—with six noncommittal words: "She went to Mr. Causton's directly."

TWELVE

A new and even more perilous mode of life, considering John's vow of celibacy, began almost immediately upon his return to Savannah. He had scarcely walked into the parsonage when an excited and highly expectant Thomas Causton appeared, "protesting his obligations" to John for taking care of his wife's niece and repeating "again and again" that whatever John "desired with regard to Miss Sophy he would consent to."

John put him off until he could consult with Sophy and then he laid down three rules:

"(1) Sophy should come to the parsonage every morning and evening,

"(2) At the Caustons' she should not have to associate with any company but of her own choice,

"(3) She should be no more upbraided with Tommy Mellichamp, nor should he be mentioned before her."

So, starting the very next day, Sophy began to spend the

161

early morning and evening hours at the parsonage. By five o'clock she was there, listening to John read prayers and a Psalm and expound the Lesson; then she walked with him in the garden and prayed. It was like old times, except there was no Elizabeth to make a threesome.

She went home shortly after breakfast but returned to the parsonage for the Society meeting, which was also attended usually by Margaret Bovey and James Burnside and others of the "inner circle." John read Ephrem Syrus to them and Dean Young's and Mr. Reeve's *Sermons* and any letters he might have written or received. That first Monday evening Sophy stayed on after the others had left and John read Valdesso to her. She returned to the Caustons' a little after nine.

Within a few days her hours at the parsonage were increased by at least two. On Tuesday, November 2, according to John's notation in his Diary, he began to teach her French, the lesson lasting, with an interval for prayers, from eight o'clock in the morning until ten. The date is important, for certainly it was too late in their friendship for Sophy to try to entice him into greater intimacy by spending more time with him; yet that is the accusation Dr. Coke and the Reverend Mr. Moore make in their biography.

"After some time," so they say, "he [John] observed she took every possible opportunity of being in his company. She also desired a greater intimacy, but modestly veiled her real motive under a request that he would assist her in attaining a perfect knowledge of the French tongue."

Could John, on his return to England, have been such an ungallant and conceited cad as to tell his friends this version of the French lessons? Surely neither Dr. Coke and the Reverend Mr. Moore, nor B. L. Tyerman and other later chroniclers who swallowed whole the Coke-Moore version realized in what an unattractive light they put the subject of their biographies.

The French lessons did give John more time to be alone

with Sophy; but his feeling for her, as we have clearly seen, had already flowered into ardent love.

However, he was fully aware that these daily, intimate hours with her were undermining his determination to remain single and realized that he must do something about it; but he was at a loss to know what. Feeling the way he did, he could not possibly stop seeing her. He should; that was plain; but how could he? He was confused, bewildered, terribly torn: How had this young woman acquired such a hold on him that she was a threat to his hold on the Lord? What magnetism did she have that his other female parishioners did not? What was it about her that made her an actual rival of Christ Himself for his affections? What . . . ? What . . . ? What . . . ?

After agonizing endlessly over these tormenting questions, he came to the conclusion that if he wrote down everything he knew and felt about her, he would have a clearer understanding of her attraction for him. By dissecting her piece by piece as a biologist would an insect under a microscope, he perhaps would be able to dissipate her power over him. Yes, he decided, the written word would serve as the magic rite to exorcise her.

So, at the top of a clean page of a notebook, he wrote the simple heading, *An Account of Miss Sophy*, and then, as if he were building a character for a novel, he put down a detailed description of her mannerisms, her bearing, her behavior, her character. . . .

(Editor Curnock says that the *Account*, which appears in his edition of *The Journal*, was written March 12, 1738, approximately a year and a half after John's systematic searching for the truth behind Sophy's relentless tug at his heart, and was done for Susannah, as "it is a perfectly fair copy, without abbreviations, which his mother's aged eyes would have no difficulty in deciphering." This is no doubt true, for John wrote several versions of his relationship with Sophy,

163

but he certainly composed the original in Savannah, for in his meticulous way he noted at the start the 1736 date, "Nov. 1, Mon." and during the following months of 1736 and 1737 he mentioned in both his Diary and Journal additions to it.)

"She was eighteen years old," he wrote. "And from the beginning of our intimate acquaintance till this day, I verily believe she used no guile, not only because even now I know of no instance to the contrary, not only because the simplicity of her behaviour was a constant voucher for her sincerity; but because the entire openness of all her conversation, answering whatever questions I proposed, without either hesitation or reserve, immediately and directly. Another thing I was much pleased with in her was, that whenever we were conversing or reading, there was such a stillness in her whole behaviour, scarce stirring head or foot, that 'she seemed to be, all but her attention, dead.' Yet at other times she was all life—active, diligent, indefatigable; always doing something, and doing with all her might whatever her hand found to do. For indeed, if the weakness of her body did not, her sense of honour would not hinder her doing anything.

"Nor did she at all favour herself on account of that weakness; if she could not remove, she would not indulge it. Softness and tenderness of this kind she would not know, having left the delicacy of the gentlewoman in England. She utterly despised those conveniences which women of condition in England would think worse than death. With bread to eat and water to drink she was content; indeed she never used any drink beside water. She was patient of labour, of cold, heat, wet, of badness of food or of want; and of pain to an eminent degree, it never making any alteration in her speech or behaviour, so that her frequent headache was only to be discerned by her paleness and dullness of her eye.

"Little of a gentlewoman in delicacy and niceness, she was still less so, if possible, in love of dress. . . . Though always neat, she was always plain. And she was equally careless of finery in other things. It was use she considered, not

164

show; nor novelty either, being as little concerned for new as for fine or pretty things. The same disregard she had for what are called diversions, such as balls, dancing, visiting; having no desire either to see or to be seen, unless in order to be wiser and better.

"Not that her love of retirement or want of curiosity was owning, as some supposed, to want of sense. . . ."

Did he hesitate here? Just who were they who supposed her "want of curiosity" was due to "want of sense"? Were they Delamotte and Benjamin? Perhaps, though certainly neither had had the temerity to come right out and say so.

"Her constant, even seriousness was very far from stupidity," he continued. "Indeed, her understanding was not of a piece with her years. Though unimproved, it was deep and strong. It reached the highest things and the lowest. It rose to the greatest, yet stooped to the least. With fine sense she had a large share of common sense, and particularly of prudence, suiting herself readily to all persons and occasions, nature in her supplying the place of experience. Her apprehension was so quick that there were scarce ever need to repeat a thing twice to her, and so clear as to conceive things the most remote from common life without any mistake or confusion. But she was by no means fond of showing her sense; seldom speaking when she could decently avoid it, and then in a few words, but such as were clear and pertinent, and contained much in little compass. . . ."

John must have felt a wave of pleasure at this point. He was expressing himself much better than at first; he was getting into the swing of what he wanted to say. His quill surely moved faster:

"One reason of her speaking so seldom was the mean opinion she had of herself, particularly of her own understanding, which was also the great cause of her constant eagerness for instruction, and indeed for improvement of every kind, as she was very sensible of her want of all. Hence too it was that she was so teachable in things either of a speculative or practical

165

nature, so readily convinced of any error in her judgment or oversight in her behaviour, and so easily persuaded to lay aside her own designs or measures and pursue those which others advised. Indeed, one would almost have thought she had no such ingredient in her nature as self-will.

"As her humility was, so was her meekness. She seemed to have been born without anger. Her soul appeared to be wholly made up of mildness, gentleness, longsuffering. Then especially, when she had to do with those who had injured her beyond the manner of men, she stayed for no entreaty before she forgave; but of one thing she was not easily convinced, that any one needed her forgiveness or had done ill either to her or any other. . . ."

Were these last lines absolutely honest? Had his judgment of her character been swept away by the flood of his adoration? Was it the whole truth that Miss Sophy "seemed to have been born without anger"? What of that frightening show of rebellion at Frederica when he had told her that she was to return to Savannah? Was that not a display of anger? Actually of rage? Yes, she had displayed anger that evening, but it was an excusable anger. She had been sorely provoked. He plunged ahead:

"She was with difficulty induced to believe any evil which she did not see. And even when she could not help believing, still she took care 'to speak evil of no man.'

"And as her greatest enemies, so much more the greatest strangers had a share in her good will and affection. She was a friend to human kind. To whomever was distressed she was all sympathy, tenderness, compassion. But to any whom she particularly called a friend her behaviour can only be conceived, not expressed. Such was the spirit of gratitude that ran through it; such the softness, the sweetness of every part of it; yet still preserving in all that yielding easiness a modesty pure as the light."

Here, he surely stood up, put his hands above his head, and stretched himself to his utmost height. The back of his neck and shoulders must have pained him. It was not, however, the amount of writing he had done that caused his discomfort; he was accustomed to doing ten times more during those hours set aside for correspondence and on those days when he served as secretary for James Oglethorpe; it was the tenseness under which he had written that knotted his nerves.

He added a few summarizing lines:

"The temper of her heart towards God is best known by Him 'who seeth in secret.' What appeared of it was a deep, even reverence, ripening into love, and a resignation unshaken in one of the severest trials which human nature is exposed to. The utmost anguish never wrung from her a murmuring word. She saw the hand of God, and was still. She said indeed, 'If it be possible, Father!' But added, 'Not as I will, but as Thou wilt!' "

Having finished the *Account* for the time being, he proclaimed in his Journal:

"Such was the woman, according to my close observation, of whom I now began to be much afraid. My desire and design was still to live single; but how long it would continue I knew not. I therefore consulted my friends [Moravians] whether it was not best to break off all intercourse with her immediately. They expressed themselves so ambiguously that I understood them to mean that I ought not to break it off. And accordingly she came to me (as had been agreed) every morning and evening.

"The time she was at my house was spent thus. Immediately after breakfast we all joined in Hickes's *Devotions*. She was then alone till eight. I taught her French between eight and nine, and at nine we joined in prayer again. She then read or wrote French till ten. In the evening I read to her and some others select parts of Ephrem Syrus, and afterwards Dean Young's and Mr. Reeve's *Sermons*. We always concluded with a psalm.

"This I began with a single eye. But it was not long before I found it a task too hard for me to preserve the same inten-

167

tion with which I began, in such intimacy of conversation as ours was."

A new solution to his problem came to him. Maybe this was the time he should make another move to go among the Indians. He had been in Georgia nine months and he was no nearer to fulfilling his mission to the savages than when he had been a Fellow at Oxford. He decided to broach the subject once more to James Oglethorpe, who was in Savannah making final preparations for another trip to England.

"You cannot leave Savannah without a minister," the Georgia leader answered emphatically.

Whether John replied verbally to this statement or only wrote it is not clear; but he did give his answer in his Journal:

"I know not that I'm under any obligation (to Savannah). I never promised to stay here one month. I openly declared before, at, and ever since my coming hither that I neither would or could take charge of the English any longer than till I could go among the Indians. If it was said 'But did not the Trustees of Georgia appoint you to be minister of Savannah?', I replied, 'They did,' but it was not done by my solicitation. It was done without either my desire or knowledge. Therefore I cannot conceive that appointment to lay me under any obligation of continuing here any longer than till a door is opened to the heathen; and this I expressly declared at the time I consented to accept that appointment."

Then John added some lines on the subject that he certainly could not have spoken to James Oglethorpe: "But though I had no other obligation not to leave Savannah now, yet that of love I could not break through; I could not resist the importunate request of the more serious parishioners 'to watch over their souls yet a little longer till some one came who might supply my place.' And this I more than willingly did because the time was not come to preach the gospel of peace to the heathen: all the nations being in a ferment. . . ."

168

John threw himself with determined enthusiasm into a
ruthless schedule. Never in all his life did he labor so diligently
and ceaselessly. He wrote a French beginner's grammar for
Sophy; he continued the study of Spanish; he continued to
compile a German grammar; he perfected himself in Byrom's
shorthand; he transcribed his hymns for the printer and arranged them in the order in which he wanted them to be set,
beginning with a verse from the *Psalms and Hymns* of Dr.
Watts:

> Ye holy souls, in God rejoice:
> Your Maker's praise becomes your voice.
>> Great is your theme; your songs be new:
> Sing of His name, His word, His ways.
> His work of nature and of grace,
>> How wise and holy, just and true!

And besides all these activities, he followed methodically
his timetable of church meetings, pastoral visits, French lessons with Sophy every morning, and devotionals every evening with her and the other "regulars" of the Society.

One evening, to John's surprise and no doubt discomfiture,
a new face appeared at the Society meeting. It was that of
William Williamson, a young man who had arrived in Savannah while John and Sophy were in Frederica and had
been taken into the Caustons' household. He had been trained
partly as a clerk by his uncle, Joseph Taylor of Bridewell.
Sizing him up as a man of "good qualifications," Thomas
employed him in "writing and transacting particular business; not publicly as a clerk in the store, but as a Domestic,
whom possibly he might have confidence in more than the
ordinary writers." It was understood that he came of good
English stock, was well educated, and sufficiently supplied
with this world's goods to pay his own way to Georgia and to
be independent of the charity of the Trustees. However, the
Earl of Egmont had reservations about William coming of
"good English stock." Writing in his diary, he claimed that

169

the young man was "the bastard son of Mr. Taylor of Bridewell and was wild when in England. . . ."

Biographer Tyerman expressed more than reservations about William's lineage. In the role of a reporter, claiming he was quoting from John's "unpublished Journal," he said this newcomer to Savannah was "a person not remarkable for handsomeness, neither for greatness, neither for wit, or knowledge, or sense and least of all for religion."

Sophy, in her warm, friendly fashion, had invited him to accompany her to the meeting; but it was the last one he attended for several months. Evidently he found August Herman Franche's *A Treatise on the Fear of Man*, upon which John expounded, much too dull for him.

In addition to all the expounding, teaching, studying, editing, arranging, visiting, John read-and-read-and-read. Just to mention one day, Monday, December 13, he listed on his reading schedule: Owen, Hickes, Nicodemis, Freylinghausen's *Gesang-Buch*, and Kempis. As Editor Curnock so aptly comments, "If close study and devotional literature could keep alive the claim of piety, Wesley in Savannah must have been a burning and shining light."

But nothing dampened the flame of love that consumed him. He was madly tempted, madly pulled apart. It was a time of severest testing. What more could he do, he asked himself, short of giving up Sophy completely? What more? What more? Finally he decided to draw up a set of resolutions. Prayerfully he put them down:

Dec. 19, 1736
In the name of God
"1—To be more watchful, before and in prayer,
"2—To strive to be thankful in eating.
"3—Not to touch even her clothes by choice; think not of her.
"4—Every hour, Have I prayed quite sincerely? Pray that you may watch, strive.

"5—Look into no book but the Bible till Christmas.

"6—From 12 to 4 o'clock, meditation or parish, no writing or reading.

"7—At Miss Bovey's start up the moment you end the paragraph. No word afterward.

"8—Speak no untended or unintended word."

Then, still restless as the sea, torn first this way and that, and heartsick, he started out a few days after Christmas to make his way through the endless snake-infested swamps, cane brakes, pine barrens, palmetto and cypress bogs, streams and rivers to Frederica. He took with him Delamotte, who was free from his school duties for the holidays, and a guide. They fortunately had horses, either loaned to them by Thomas or rented from some other source.

"Dec. 28th. Mr. Delamotte and I with a better guide set out for Frederica by land," he recorded. "We stayed that night and the next morning at the Cowpen and in the evening came to Fort Argyle. It stands pleasantly on the high bank of the river Ogeechy [Ogeechee]. Then we went on to Cooan-oochi River, over which we swam our horses by the side of a small canoe in which we crossed it. We made a fire on the bank, set up our blankets for a tent, commended ourselves to God, and not withstanding the rain, slept quietly till morning.

"Friday 31st. After riding through the woods between thirty and forty miles, we made a good fire and cheerfully ended the old year.

"Jan. 1st. Our provisions fell short, our journey being longer than we expected; but having a little barbecued bear flesh (that is dried in the sun) which we had reserved for such an occasion, we boiled it and found it very wholesome."

On Sunday, the second, they reached the settlement of the Scotch Highlanders at Darien and from there by periagua the twenty miles to Frederica were fairly easy going.

171

After John had been in Frederica for twenty days, he heard from a Captain Ellis, whose sloop had just arrived off St. Simons from Charles-Town, that Tommy Mellichamp had been let out of jail and was on his way to Savannah. Immediately, so John wrote in his Journal, he was "determined to be there" himself as soon as he could.

"Having beaten the air in this unhappy place," he took his "final leave of Frederica." It was final, he explained, "not because of any apprehensions of my own danger, though my life had been threatened many times, but an utter despair of doing any good there, which made me content with the thought of seeing it no more."

He was apprehensive for a miserable while that he would never reach Savannah, for the mists and contrary winds detained him for several days on the island of Sapelo; but even after he did arrive, he did not find Sophy. She was with Mary Musgrove at the Hog Crawl. More frantic than ever—for he did not consider Mary proper company for Sophy—he straightway took another boat and rowed with every ounce of his strength up the river to fetch her.

That evening he wrote in his Journal these exultant lines:

"She took the boat and came down with me immediately, as it was not her custom to deny me anything. For indeed from March 13, 1736, the day I first spoke to her, till that hour, I cannot recollect so much as a single instance of my proposing anything to her, or expressing any desire, which she did not fully comply with."

The next day John's mind was diverted briefly from Sophy. He heard that Margaret Bovey was planning to marry James Burnside and quickly he went to her and "told her with all plainness" his "thoughts of Mr. Burnside and of the whole affair." She "did not entirely agree with him," but "took it as it was intended."

John did not elaborate on his objections to James; they were possibly of minor importance. It seems most likely that

172

he wanted Margaret to remain unmarried so she could be a more devout and devoted "deaconess" of the church.

Then rapidly his thoughts turned back to Sophy and he was again covering pages of his Journal about her.

"I was now in a great strait," he lamented. "I still thought it was best for me to live single. And this was still my design; but I felt the foundations of it shaken more and more every day. Insomuch that I again hinted at a desire of marriage, though I made no direct proposal. For indeed it was only a sudden thought, which had not the consent of my own mind. Yet I firmly believe, had she (Miss Sophy) closed with me at this time, my judgement would have made but faint resistance. But she said she thought 'it was best for the clergy not to be encumbered with worldly cares and that it was best for her, too, to live single, and she was accordingly resolved never to marry.' I used no argument to induce her to change her mind."

Possibly at this juncture Sophy was still in love with Tommy and, now that he was out of jail, her inclination to marry John, if she had had one on the trip from Frederica, was considerably weakened. In spite of Tommy's criminal record—perhaps even because of it—he strongly appealed to her gentle, tender-hearted, sympathetic nature. Then, too, he was a youthful, dashing, devil-may-care character. Compared to the older strict-living parson, Tommy might hold all the trumps in Sophy's romantic eighteen-year-old eyes.

John admitted he "used no argument to induce her to alter her resolution" and "upon reflection" thought he had had a very narrow escape. What he needed, he decided, was some sober, wise counsel. While it was yet in his power, he had best go to the House of the Moravians and ask his friend Herr Toltschig, whether he should "break off so dangerous an acquaintance."

"What do you think would be the consequence if you should?" questioned Herr Toltschig calmly.

173

"I fear, sir," answered John with no hesitancy, "her soul would be lost, being surrounded with dangers, and having no other person to warn her of and arm her against them."

"And what do you think would be the consequence if you should not break it off?"

"I fear I should marry her."

"I don't see why you should not," answered the Moravian pastor impatiently.

John was shocked and, with disarming frankness, bared his reaction in his Journal:

"I went home amazed to the last degree; and it was now first that I had the least doubt whether it was best for me to marry or not, which I never before thought would bear a question. I immediately related what had occured to Mr. Ingham and Delamotte. They utterly disapproved of Mr. Toltschig's judgment, and in the evening went, as I desired they would, and talked largely with him and Anton (the Moravian Bishop Seifart) about it. It was midnight when I went to them; but even then they did not seem to be fully assured. Mr. Ingham still insisted I had not sufficient proof of her sincerity and religion, since the appearance of it might be owing partly to an excellent natural temper and partly to her desire of marrying me."

To which John impatiently retorted, "How can you reconcile your statement with what she told me on Thursday?"

Benjamin's cynical reply suggests that he had not taken seriously Sophy's resolve never to marry. "Very well," he answered, "she would soon recall those words if you made her a direct proposal."

Then he advised John to leave Savannah for a few days, arguing that he could not think clearly about the situation while constantly seeing Sophy. John, as he said himself, "saw the wisdom of this advice" and decided to go to Benjamin's school at Irene for a while. Before he left, though, he wrote Sophy a brief note that he gave to Margaret Bovey to deliver after he had gone. It said:

"Feb. 6. I find, Miss Sophy, I can't take fire into my bosom, and not be burnt. I am therefore retiring for a while to desire the direction of God. Join with me, my friend, in fervent prayer, that He would show me what is best to be done."

Then he traveled to Irene with Mary Musgrove, who happened to be returning to her Hog Crawl from Savannah. And until February 11 this is practically the last notation that appears to have been written with a fairly calm mind.

He was split into two persons: one, the very human, affectionate, sexually aroused lover of a woman; the other, the ascetic, overdisciplined, earnest, dedicated lover of God, His Son, and the Holy Ghost. And the two warred fiercely and continuously with each other.

In the struggle to dam the raging torrent of his passion, John cut down trees, blasted paths through the woods, caulked a boat; he read, he meditated, and, after the first day, he wrestled mightily with his God in prayer. All this and more he did; yet, between these labors, he unconsciously increased the tempestuous flood by reading over *An Account of Miss Sophy* and adding to it.

"When I came to Irene, I did not care to ask counsel of God immediately, being 'a man of unclean lips,'" he wrote. "I therefore set aside Monday the 7th for self-examination; adding only that general prayer, whenever thoughts arose in my heart concerning the issue of things, 'Lord, Thou knowest! If it be best, let nothing be allowed to hinder; if not, let nothing be allowed to affect it.' And this exercise I continued for several hours with some measure of cheerfulness. But towards evening God hid His face, and I was troubled. My heart sank in me like a stone. I felt how bitter a thing it is for a spirit of an unbounded appetite to be left a prey of his own desires. But it was not long. For I no sooner stretched out my hands to Heaven and bewailed my having parted from Him, than God sent me help from His holy place, and my soul received comfort.

175

"Tues. 8.—The next morning I was obliged to go down to Savannah. There I stayed about an hour; and there again I felt, and groaned under the weight of, an unholy desire. My heart was with Miss Sophy all the time. I longed to see her, were it but for a moment. And when I was called to take boat, it was as the sentence of death; but believing it was the call of God, I obeyed. I walked awhile to and fro on the edge of the water, heavy laden and pierced through with many sorrows."

What a lonely, small figure he must have been, pacing along the bank of the swift-flowing Savannah. Above him, on the Bluff, just a few blocks away, was his dearly beloved. How often his piercingly bright, yet mournfully sad eyes must have scanned that upper rim for a glimpse of her. And every time he looked, his breath shallow, his heart thudding, and his whole aching being reaching out for her, he prayed that she would be standing there, calm and sweetly serene, as was her way, a gentle smile on her lovely young face.

But she never came. The pain of his disappointment was so intense that there, on the river bank, he experienced a kind of vision. He recounted it simply:

"There One came to me and said, 'You are still in doubt what is best to be done. First, then, cry to God that you may be wholly resigned, whatever shall appear to be His will.' I instantly cried to God for resignation. And I found that and peace together. I said, 'Sure it is a dream.' I was in a new world. The change was as from death to life. I went back to Irene wondering and rejoicing; but withal exceeding fearful, lest my want of thankfulness for this blessing, or the care to improve it, might occasion its being taken away."

In the days that followed, his mind became clearer and his judgment surer. Besides believing Sophy's resolve never to marry, he was convinced marriage was not "expedient" for him "for two weighty reasons." He wrote them down: "(1) because it would probably obstruct the design of my coming into America, the going among the Indians; and (2) because I was not strong enough to bear the complicated temptations

176

of a married state." The second had to be the weightier reason. Worshiping Sophy as he did with all his heart would "make" him "know her after the flesh" and delight in that knowledge to the neglect of his Master.

The issue being settled once and for all, as he thought, he returned leisurely by land to Savannah, even indulging himself in a bowl of rice before he left Irene and taking two hours out of the journey to repair the path; but on reaching Savannah, he directly confided his decision to Benjamin, Delamotte, James Burnside, Herr Toltschig, and other Moravian friends.

He waited two days, however, before bringing himself to break the news to Sophy. He reported bluntly in *An Account:* "About seven in the morning, I told her in my own garden, 'I am resolved, Miss Sophy, if I marry at all, not to do it till I have been among the Indians.'" But in the Diary he added a very telling detail:

"8 Explained with Miss Sophy, private prayer, uneasy.

"9 In talk with Delamotte, diary; more uneasy . . ."

He had every right to be uneasy. Judging from Sophy's quick reaction, his decision had shocked and wounded her. The very next morning she told him, "People wonder what I can do for so long at your house; I am resolved not to breakfast with you any more. And I won't come to you any more alone."

This declaration is the most meaningful hint we have had as to Sophy's attitude toward John at that time. Whether she had finally managed to get over her love for Tommy we have no way of knowing; John, just two weeks before, had mentioned that after morning prayers he "conversed with Miss Sophy respecting Mellichamp, who being released from prison had become dangerous"; but failed to record what Sophy said. But no matter how she now felt about the erstwhile counterfeiter, the remark would indicate that she did want to prod John into marrying her. She needed the peace and security of his home and the comforting affection he so

177

obviously had for her, and reasoned that her ultimatum of no more breakfasts with him and no more visits to the parsonage alone would compel him into reconsidering his decision not to marry, if at all, until after he had been among the Indians.

When it did not, she took another drastic step. The next morning she declared, "I don't think it signifies for me to learn French any longer." But then, sensitive and soft-hearted as she was, her resolve weakened and she hurriedly added, "My uncle and aunt, as well as I, will be glad of your coming to our house as often as you please."

Instantly John protested, "You know, Miss Sophy, I don't love a crowd, and there is always one there."

"But," she reminded him sweetly and pointedly, "we needn't be in it."

She did continue, however, to come to the parsonage for the devotional meetings and prayer services. The very day she announced giving up the French lessons, she was back with John by one o'clock. The Diary records:

"1. Mr. Campbell, Mrs. Gilbert, Miss Sophy, sung, prayed, sung, prayed, sung.

"2. Garden, conversed, she [Sophy] quite open; got no good; meditated. She would breakfast with me no more." (Evidently John had urged her to change her mind on this matter.)

Then she was back for evening prayers and after the prayers she and the other members of the Little Society stayed on "for reading, conversation and singing." And the next day she not only came for early prayers; she also took a French lesson, though not at the parsonage, but "after tea in her own house," as John carefully noted, and she again attended the evening Society meeting.

So, in spite of her seemingly purposeful moves to push John into an out-and-out proposal, their close association continued smoothly for three days. Then, still having received no declaration of love, the strain apparently became too much for her and her poise collapsed. Once more John shows his naïveté in the following account:

"Sat. 19—I called upon her at Mr. Causton's, and we walked together in the garden. She did not seem to be affected with anything I said, but was in such a temper as I never saw her before, sharp, fretful, and disputatious. Yet in an hour she awaked as out of sleep, told me she had been very ill all day, and indeed scarce in her senses, and feared she had given a sufficient proof of it in her behaviour, which she begged I would not impute to her, but solely to her disorder."

The poor, blind man.

THIRTEEN

A couple of days later John's thoughts were partly distracted from his grievous problem by the threat of a Spanish invasion and the unexpected predicament in which it placed his Moravian friends and Thomas Causton.

From Charles-Town, the First Bailiff received letters informing him that the Spaniards in Florida were preparing to invade Savannah at an early hour. The Florida Governor and Council, so the dispatches said, had already sent orders to their agents in the Creek and other Indian nations to raise eight hundred volunteers to join the Spanish troops and to buy sufficient corn and rice to provision them.

Thomas, highly alarmed, called a meeting of the leading citizens to discuss what was best to do. Two plans evolved: They must immediately build a fort on the Bluff of the Savannah River at the southeast corner of the town, and they must take a city-wide census.

On the twentieth of February, according to Adelaide Fries's *Moravians*, "officers went through the town, taking the names of all who could bear arms, freeholders and serv-ants alike." Three of them appeared at the House of the Mo-ravians and demanded from Joseph Toltschig a list of the able-bodied men there.

"There is no one among us who can bear arms," Joseph told them, meaning, of course, that their religion forbade them to do so.

"It is remarkable that in a house full of strong men none can bear arms," answered one of the census takers sarcasti-cally. "Hurry up and give us the names; we can't wait."

Joseph quietly stood his ground. He said if any of the Mo-ravian household desired to go to the defense of Savannah, none would stop him, but he would furnish no names.

The census taker, his patience at an end, snapped he would report him to Bailiff Causton.

It was a good idea, Joseph agreed. He, too, would report the matter to the Bailiff.

Benjamin accompanied Joseph to see the First Bailiff; but since Joseph was fully capable of taking care of himself in the argument that ensued, Benjamin kept quiet except to translate.

"Everybody must go to war and fight for his own safety," declared Thomas, "and if you will not join the army, the town's people will burn down your house and will kill you all."

"That may happen, but we cannot help it," said Joseph. "It is against our conscience to fight."

Thomas grew more threatening. "If you do not mean to fight, you had better go and hide in the woods, out of sight of the people, or it will be worse for you; and you had better go before the enemy comes, for then it will be too late to escape, the town's people will certainly kill you."

"You forget that Oglethorpe promised us exemption from military service and we claim the liberty he pledged."

Thomas replied testily, "If the Count [Count Zinzendorf] and the Trustees, and the King himself had agreed on that in

London it would count for nothing here. If war comes it will be fight or die. If I were an officer on a march and met people who would not join me, I would shoot them with my own hand, and you can expect no other treatment from the officers here."

"We are all servants and can not be legally impressed," the Moravian bishop pointed out.

"If the Count himself were here, he would have to take his gun on his shoulder and all his servants with him. If he were living on his estate at Old Fort it would make no difference, for the order of the Magistrates must be obeyed. If the English to whom the country belongs must fight, shall others go free?"

Thomas finally wore Joseph down to the point of giving the number of able-bodied Moravians. Why not? Joseph reasoned. They could be counted any time. But the names he refused to give.

Thomas was right about the settlers' reaction to the Moravians' pacifism. They vowed that before they would fight to defend them, they would mob and kill them. The Germans were injurious to the Colony anyway, they railed. They worked so cheaply, they lowered the wage scale, and they spent no money in the shops, for they made everything for themselves.

After three days of angry protestations, the freeholders in charge of erecting the new defenses hit upon what they considered a brilliant idea. They asked the Moravians to lend them their oxen and wagon and to supply the men to haul logs for the fort. The Moravians replied that they would lend their oxen and wagon without charge and they would supply the food for the animals; but none of their number would lift a hand in preparation for war.

This infuriated the settlers to such a pitch that several of the Brethren began to consider the advisability of offering to hew logs for the fort just as a matter of friendship. They argued they could do it in the depths of the forest without ever seeing to what use the logs were being put. The suggestion gained so much favor that the head Moravians decided to settle the argument by drawing lots. The slip that was drawn forbade any compromise.

The tension grew. Mobs gathered in front of the House to double their fists and call out curses. When the situation appeared to be on the verge of serious violence, Joseph held a meeting of the Brethren to decide whether they should wait for the storm to pass or pack their belongings and move to North Carolina or Pennsylvania. After a long discussion, this question, too, was referred to the lot. The drawn slip read, "Go out from among them."

Following up this directive, John wrote a letter that Joseph dictated to the First Bailiff, reminding him that the Moravians' main reason for coming to Georgia was to enjoy freedom of conscience and of worship.

"But if this cannot be allowed," said Joseph, "and our remaining here in Savannah be burdensome to the people, as we already perceive it begins to be, we are willing, with the approbation of the Magistrates, to remove from this place; by this means any tumult that might ensue on our account will be avoided, and [any] occasion of offense cut off from those who now reproach us that they are obliged to fight for us."

The letter came as a terrible blow to Thomas. He had never intended to push the Moravians to such lengths that they would abandon the Colony. He knew that James Oglethorpe and the Trustees admired these people greatly, considering them well-behaved, industrious, worthwhile colonizers.

Hurriedly he summoned Joseph to another conference and explained ingratiatingly that since Joseph's people trusted in God, he doubted seriously that God would allow their House to be burned over their heads.

That was the least of their worries, replied Joseph with

183

some hauteur; they had come to the Colony for religious freedom and now the people were attempting to force them to act contrary to the dictates of their conscience.

Realizing that the Moravian leader was adamant, the First Bailiff's thoughts began to run frantically in circles. What could he say to hold them in Georgia until, perhaps, an opportunity arose to change their minds? What could he say to halt this damaging move and yet save his face? Finally he declared he had no power in the matter of their leaving; that must be settled among Count Zinzendorf, the Trustees, and themselves. However, he could not permit them to leave until he received an order from the Trustees. Meanwhile, he would do all he could to "quiet the people's indignation."

Though the Spanish invasion did not materialize at this juncture and the antagonism of the settlers subsided, the Moravians did not alter their resolve to leave Georgia. In their own good time they would make the move.

During the early days of the confrontation, John decided that either he or Benjamin should go to England to try to persuade James Oglethorpe, who had been there for several months, and the Trustees to assure the Germans that their freedom of conscience would not be violated, as well as to see if some new missionary workers might be secured for this wilderness vineyard of the New World.

Originally John thought he should be the one to go; but before definitely making up his mind he wanted to discuss it with Sophy. He found her and Martha together and, with no polite chatter, broke the news that he probably would depart for London shortly. Sophy was stunned. Her face paled, then flooded with color, then went white again, and she stared fixedly at John until he finished speaking.

"What, are you going to England?" she blurted out as if she could not believe her own ears. "Then I have no tie with America left."

Martha, evidently realizing instantly that it would never

do for Sophy and John to be separated at this crucial point in their love affair, spoke up: "Indeed, I think I must go, too. Phiky [this was her pet name for her niece], will you go with me?"

"Yes, with all my heart," Sophy declared.

Then, hoping apparently to point out to John just how deep an effect his threatened departure had had on her niece, Martha said to Sophy, "[But] last night you said you would not [go.]

"True, but now all the world is alike to me," Sophy replied.

These words were unmistakably music to John's ears, music he longed to hear repeated again and again, for that very evening, walking Sophy home from the parsonage after the Society meeting, he reintroduced the subject. "Miss Sophy, what did you mean this afternoon by saying if I went to England, you had no tie to America left?"

With tears in her eyes, she answered, "You are the best friend I ever had in the world. You showed yourself a friend indeed when no one else would have afforded me any more than common pity."

"You would hardly confess this if the Trustees should be set against me, and take away all I have here."

"Indeed, I would," she replied fervently, "and you or your friends can never want while I have anything."

John decided not to go after all; he would send Benjamin. And so Benjamin embarked the very next afternoon. The Moravian, Peter Rose, and his wife would be in charge of the Indian school at Irene during his absence. They had been working there almost from the school's beginning.

John did not see Sophy on the day of Benjamin's departure until after the ship sailed; but then he hurried to the Caustons' where she happened to be alone. "This was indeed an hour of trial," he wrote. "Her words, her eyes, her air, her every motion and gesture were full of such a softness and sweetness I know not what might have been the consequences had I then but touched her hand. And how I avoided it, I know not. God is surely over all!"

The next day he was alone with her again—this time at the parsonage—and again in acute pain he added to *An Account:* "Finding her still the same, my resolution failed. At the end of a very serious conversation I took her by the hand and, perceiving she was not displeased, I was so utterly disarmed that that hour I should have engaged myself for life, had it not been for the full persuasion I had of her entire sincerity, and in consequence of which, I doubted not but she was resolved (as she had said) 'never to marry while she lived.'

"A moment's reflection when she was gone convinced me that I had done foolishly. And I once more resolved by God's help to be more wary for the future. Accordingly, though I saw her every day in the following week, I touched her not."

Delamotte, apparently ignorant of the restraining vise into which John had locked his emotions, grew alarmed at the state of affairs. Indeed, so John reported, he "had never seen him in such uneasiness before." Weeping broken-heartedly, Delamotte said to his idol, "I find we must part, for I can not live in this house when you are married to Miss Sophy."

Surprised, John answered, "I have no intention to marry her."

"You do not know your own heart, sir," Delamotte protested. "I can see clearly you will marry her very soon unless you break off all intercourse with her."

John had not expected his young, doting companion to speak so bluntly. He answered quite stiffly, "That's a point of great importance and therefore not to be determined suddenly."

Delamotte was not to be put off. "You ought to determine it as soon as possible," he argued, "for you are losing ground daily."

John admitted frankly that there was truth in the remark and so readily consented to set aside the next day so that he and Delamotte might arrive at a decision. He described the session in *An Account:*

"March 4, Fri.—Having both of us sought God by deep consideration, fasting, and prayer, in the afternoon we conferred together, but could not come to any decision. We both apprehended Mr. Ingham's objection to be the strongest, the doubt whether she was what she appeared. But this doubt was too hard for us to solve. At length we agreed to appeal to the Searcher of hearts. I accordingly made three lots. In one was writ, 'Marry'; in the second, 'Think not of it this year.' After we had prayed to God to 'give a perfect lot', Mr. Delamotte drew the third, in which were these words, 'Think of it no more.' Instead of the agony I had reason to expect, I was enabled to say cheerfully, 'Thy will be done.' We cast lots once again to know whether I ought to converse with her any more; and the direction I received from God was, 'Only in the presence of Mr. Delamotte.'

"I saw and adored the goodness of God, though what He required of me was a costly sacrifice. It was indeed the giving up at once whatever this world affords of agreeable—not only honour, fortune, power (which indeed were nothing to me, who despised them as clay in the streets), but all the truly desirable conveniences of life—a pleasant house, a delightful garden, on the brow of a hill at a small distance from the town; another house and garden in the town; and a third a few miles off, with a large tract of fruitful land adjoining to it. And above all, what to me made all things else vile and utterly beneath a thought, such a companion as I never expected to find again, should I live one thousand years twice told. So that I could not but cry out: 'O Lord God, Thou God of my fathers, plenteous in mercy and truth, behold I give Thee, not thousands of rams or ten thousands of rivers of oil, but the desire of my eyes, the joy of my heart, the one thing upon earth which I longed for! O give me Wisdom which sitteth by Thy throne, and reject me not from among Thy children!' "

In listing the world's goods he was sacrificing, John was calculating that by marriage he would come into possession of—or at least the use of—Sophy's land, which he frequently referred to in the Diary and Journal, and would in time inherit some of Thomas' houses and five hundred acres. Several months back Thomas had built a commodious country house, which he called Ocstead, on a high bluff overlooking the Wilmington River and the wide stretches of marsh near Thunderbolt. John had seen Ocstead at least once; he had accompanied James Oglethorpe that far when the Georgia founder had last left for England; but it was not until the day after the decision by sortilege that he seems to have appreciated the place fully. He described it thusly:

"Mon. 7.—Mr. Causton asked me to ride with him to his plantation, four miles from Savannah. I was quite struck with the pleasantness of the situation: the hill, the river, the woods were delightful, and shot a softness into my soul which had not left me when at our return he asked me to drink a dish of tea at his house."

Sophy was at the town house, for John continued his report of the afternoon with a puzzling account of his encounter with her—the first since the decree to think of marriage "no more":

"Soon after I came in, Miss Sophy went out, and walked to and fro between the door and the garden. I saw she wanted to speak to me, but remembered my resolutions, especially that to converse with her only in Mr. Delamotte's presence. Yet after a short struggle, the evil soul prevailed in me, and I went. Immediately she catched hold of both my hands, and with the most engaging gesture, look, and tone of voice said, 'You never denied me anything that I desired yet, and you shall not deny me what I desire now.' I said, 'Miss Sophy, I

188

will not; what is it?' She answered, 'Don't say anything to her that offered me the letter the other day. My refusing it has given her pain enough already.' I replied, 'I will not. And if you had told me of it before, I would not have told your uncle of it, as Mr. Williamson did.' She said, 'Did he? Well, I find what you have often said is true. There is no trusting any but a Christian. And for my part, I am resolved never to trust any one again who is not so.' I looked upon her, and should have said too much had we had a moment longer. But in the instant Mr. Causton called us in. So I was once more 'snatched as a brand out of the fire.' "

The letter Sophy refused to accept must have been from Tommy, who was still in Savannah and still out of jail. (John just two days before had noted that Tommy had come to see him, though what he had come about John failed to say.) No doubt because of his criminal record and the watchful eye of the First Bailiff, Tommy was afraid to approach Sophy openly and so had written her a letter that one of his cousins or friends had tried to give her.

The conversation that John had with Sophy the next morning gives credence to this supposition because he quickly brought up Tom's name while breakfasting with her (she apparently had backed down from her resolution never to have breakfast with him again) and with Delamotte.

"Miss Sophy, what do you think of Mr. Mellichamp?" he asked point-blank.

"I thank God," she answered, "I have entirely conquered that inclination."

One might think this answer would have contented John for the time being; but not at all. After a little more talk, he remarked, "I hear Mr. Williamson pays his addresses to you. Is it true?"

This took Sophy by surprise, for there was a "little pause" before she replied, "If it were not [true] I would have told you so."

189

"How do you like him?"

"I don't know; there is a great deal in being in the house with one. But I have no inclination for him."

"Miss Sophy, if you ever deceive me, I shall scarce ever believe any one again."

Sophy looked up at him and answered with a smile, "You will never have that reason for distrusting any one; I shall never deceive you."

She got up to leave then, but "turned back" and added, "Of one thing, sir, be assured: I will never take any step in anything of importance without first consulting you."

"She went, and I saw myself in the toils," John wrote in *An Account*. "But how to escape I saw not. If I continued to converse with her, though not alone, I found I should love her more and more. And the time to break it off was past. I felt it was now beyond my strength. My resolutions indeed remained. But how long? Yet a little longer, till another shock of temptation, and then I well knew they would break in sunder as a thread of tow that has touched the fire. I had many times prayed that if it was best our intercourse should break off, and that if I could not do it she might. But this too I saw less and less reason to expect. So that all these things were against me, and I lay struggling in the net; nay, scarcely struggling, as even fearing to be delivered."

That very evening, after Sophy had left the prayer service and gone home, she returned "in the utmost consternation" to the parsonage with Margaret Bovey and urged John to go to her aunt and try to quiet her. John found Martha "with an open letter in her hand," which she gave him to read. It was from Tommy to Sophy—perhaps the very letter Sophy had refused to accept some days before. In some unexplained fashion, Martha had "intercepted it."

John did not put down in *An Account* the contents of the letter, but whatever they were, they threw Martha into a terrible state, for John told her, "I hope things are not so ill as you apprehend," and only departed "when she was a little more composed" in order "at her desire to make some further inquiries."

On his return in half an hour, Martha was "chiding Miss Sophy very sharply." Among many other denunciations, she screamed, "Get out of my home; I will be plagued with ye no longer." Then, turning to John, she cried, "Mr. Wesley, I wish you would take her; take her away with ye."

Amazingly calm, considering the stormy circumstances, John replied, "Miss Sophy is welcome to my house, or anything that I have."

It is clear from that remark that there was nothing in Tommy's letter that incriminated Sophy. John certainly would not have offered her his home or "anything" he had if the letter had suggested she was guilty of a wrongful act. His feelings toward her had not altered the fraction of a heartbeat.

Sophy, however, did not grasp at his offer. Apparently stunned into a cowering silence by Martha's onslaught and John's rather pompous statement, she, as John reported "answered only with tears." Once again the question intrudes: But how else could she have answered? John had made no declaration of love, no proposal of marriage. Why had he not stepped forward quickly, taken her into his arms, and assured her that he wanted her for his wife? Why, why had he not spoken out? Could she, at eighteen, understand that his vows of chastity were more compelling than his passion for her?

John understood it and was in abject misery. He returned to the parsonage about ten that same evening with, so he expressed it, "such an unwillingness and heaviness as I had scarce ever felt before."

Very early the next morning, a mean, rainy morning, he was already on his way back to the Caustons'. What he hoped to accomplish will always remain a mystery, for he was met at the door by a completely changed, smiling, smug Martha who opened the conversation with this bomb shell:

"Sir, Mr. Causton and I are exceedingly obliged to you for all the pains you have taken about Sophy. And so is Sophy too; and she desires you would publish the banns of marriage between her and Mr. Williamson on Sunday."

John's reply, if any, received no space on any sheet of paper; but that he was stunned and sickened is apparent from Martha's next words: "Sir, you don't seem to be well pleased. Have you any objection to it?"

"Madam, I don't seem to be awake," John finally managed to get out. "Surely I am in a dream."

Martha assured him it was no dream. "They agreed on it last night between themselves after you was gone. And afterwards Mr. Williamson asked Mr. Causton's and my consent, which we gave him; but if you have any objection to it, pray speak. Speak to her. She is at the Lot. Go to her. She will be very glad to hear anything Mr. Wesley has to say. Pray go and talk to her yourself."

"No, madam," John said stiffly, struggling with all his might to keep from breaking down, "if Miss Sophy is engaged, I have nothing to say. It will not signify for me to see her any more."

Then, still stunned and at a loss for words, he suggested leaving; but Martha insisted on his staying at least until the rain let up. While he waited, the burden of her conversation was: Why was he so uneasy? And why didn't he go and talk with Sophy himself? Which prompted him to write in *An Account:* "I doubted whether all this were not artifice, merely designed to quicken me. But though I was uneasy at the very thought of her marrying one who, I believed, would make her very unhappy, yet I could not resolve to save her from him by marrying her myself. Besides, I reasoned thus, 'Either she is engaged or not; if she is, I could not have her if I might: if not, there is nothing in this show which ought to alter my preceding resolution.' "

Nevertheless, in the very next paragraph he flatly contradicted his own assertion that he "could not save her . . . by marrying her." As some biographers have suggested, he could have inserted the paragraph later in *An Account;* but he was in such a frantic, upset frame of mind, he could have written at that very hour practically anything. What he did write either then or later was: ". . . Had I seen the real case to be this—'She is engaged, but conditionally only, Mr. Williamson shall marry her if you will not' I could not have stood that shock. I should have incurred any loss rather than she should have run that hazard, of losing both her body and soul in hell."

In this wild turmoil, he prayed awhile, then, as he understated it, "still full of perplexity," he felt he must see Sophy and talk to her at least once more. Pitifully meek, he persuaded Delamotte to walk approximately five miles to Sophy's Lot and ask her if John's company would be agreeable to her. After what must have seemed like an eternity to John, Delamotte returned with the assurance that Sophy would be happy to see him. Immediately, he set out and found her and William together, sheltered from the rain by a lean-to for tools and hay and bags of grain for the animals. The three entered into a session of talk and of long silences, the details of which may be read in John's own words.

"She began with her usual sweetness," he wrote. " 'Why would you put yourself to the trouble of sending? What need of that ceremony between us? You know your conversation is always welcome to me.' Then silence ensued, which Mr. Williamson broke thus: 'I suppose, sir, you know what was agreed on last night between Miss Sophy and me?' I answered, 'I have heard something; but I could not believe it, unless I should hear it from Miss Sophy herself.' She replied, 'Sir, I have given Mr. Williamson my consent—unless you have anything to object.' It started in my mind, 'What if she means, unless you will marry me?' But I checked the thought with, 'Miss Sophy is so sincere: if she meant so, she would say so'; and replied, 'If you have given your consent, the time is past; I have nothing to object.' Mr. Williamson desired me, if I had, to speak, and then left her and me together."

Together in that little windowless shed, with the gray, misty rain outside like thinned moss swaying on the live oaks in the fickle puffs of wind from across the pale yellow marshes and mud flats of the Wilmington River. Intimately together in that small shadowy space, yet inwardly, achingly tense, apprehensive, and shy as strangers stranded on some deserted shore.

" 'Tis hard to describe" John continued, "the complication of passions and tumult of thought which I then felt: fear of her approaching misery, and tender pity; grief for my own loss; love shooting through all the recesses of my soul, and sharpening every thought and passion. Underneath there was a faint desire to do and suffer the will of God, which, joined to a doubt whether that proposal [of marriage] would be accepted, was just strong enough to prevent my saying plainly (which I wonder to this hour I did not say) 'Miss Sophy, will you marry me?' As soon as I could speak, I reminded her of her resolution, 'If she married at all, to marry none but a religious man,' and desired her to consider whether Mr. Williamson was such. She said, 'She had no proof to the contrary.' I told her, 'That was not enough. Before she staked so much upon it, she ought to have full, positive proof that he was religious. She said again, 'I no otherwise consented, than if you had nothing to object.' Little more was said, tears in both supplying the place of words. More than an hour was spent thus."

An hour is a long, long time.

Just before William returned, Sophy said to John, "I hope I shall always have your friendship."

John answered yes, he could "still be her friend," even though he left America.

"I hope you won't leave us," she begged.

"I can't at all judge of how God will dispose of me." It was

194

a stiff, formal remark. Perhaps he was afraid to try to utter any other kind.

Nevertheless, Sophy gently persisted. "However, you will let me have your correspondence."

"I doubt it cannot be."

Upon William's return, John recounted, he "exhorted them both to 'assist each other in serving God with all their strength' and her in particular 'to remember the many instructions and advices I had given her.'" He then kissed them both and took his leave of her "as one I was to see no more."

On reaching the parsonage, he went into the garden and strode back and forth, struggling to find surcease for his tortured body and mind. He felt crucified. He, too, was giving his blood, his heart's blood, to serve God in the only way he believed right. Once again his own words give us the most vivid and poignant account of his ordeal:

"From the beginning of my life to this hour I had not known one such as this. God let loose my inordinate affection upon me, and the poison thereof drank up my spirit. I was as stupid as if half awake, and yet in the sharpest pain I ever felt. To see her no more: that thought was as the piercings of a sword; it was not to be bourne, nor shaken off. I was weary of the world, of light, of life. Yet one way remained, to seek God—a very present help in time of trouble. And I did seek after God, but I found Him not. I forsook Him before; now He forsook me. I could not pray. Then indeed the snares of death were about me. The pains of hell overtook me. Yet I struggled for life; and though I had neither words or thoughts, I lifted up my eyes to the Prince that is highly exalted, and supplied the place of them as I could: and about four o'clock He so far took the cup from me that I drank so deeply of it no more."

Still, the dregs were bitter. His next move proves even more plainly than his words how utterly desperate he felt. He had to do something; he had to talk to somebody. So he wrote a note to the First Bailiff, asking him to come to see him. Around five o'clock—to John it must have seemed like midnight by this time—he came.

"I don't approve of this match," Thomas said right off. "Mr. Williamson asked my consent this morning; but I have neither denied nor given it. Indeed I have often promised Sophy, so she would not have Mellichamp, she should have whom she would beside. But what passed between her and you at the Lot?"

John told him, as he noted, "without any disguise," to which Thomas exclaimed, "If you loved her, how could you possibly be so overseen as not to press her when she was so much moved?"

What John answered to this he omitted from *An Account;* perhaps he did not understand himself how he had managed not to "press her."

Now Thomas said wearily, "I will tell her my thoughts of it once more, and, if you please, so may you. But if she is not then convinced I must leave her to herself."

When he had gone, John asked himself what he would have done if Thomas had said plainly, "If you please, you may have her still; but if you won't, another will." If . . . if . . . if . . . ? Did John regret that the First Bailiff had not forced the issue? Did he long for someone, anyone, to tell him he must marry her? Someone to assure him it was the right thing to do? Right in the sight of God?

Thomas apparently carried out his part of the bargain to tell Sophy his "thoughts," which certainly meant that he urged her to try once more to bring John to the point of proposing. For when, that evening, she and William came to the prayer service and John asked her to stay after the rest of the company had left, she "readily" agreed, waving aside William's objections.

What a graphic detail is illuminated by just one sentence in *An Account!* Referring to William, John noted: "He

196

walked to and fro on the outside of the house, with all the signs of uneasiness."

But in spite of William's pacing in front of the parlor windows and of Delamotte's refusal to move out of hearing distance, John angrily accused Sophy of lying to him. "Miss Sophy, you said yesterday you would take no steps in anything of importance without first consulting me."

"Why, what could I do?" she asked imploringly. "What could I do? Just what could I do? I can't live in that house. I can't bear these shocks. This is quite a sudden thing. I have no particular inclination for Mr. Williamson. I only promised if no objection appeared. But what can I do?"

And she might have continued repeating this pitiful, pointed question, praying to get the answer she and Thomas wanted, if William, his patience exhausted, had not come in "abruptly" and "took her away."

We only have to glance at the wavering, messy, frequently corrected writing on the page of John's Diary for March ninth and to read the transliteration to know that this day was the most terrible he had experienced. Beginning with the hour Martha broke the news of the engagement to him, here is that page:

"10 Mrs. Causton's, in talk with her. Miss Sophy to be married; meditation.

"12 At the Lot, within with her, quite distressed!

"1 Within. Confounded!

"2 Took leave of her, ½ [an hour] at home. Could not pray!

"3 Tried to pray, lost, sunk!

"4 Bread, conversed with Delamotte. Little better!

"5 Mr. Causton came, in talk, tea.

"6 Kempis; German, Easier!

"7 Prayers.

"8 Miss Sophy et cetera, ½ within with her, ¾ with Delamotte, prayer.

197

"No such day since I first saw the sun!

"O deal tenderly with Thy servant!

"Let me not see such another!"

The next day he was still in a frenzy of indecision. He could not let the engagement stand, yet, when given the chance, he could not ask Sophy to break it. William, foolishly or magnanimously, had given him two opportunities to persuade Sophy to change her mind and marry him; but both times it had been impossible for John to bring himself to the point where he was willing to throw off the heavy, burdensome, restraining yoke of celibacy.

John Naylor, in his biography *Charles Delamotte, John Wesley's Companion*, agrees that this is the only excuse for John's erratic behavior; however, there were no actions or words of Sophy's that support his conclusion that she, too, was influenced by John's ideology. Maybe, in the beginning, she was swayed by his beliefs; but for weeks now she had been influenced only by her urge to marry him. Mr. Naylor writes: "This love story is sad and perplexing. The reader grows impatient. Such chopping and changing—now hot, now cold—doubts and endless consultations—all this seems absurd until we realize that to both lovers the sacredness of the minister's calling is the supreme consideration."

Despite John's "supreme consideration," he still desired another chance to argue with Sophy. He might not be able to propose marriage; but he might be able to stop her from a marriage with William. Then who could tell what might happen? Maybe in time he could see his way clear to make her his wife; maybe his passion might cool and there would be no longer the danger of her usurping the Church's role in his life. So he called again at the Caustons', evidently quite early, for he caught both William and Thomas at home.

"I wish to speak with Miss Sophy," he announced, surely holding his small figure as stiff as the bole of a pine sapling and staring unflinchingly with his piercing eyes at the two men and Martha.

"Sir, you shall speak with her no more till we are married," declared William. "You can persuade her to anything. After you went from the Lot yesterday, she would neither eat nor drink for two hours; but was crying continually, and in such an agony she was fit for nothing."

John answered with considerable arrogance in light of the delicate situation. "To-morrow, sir, you may be her director, but today she is to direct herself."

Then he asked for a piece of paper, and when it was provided, he "writ" these words: "Miss Sophy, will you see me or not?"

Sophy immediately came down. She and John went into the garden.

"Are you fully determined?" John asked her.

"I am," she answered.

"Take care you act upon a right motive," he warned. "The desire of avoiding crosses is not so. Beside, you can't avoid them. They will follow and overtake you in every state."

In understandable haste William joined them, forcing John to include him in the conversation. John advised them "to have the banns regularly published, exhorted them to love and serve God"; then assured them they could always count on his "friendship and assistance"; then returned to the parsonage "easy and satisfied."

Nevertheless, obsessed with love, he sought Sophy out again that very afternoon. He went to her Lot, accompanied by Delamotte, and read to her and William *Meditation on Heaven* by Bishop Hall, during which, according to John's notes, "Miss Sophy fixed her eyes on Mr. Williamson and me alternately for above half an hour, with as steady an observation as if she had been drawing our pictures."

When the reading was over, William, acting the perfect gentleman, said graciously to John, "I shall always be glad of your advice and hope you will favour us with your conversation, which I shall look upon as a particular happiness both to Sophy and me."

John could not unbend. Holding himself rigid, he answered, "I hope we shall all be happy in the place we have been reading of."

And so confident was he that this hope would someday be realized, he returned to the parsonage "rejoicing and wondering" at himself.

FOURTEEN

Sophy and William, accompanied by Margaret Bovey and
James Burnside, set out the next morning by boat for Purrysburg, South Carolina, and the next day—exactly a year from
the day John first spoke to Sophy—the two couples were
married.

The news of the trip made John actually ill. Indeed, from
the moment he learned that the four had left for Purrysburg,
he was in acute mental and physical distress. Suffering far
too greatly to write at any length, he jotted down sparse notes
in his Diary. He mentioned that he began the morning as
usual with prayer and singing; then wrote the one word,
"Pain." He then noted that he read prayers twice and twice
drank coffee, which he rarely ever touched; and talked with
Thomas. He found some relief in working on the German
dictionary, then, at ten o'clock, was in "much more pain." At
eleven, he was still in "much pain," but in spite of it, read the
book of Job and felt somewhat easier. In the afternoon he had
a visit from John Brownfield who, hearing of the double

201

elopement, hurried to spill all he knew and to find out all John knew. When night finally came, John went to the House of the Moravians and spent the whole evening talking about Sophy.

But the wedding day itself was the worst. He was in so much pain that he thought—even hoped—he was going to die. So he wrote his will, after which he managed to add one line to his Diary: "Today Miss Bovey and Miss Sophy were married at Purrysburg!!!"

He must have gone over and over the things he had done and not done; the words he had spoken and those he had left unspoken; but we have a record of only one incident for which he reproached himself. In early December he had suggested to Sophy that she "sup earlier and not immediately before she went to bed," which threw her into William's company, and "on this little circumstance," John mourned, hung "an inconceivable train of consequences. . . . All the colour of remaining life for her; but, perhaps all my happiness, too, 'in time and eternity.' "

Although the tragic fact that Sophy was married sickened him almost beyond bearing, he was also enraged and infuriated that a minister of the Church of England had married her and William before the banns were published. He made a solemn oath that he would protest the "carelessness" and "illegality" of the minister's action to the Reverend Mr. Gardner, the Bishop of London's Commissary at Charles-Town.

Thus John refused to recognize the marriage as valid. Sophy was still Miss Sophy to him, not Mrs. Williamson, though Margaret, from that day forth, became Mrs. Burnside. There was no question in his mind of the legality of Margaret's union with James. When he had objected to their marrying, they had had the banns published in South Carolina.

Immediately after the wedding ceremony, the two couples returned to Savannah, arriving at three o'clock in the morning. In spite of the late hour at which Sophy went to bed, she came that very day, a Sunday, to early-morning prayers. Thirty-nine others were present; but in his Diary John mentioned only Sophy by name. She also came to the afternoon class with the usual small group. And again the next evening.

At first John refrained from speaking to her about the legality of her marriage; but he discussed it freely with Margaret and James and others; and, when three days had passed, he sent for William so he could have it out with him.

William came, but not in the pliable mood for which John had hoped. William was already exceedingly angry over the pastor's remarks, which had been repeated to him, and he accused John of hating both Sophy and him and doing all in his power to cause trouble for them. The necessity of publishing the banns he simply brushed aside. He said he had looked upon Sophy as his wife for about six weeks—almost from the minute he had laid eyes on her—and he felt that was sufficient notice of his intentions.

"Furthermore, Mr. Wesley," he continued with considerable heat, "my wife has declared she will never come within your house again and she has begged me not to do it; nay not to go out alone, for she believes if either Mr. Delamotte or you caught me I would be murdered."

Without denying or affirming this danger to William's life, John said, "I would like to talk to her myself."

"She would never consent to it," William replied emphatically. Nevertheless, four days later he told John he could see her if he still so desired.

He desired it very much. He was considering refusing her the Lord's Supper, but he wanted to talk to her first. He arranged a meeting for Saturday evening at the Burnsides'. Only he, Margaret, and Sophy were present. Hurt and bitter as he had been for days, he taxed Sophy with insincerity before her marriage and with ingratitude since.

"I was never insincere with you," she protested. "On the noon of that day when the letter [Tommy's] was taken I told

203

Mr. Williamson that I should be glad to serve him as a friend, but resolved never to admit him as a lover."

Then, quite frankly, she admitted that if John had "pressed" her to marry him at any time her "temper was ruffled," she could not have refused him. She also said it was Tommy whom she feared would kill William if he ventured out alone, not John. Not for a moment had she seriously considered that John would treat her unkindly or speak an unkind word about her.

"Indeed, many instances of your anger and resentment have been related to me since my marriage," she elaborated, "but I could hardly believe them. Nor could they ever provoke me to say anything disrespectful of you. The most I've ever said was, 'Well, whatever he may say or do, now or hereafter, I will always own the man has been my friend and done me more service than any person living!' "

John was appeased for the time being. As he wrote in his Journal, "I believed what she said, and received her as a communicant the next day."

The Communion service over and the congregation dismissed, he dashed out of the courthouse-church and raced after her, his long black cassock whipping about his short, slender legs in the high March wind, until he overtook her. "Miss Sophy, I want to exhort you not to be weary of well-doing," he blurted out.

She listened quietly while he poured out further words of admonition; then she announced with shocking directness, "Mr. Williamson thinks it makes me uneasy to speak to you and therefore desires me to do it no more."

John realized immediately this was no whim of William's, but a serious command and so, the very next Sunday, he told Margaret and James that they would have to take over Sophy's religious training, as he could no longer see to it. They agreed to do their best and for three weeks he conveyed through them the counsel he deemed she was most in need of.

The fact that she was out of sight did not mean, however, that she was out of mind. He continued to think of her constantly. He read *An Account of Miss Sophy* to Margaret; he wrote to his brother Samuel about her and received in reply this sibling-like sentence of consolation: "I am sorry you are disappointed in one match because you are very unlikely to find another"; he spent an hour in private prayer for Sophy; he transcribed and sent to her a verse, written by a bond servant who had committed suicide, the last two lines of which certainly expressed his own despairing mood:

> Death could not a more sad retinue find:
> Sickness and pain before, and darkness all behind!

On the day he transcribed the verse, his Diary carried these exciting lines:

"8. Mr. Causton's, he out, conversed with Miss Sophy, Mrs. Causton, Mr. Williamson. . . .

"10. Could not sleep. . . . Could not sleep. 12. . . ."

That conversation with Sophy broke the arid spell of no communication with her that he had endured these weeks. On this day (it was Good Friday) he decided that the Burnsides' secondhand advice was "having little effect" and that he should resume speaking to her himself. They talked under the Caustons' shed, a sort of lean-to like a temporary porch, on the garden side of the house.

"This was our third conversation since her marriage," John recorded, "and lasted half an hour; but no private one, four or five persons being in the house within sight of us, and, if they pleased, hearing, too. She professed large obligations to me; I exhorted her to fulfill all righteousness."

Then, because Margaret had evidently told him that Sophy laid at William's door her slackening off of attendance at church services, devotionals, Society meetings, and other religious observances, John gave her a piece of advice that caused widespread discussion; in fact, he called it "that much controverted advice." Professing he would "avow it before all

205

the world," he told her: "In things of an indifferent nature you cannot be too obedient to your husband; but if his will should be contrary to the will of God, you are to obey God rather than man."

In the next sentence John gloated: "It may be observed that this day, of her own free choice, she fasted till evening."

This encounter apparently whetted John's appetite for more encounters because, the day following, after the Easter eve Communion, he spoke to her again "to the same effect," and this time Sophy told him in so many words, "Mr. Williamson is unwilling I should talk to you not because he thinks it makes me uneasy, but because he is afraid it would make me too strict."

More incensed now than ever that, without banns and by an irresponsible minister, she had been joined in matrimony to a man with no more Christianity than William, John, two days after Easter, set out in a sloop for Charles-Town to report the case to the Reverend Mr. Gardner. The Bishop assured him that no such irregularity would take place in the future. He felt certain, he said, that the clergyman in Purrysburg was the only one guilty of such lapses, but to be on the safe side he would caution all ministers of South Carolina under his jurisdiction at a meeting to be held the following week.

John remained in Charles-Town until the meeting convened so that he personally could take the matter up with the members. And for his pains several of them promised "they would never interfere with him in anything, nor (in particular) marry any persons of the Georgia Province without a letter from him, desiring them so to do."

On his way back to Savannah he passed through Purrysburg. So hateful were the connotations the town held for him that he was impelled to scourge it with his pen, though in his frenzied state he could not even express himself gramatically: ". . . a town the most without the appearance of a town I ever saw, with no form of comeliness or regularity.

. . . O, how God hath stretched over this place 'the lines of confusion and the stones of emptiness.' Alas for those whose lives were here vilely cast away, through oppression, through divers plagues and trouble! O, earth! How long wilt thou hide blood? How long wilt thou cover thy slain?"

Returning to Savannah, he pondered a dilemma that had engrossed him even before he left—"whether he could admit Miss Sophy to the Communion till she had in some manner or other owned her fault and declared her repentance." As we know, this was the second time he had faced this problem. But this time Sophy's fault was different. He gravely doubted he could admit her because he had been informed "she had left off fasting, and because she neglected all the morning prayers, though still acknowledging her obligation to both, which made a wide difference between her neglect and that of others."

Before the trip to Charles-Town, he had discussed with Delamotte repelling her from the Table. Amazingly, considering his former uncertainty of Sophy's sincerity, Delamotte urged John "to bear with her till he had spoken with her once more" and this, "after much consideration," John had decided to do. The trip, however, had delayed the conversation and on his return other matters delayed it a little longer. Among the other matters was Sophy's presence at morning prayers; he must have found it a bit difficult to discuss denying her the Lord's Supper when on Thursday, May 12, less than a week after his return, she appeared at that very early-morning service. Another matter that might have delayed him was his heavy paper work. On that same Thursday, after three hours with his Journal, he sorted papers, and "dinner over" at noon, he "writ Miss Sophy's Case until 5 o'clock."

Now, instead of *An Account of Miss Sophy* obsessing him, it was the *Case*. On Friday the thirteenth, he worked the entire morning on the Case; discussed it with the Moravians, who had not yet pulled up their Savannah stakes, and "writ" on it some more. That evening he talked with William, but, alas, never mentioned on what subject. But it must have been about Sophy, for they had no other topic in common.

And the following day, except for felling trees, which was the most strenuous physical exercise he knew, he continued to think about her and to talk with William about her. On Monday, the sixteenth, he wrote on the Case for two hours, bringing it up to date. Then he had the conversation with Sophy for which he had been waiting for two weeks. He reported it thusly: ". . . I did speak to her under the shed at Mr. Causton's from seven until evening prayers. This was our fifth conversation in which I honestly exhorted her to avoid all insincerity as she would avoid fire; to hold fast all the means of grace; and never to give way to so vain a thought as that she could attend the end without them. I hoped my labour was not in vain, for she promised fair and appeared deeply serious."

Still he continued to be ridden by thoughts of her and to be impelled into discussions about her with practically everyone with whom he came in contact, especially with Martha and Thomas. Again and again they had tea with him or he had tea with them, the main subject of their conversation being Sophy or John himself. He wrote in *Another Version of the Williamson Case:* "March 29, drinking tea at my house, after talking at least an hour and a half in praise of Mrs. Williamson, she [Martha] said and to the same effect she said two or three months after, both at her house and at Hogshead [Ocstead], 'Why couldn't you have told me you liked her—O! I should have been too happy!' And on Monday, May 23, speaking at Hogshead on the same head, after expressing several times her wish that I had married her, she added, 'What could I do more? I bid you take her—take her away with you.' I answered, 'Madam, I told her she was welcome to my house.' She said, again, 'Aye, but you didn't take her.' "

Then, after a river of words had flowed from the lips of the three of them, Thomas began criticizing William with considerable bitterness concluding his diatribe with the suggestion that Sophy should be free of him. "Since happiness is the end of marriage, where that can't be attained, the marriage is certainly null and void, and consequently both parties at liberty to marry where they can be happy," he expounded. "Why now there is poor Sophy. She can never be happy with that man."

John cut him short by saying, "I grant unhappy couples are at liberty to live asunder. But not to marry elsewhere. There is no law of God or man which will justify that."

Thomas answered, "If there is not a law for it, there ought to be, that the community may not lose so many children."

In an account of still another conversation of June 4, John reveals with pitiful clarity his complete subjection to thoughts of Sophy: "Going to speak to Mr. Brownfield, and not finding him at home, I fell into a conversation with Mrs. Brownfield upon Mrs. Williamson."

This is the first time John referred to Sophy as Mrs. Williamson in writing. The information Polly Brownfield imparted must have made Sophy suddenly seem like a stranger to him, a stranger whose coils he had been fortunate to escape. In fact, the paragraph preceding the account of the session with Polly reads:

"God showed me yet more of the greatness of my deliverance, by opening to me a new and unexpected scene of M.S.'s [Miss Sophy's] dissimulation. O never give me over to my own heart's desires, nor let me follow my own imagination!"

Polly, aware of the hurt and bitterness that gnawed at John, thought apparently to work her way into his good graces by declaring that her husband had warned her of Sophy long before "in words to this effect, 'Polly, take care [beware] of Miss Sophy; she is above your match.'"

She then related that on a Sunday night when she was at the Caustons (a Sunday night before Sophy was married to William and while Tommy was a free man in Savannah) she taxed Sophy with inconstancy to Tommy, which Sophy emphatically denied. She declared she loved him as well as ever and would come to Polly's to talk to her about him.

"On Tuesday she came," so Polly recounted, "and desired me to send a letter for her to Dolly Mellichamp [a relative of Tommy's], to give poor Tommy an opportunity of clearing himself. I told her I would not do it for the world without first asking Mr. Brownfield's advice, which I did. His advice was to have nothing to do with it. The next day she came to me crying and saying, 'I am ruined; my uncle says they have put Tommy in jail again.' "

Though this incident, if it happened at all, was approximately now three months past, it threw John into the wildest excitement. The account he wrote in his Journal shows his near madness:

"What could I do now? Go, and tell her of her fault between me and her alone? So I should have chosen, either as a friend or a pastor; but being cut off from this, all that remained was to inquire of others as diligently as I could whether this were not a false accusation. First then, I asked Mr. Brownfield to tell me frankly how far one might depend on Mrs. Brownfield's word? He answered, 'Perhaps she may not tell you all the truth she knows; but be assured she will tell you nothing but the truth.' I asked him next if he had ever advised her to have a care of Miss Sophy. He said he had, and repeated the words. I inquired further if she had ever asked his advice about sending a letter from Miss Sophy to Dolly Mellichamp. He said 'Yes; and he had advised her to have nothing at all to do with it.'

"I could think of but one thing more, which was to hear what Mrs. Causton, who knew her [Sophy] best, had to say in her defense. I went therefore to Hogshead, where she was, and told her so much of my objections against Mrs. Williamson as I could without betraying my authors to the resentment of the family. She strenuously maintained that Mrs. Williamson had never said anything false, or dissembled with me at all. Some of the words she spoke, leaning her head

210

back and lifting up both hands, were, 'By the Lord God, Sophy is as innocent as a new-born child; and I know she has as great a value for you as for any person living, except Mr. Williamson.' "

John apparently dismissed Martha's fervent protestations in favor of Polly's story, for he decided that the time had now really come for him to banish Sophy from the Holy Communion. Once again, however, Delamotte, having heard the full account, persuaded him "still to admit her."

"But a new hindrance now occurred," John complained bitterly in his Journal; "she would not admit herself." Looking over the Register, he found she had absented herself five times in April and May alone; and in this month, June, four times more, *viz*, the 11, 12, 24 and 29. (Though John might not have been aware of her condition, which may or may not have had anything to do with her absences, Sophy was pregnant.) Once more he determined to speak to her.

Nevertheless, almost a month went by before an opportunity presented itself. On John's part it was a month of constant activity: of "business" that had to do with the *Case of Miss Sophy*—of pastoral visits; of funerals, and of illness. Among the ill was John himself. Several times in his Diary he mentioned that John [Reigner] came, and frequently he noted he slept during the day, which, in his case, must be considered a serious symptom.

On Sunday, July 3, he found his chance. Sophy, in spite of her pregnant condition and the humid heat that lay over Savannah, was at the morning service and so, immediately after the Holy Communion, John caught up with her on the way home. "Mrs. Williamson," he began quite formally, "have you any reason to believe that from the day I first saw you till this hour, I have dissembled with you?"

"Indeed, I don't believe you have," she answered. "But you seem to think I have dissembled with you."

He told her he most assuredly did and began to elaborate on the reasons for his belief. But Sophy did not listen patiently as in times past. Edgy, either because of the heat or her condition, or because she resented what he was saying, she grew more and more angry, "till after a few minutes," as John reported, "she turned and went abruptly away."

Astounded, John must have stood rooted to the street, staring after her. He was at a loss to understand such behavior in Sophy, of all people. Was she wholly without remorse? Was she completely indifferent to her guilt? Was she hardened? Lost? It certainly appeared that way to him, but he was unwilling "to trust his own judgment and so went to see James Burnside to tell him everything and to ask how he "ought to act."

James, taking his cue from John's presentation of the "case," answered, "Sir, the case is clear. While things appear to you as they do now, you cannot admit her to the Holy Communion. The consequences of rejecting her, you know; but be they what they will, that does not alter your duty."

"Hereon I determined to do what I judged my duty," John confided in his Journal, "but with all the mildness and prudence God should give me."

Though he wrote that his mind was made up, he nevertheless felt he should give her "another opportunity, either of clearing herself or owning her fault," and went the very next evening to the Caustons' to interrogate her. But she would say nothing at all. Nothing! It was Martha who had all the answers. Inviting him to walk in the garden, she "talked largely of Sophy's innocence"; apologized for Sophy's rudeness of the day before, and urged him "more than once" to write to Sophy and tell her what he disliked in her behavior.

This he agreed to do.

But before he wrote to Sophy, he wrote to Thomas:

"Sir,
"To this hour you have shown yourself my friend; I ever have and ever shall acknowledge it. And it is my earnest de-

212

sire that He who hath hitherto given me this blessing would continue it still.

"But this cannot be, unless you will allow me one request, which is not so easy as it appears. Do not condemn me for doing in the execution of my office what I think it my duty to do.

"If you can prevail upon yourself to allow me this, even when I act without respect of persons, I am persuaded there will never be, at least not long, any misunderstanding between us. For even those who seek it, shall, I trust, find no occasions against me, except it be concerning the law of my God. I am, &c

July 5, 1737."

An hour later he sat down to compose the letter to Sophy. He must write it in the most calm and friendly manner, he reminded himself, not only "in pursuance" of his resolution "to proceed with all mildness," but because Sophy had told him "she was so much grieved already." He wrote:

"If the sincerity of friendship is best to be known from the painful offices, then there could be no stronger proof of mine than that I gave you on Sunday; except that which I'm going to give you now, and which you may perhaps equally misinterpret.

"Would you know what I dislike in your past or present behaviour? You have always heard my thoughts as freely as you asked them. Nay, much more freely; you know it well, and so you shall do, as long as I can speak or write.

"In your present behaviour I dislike (1) your neglect of half the public service, which no man living can compel you to; (2) your neglect of fasting, which you once knew to be a help to the mind, without any prejudice to the body; (3) your neglect of almost half the opportunity of communicating which you have lately had.

"But these things are small in comparison of what I dislike

213

in your past behaviour. For, (1) You told me over and over you had entirely conquered your inclination for Mr. Mellichamp. Yet at that very time you had not conquered it. (2) You told me frequently, you had no design to marry Mr. Williamson. Yet at the very time you spoke you had the design. (3) In order to conceal both these things from me, you went through a course of deliberate dissimulation. Oh how fallen! How changed! Surely there was a time when in Miss Sophy's life there was no guile.

"Own these facts, and own your fault, and you will be in my thoughts as if they had never been. If you are otherwise minded, I shall still be your friend, though I cannot expect you should be mine."

It could not have been an easy letter to write. As it so plainly shows, he was consumed with jealousy—the neglect of her religious duties was "small," he baldly admitted, "in comparison" with her conduct in matters of the heart—and so listing what he considered her acts of "deliberate dissimulation" must have made him weep inwardly, if not outwardly. How he unintentionally pitied himself! He felt himself more wronged than any of God's creatures.

Even his Diary of that July 5 showed signs of distress, as well as bearing evidence of his continued preoccupation with the "case." He talked of "Miss Sophy" with John Brownfield, the Moravians, and James.

The next morning he was still apparently highly nervous and full of anxieties, for, to relieve "the tension," he walked the five miles to Thunderbolt, reading Archbishop Usher and composing verses all the way there and back. And he was still composing verses in the afternoon when Thomas, Henry Parker, and Recorder Christie arrived at the parsonage.

"Mr. Wesley, you have sent me a letter that I can not understand," the First Bailiff declared excitedly. "How can you possibly entertain such a thought of me as that I would oppose you in executing any part of your office?"

"Sir, what if I should think it the duty of my office to repel one of your family from the Holy Communion?" John asked bluntly.

"If you repel me or my wife, I shall require a legal reason," Thomas answered, as if he were discussing a hypothetical question. "But I shall trouble myself about none else. Let them look to themselves."

Five days later, Sophy miscarried. Mrs. Causton told some friends it was because John had chided her dear niece eight days before, but she told others it was because of his unkind letter. Sophy, however, said it was because of her "hurry and concern for Mr. Williamson," who had come down with a fever.

The news of the miscarriage did not change John's "case" against Sophy. In fact, the "business" was fast becoming more urgent. Even on a trip to Ebenezer, where the Salzburgers were settled, he poured every detail of it into the ears of his old friend, August Gottlieb Spangenberg, who, after a long absence from Georgia, was back to look into the uneasy truce between the Moravians and the Savannah Magistrates.

"The calm we have so long enjoyed is drawing to an end," John told him, referring to the calm of his own parish. "You will shortly see that I am not, as some might have told you, a respecter of persons. I am determined, God being my helper, to behave indifferently to all, rich or poor, friends or enemies."

The very next Sunday, August 7, John took the step over which he had been agonizing so long. In front of the assembled congregation, as Sophy knelt at the rail, he refused her the Lord's Supper. He wrote that he had wanted to warn her privately beforehand, but having had no opportunity to do so, he was "reduced to the necessity of telling her in the church (indeed, so softly that none heard it but herself) and in the mildest manner" he was capable of, "I can't administer the Holy Communion to you before I have spoken with you."

FIFTEEN

Sophy did not take her expulsion from the Communion Table meekly. Her usually gentle, even-tempered, submissive nature erupted as furiously as a volcano. Those expressive eyes, which John so loved, must have flashed like lightning, and her lovely face with its wondrously sweet smile was grim. That very afternoon she hurried to the Burnsides' to give vent to her indignation; but for once she received no sympathy.

Margaret told her quite frankly: "Sophy, you was much to blame, after receiving that letter from Mr. Wesley, to offer yourself at the Table before you had cleared yourself to him. But you can easily put an end to this by going to Mr. Wesley now and clearing yourself of what you are charged with."

Sophy answered curtly, "No. I will not show such meanness of spirit as to speak with him about it myself; but somebody else shall."

Two days later, at seven o'clock in the morning, Noble Jones, one of the four constables of Savannah, served a warrant on John, issued the day before by Recorder Christie. It read:

"Georgia, Savannah Ss [Abbreviation of *scilicet*, meaning to wit, namely, etc.]

"To all Constables, Tithingmen and others, whom these may concern:

"You, and each of you, are hereby required to take the body of John Wesley, Clerk:

"And bring him before one of the bailiffs of the said town to answer the complaint of William Williamson and Sophia, his wife, for defaming the said Sophia, and refusing to administer to her the Sacrament of the Lord's Supper, in a public congregation, without cause; by which the said William Williamson is damaged one thousand pounds sterling: And for so doing, this is your warrant, certifying what you are to do in the premises. Given under my hand and seal of the 8th day of August, Anno Domino 1737.

Tho. Christie."

Constable Jones took John before the Second Bailiff, Henry Parker, and Recorder Christie. Since lawyers were not allowed to appear for a defendant in any Georgia court, John stood alone just a few feet below the dais at which he was accustomed to conduct the church services. William's charges against him were: (1) that John had defamed William's wife; (2) that he had repelled her without cause from the Holy Communion.

The first article John denied and the second he refused to answer to. "It being purely ecclesiastical," he said. "I cannot acknowledge the Court's power to interrogate me."

This statement must have baffled Henry completely; he had no training in the law. He only knew how to saw a little timber and float it downstream to be loaded for the West Indies and how to raise a few cows, pigs, chickens, fruit, and vegetables. He doubtless stared in consternation at John for

217

several minutes; then glanced inquiringly at Recorder Christie. The Recorder certainly pretended not to notice Henry's appeal, for he was as ignorant of the law as was the Second Bailiff.

Realizing that he could expect no help from the Recorder, Henry declared, "Nevertheless, Mr. Wesley, you are ordered to appear at the next Court holden for Savannah."

At that point William stepped forward. "Gentlemen," he said ingratiatingly, "I desire Mr. Wesley may give bail for his appearance."

To which Henry replied with considerable dignity, "Sir, Mr. Wesley's word is sufficient."

William stalked out in anger and shortly tacked a notice on the public bulletin board in Percival Square, forbidding anyone to carry John out of the Province, as he was "guilty of divers, notorious offences, under the penalty of 1,000 pounds."

Thomas at this juncture was less hotheaded than either his nephew-in-law or Sophy. Perhaps a warning of James Oglethorpe's echoed in his ears. According to John's biographer, the Reverend Mr. Moore, the Georgia leader, on the eve of his departure for England, had said to Thomas, "Causton, whatever you do, take heed, if you regard my favour, that you do not quarrel with Mr. Wesley." Furthermore, as First Bailiff, he was answerable to the Trustees for his actions and acutely conscious of the fact that they had appointed John to the Savannah ministry and would look with disapproval at court proceedings against him. So Thomas decided to extend an olive branch. He wrote John a letter, prompted, so he explained, "from a just regard of the friendship which had subsisted till this affair," asking him to appear at four o'clock that afternoon before all the people at the courthouse-church to give his reasons for repelling Sophy.

John carefully considered the proposal and rejected it on three grounds, which he set down in his Journal: "(1) because all the people were not proper judges of ecclesiastical matters; (2) because I was unwilling to expose her; and (3) because I foresaw that Mr. Causton himself would probably be insulted by the people."

The last "because" was a very real possibility. The settlers' wrath against the First Bailiff had been building up ever since he had become so affluent—the fine, new country house was the most glaring evidence—while their penury continued.

One bitter complaint to the Trustees was made by Robert Parker, a rather well-to-do trader in lumber, fish, and other Georgia commodities. "There is such an alteration of people," he wrote, "especially amongst them that have to do with the store, Mr. Oglethorpe would not know them. He has been witness of their poverty; [now] they never appear without their ruffles and their houses are well furnished with plenty of everything to profuseness."

Another was from Peter Gordon, Savannah's first First Bailiff, who, after a visit back to England, had returned to Georgia with Tomochichi and his party of Indians and with the original group of fifty Salzburgers. He reported to the Trustees that he "found the affairs of the Colony in the utmost confusion and so general a dislike that many of them had actually a design of sending Mr. Causton home to England in irons."

But Biographer Tyerman waxed more indignant over Thomas' blossoming of power and riches than either of these two: "By clever rascality he wiggled himself into Oglethorpe's favour and . . . was appointed a sort of dictator of the infant settlement, and had charge of the stores which the trustees sent over for the use of the colonists."

Then, after pointing out that in 1737 there were only 518 inhabitants in Savannah, of whom only 369 were adult males and females, the Reverend Mr. Tyerman continued his denunciations: "This was no large kingdom, but Thomas

219

Causton was a large man, because he was at the head of it. Indeed, the molehill empire seems to have magnified itself to the utmost extent possible, by the introduction of law, the establishment of courts, the appointment of officers, the election of juries and the adoption of everything else within its power which was likely to make a pompous minikin miniature of the great system of government at home. Causton was 'chief magistrate' and of course a 'chief' had subordinates under him. There was a recorder, also a bailiff. There were constables, tithing men and other great functionaries, all armed with solemn authority to rule, govern and keep in order, first themselves, and the above five hundred men, women and children, including John Wesley, the Oxford priest, and Charles Delamotte, the merchant master of almost a ragged school.

"Of all the great powers, however, in this log-built [Savannah, as we have already noted, was built of clapboards] village of five hundred souls, Thomas Causton in his own estimation, and in fact, was greatest."

John, in refusing Thomas' offer, did not list his reasons, but simply wrote: "I apprehend many ill consequences may arise from doing so. Let the case be laid before the Trustees."

The next morning, when the town bell rang as usual at seven o'clock to relieve the tithingmen on guard, the rumor spread like a wave across a beach that it was being rung for John's trial. In an unbelievably brief time the streets and squares were swarming with Savannahians on the way to the courthouse-church.

John, though, knowing better, remained quietly in the parsonage and Thomas, already in receipt of his letter, hurried there to see him. Immediately John realized that the First Bailiff's heart was no longer warmed by the spirit of reconciliation. He was in a fine fury and, by the time he finished telling John what he thought of his reckless, inconsiderate lack of co-operation, John understood that the fire he had lit was beyond control. (Indeed, in *Another Version of the William-son Case*, after recounting the bare facts of Sophy's expulsion from the Communion Table, John added: "Behold how much matter a small fire kindleth!")

Nevertheless, Thomas arrived at the parsonage again the next morning to try to arrange for a settlement of the case out of court. "Make an end of this matter," he thundered. "Thou hadst best. My niece to be used thus! I have drawn the sword, and I will never sheathe it till I have satisfaction." Then, catching his breath, he added, "Give the reasons of your repelling her before the whole congregation."

"Sir, if you insist upon it, I will," John answered, "and so you may be pleased to tell her."

"Write her and tell her yourself," Thomas snapped.

"I will."

So, as soon as Thomas was gone, John sat down and composed the following:

"To Mrs. Sophia Williamson,

"At Mr. Causton's request, I write once more. The rules whereby I proceed are these:

" 'So many as intended to be partakers of the Holy Communion, shall signify their names to the Curate, at least some time the day before.' This you did not do." (Even the most ardent admirer of John Wesley must wonder what this rule had to do with Sophy's expulsion when he had decided upon it a week before.)

" 'And if any of these . . . have done wrong to his neighbours, by word or deed, so that the congregation be thereby offended, the Curate . . . shall advertise him, that in any wise he presume not to come to the Lord's Table until he hath declared himself truly repented.'

"If you offer yourself at the Lord's Table on Sunday, I will advertise you, as I have done more than once, wherein you have done wrong. And when you have openly declared yourself to have truly repented, I will administer to you the mysteries of God.

John Wesley
August 11, 1737"

John meant exactly what he said. Though he had been pushed beyond the limit of his endurance by jealousy and love, he was now willing and ready to forgive. He was impetuous and instantly condemned what he judged wrong-doing, but he had a quick, let-bygones-be-bygones nature.

John's biographer, John Hampson, testified to this forgiving quality. Writing about his character in general, he said: "A remarkable feature in Mr. Wesley's character was his placability. . . . Persecution from without, he bore not only without anger, but without the least apparent emotion. . . . He had a great facility in forgiving injuries. Submission on the part of the offender, presently disarmed his resentment, and he would treat him with great kindness and cordiality."

When Delamotte delivered John's letter into Thomas' hands, Thomas, on the other hand, showed no let-bygones-be-bygones spirit. Indeed, Thomas flew into a rage and said "many warm things." "I am the person that am injured," he shouted. "The affront is offered to me; and I will espouse the cause of my niece. I am ill-used; and I will have the satisfaction, if it be to be had in the world."

And in the days that followed, he did begin in his own fashion to get satisfaction. He coaxed from Sophy all the letters John had written during the seventeen months of their acquaintance and read aloud the personal, intimate paragraphs, "even," according to John's Journal, "making here and there a few words to make things more clear" to friends and acquaintances on the street corners, in coffee shops, in taverns, in the Store, along the waterfront, everywhere. And while he was spreading the contents of the letters, Martha and William were telling everyone that Mr. Wesley had done this "merely out of revenge because Sophy would not have him."

William and Martha were not the only ones who were convinced that John had repelled Sophy out of revenge. One woman or man—John simply wrote "one"—who was familiar with John's "whole intercourse with Miss Sophy from the beginning," told him he was "wholly in the wrong." John believed the person had been influenced against him by Thomas.

The northern part of the Colony was split wide open, as is clearly apparent from the pages of the Journal of Colonel William Stephens, who arrived in Savannah November 1 to be the secretary of the Georgia Trustees and in that capacity keep them informed of all matters pertaining to the Colony. Though he did not arrive until three months after Sophy was refused Communion, the controversy was still raging, according to his report:

"Thursday, Nov. 3, 1737. I had from different Hands a long Detail of the Cause of Discord between Mr. Causton and the Parson, ever since Mr. Williamson married Miss Hopkins (niece of Mr. Causton) which was told me variously, as the Relators inclined; but it was carried now to that height as to engage a great part of the Town, which was so divided that Mr. Causton and Mr. Wesley drew their greatest Attention and the Partisans of both sides did not stick to throw Plenty of Scandal against their Adversaries. . . ."

Then again, on November 7, Colonel Stephens wrote, "Went in the morning and took my Breakfast with Mr. Wesley. . . . I've had some Talk about the Differences betwixt him and Mr. Causton, which he put in another Light than which I had it on the other Side.

"I desired him to be free, assuring him that my Ears were equally open, and I should be glad to be instrumental (if it lay in my power) to reconcile those Animosities, which began first between two Friends and had now drawn almost the whole Town into Parties in the Quarrel. I found it manifest the first Rise of it was upon young Williamson marrying Mr. Causton's niece, whom the Parson had a Liking to for himself; and who, whilst she was unmarried, used constantly to receive the Sacrament, which is here administered weekly to some few, who frequently resort to Mr. Wesley for their better edification, in private; but upon Miss Hopkey's entering into the State of Wedlock, she refrain'd from such private Lectures and refused to go to him when sent for; probably by Direction from her Husband; for which Reason (or some other unknown to me) Mr. Wesley refused her the Sacrament at the next Communion, and she went home from the Table: So far Mr. Wesley acknowledged to me, but in his own Justification said, he had given her Notice before not to offer herself there, till she had first conferr'd with him in private. Mr. Wesley told me further he would at some other opportunity explain these Things more fully, and I believed I would hear it impartially."

Years later, in far-away England, several of John's biographers were as scathing of John's stand in refusing the Lord's Supper to Sophy as were his detractors in Savannah in 1737.

The historian Robert F. Wearmouth, in his work, *Methodism and the Common People of the Eighteenth Century*, is most critical. Though he describes John as the "founder," the "genius," the "guide and leader" of the Methodist movement, he laments this performance of John's thusly: "His love-affair with Sophia Christiana Hopkey in Georgia was a strange story, simple-mindedness and emotions of revenge, naïveté, and annoyance weaving in a quaint tapestry. . . . When the girl herself had lost patience with his dalliance and married another, there were signs of vindictiveness in the ecclesiastical penalties Wesley imposed upon her for assumed spiritual delinquency. His behavior was inexcusable and several charges were laid against him, unfriendly and hostile discussions ensued, and he found it necessary to flee from the settlement."

In spite of ignoring almost completely the romance of John and Sophy, as did the majority of the Wesley followers producing "lives" of the father of Methodism, John Hampson does enter the fray long enough to declare that if the charge that John "had made his address to this lady . . . was false," John "ought to have contradicted it in the most express terms"; otherwise, "his behavior will be naturally ascribed to a phrenzy of disappointed love."

V.H.H. Green, in his biography *The Young Mr. Wesley*, denounces John's conduct quite harshly. "There seemed no escape from [his] growing unpopularity," Mr. Green writes, "which reached its climax when Wesley, at the close of an incredibily indiscreet relationship with Sophy Hopkey, used ecclesiastical discipline, as it appeared to the colonists, to forward his personal ends. The repercussions of the unfortunate affair between the high-minded don and the sensitive Sophy re-echoed through the Colony and the Mother Country."

Still another critic, Richard Watson, author of *The Life of the Rev. John Wesley, A.M. Sometimes Fellow of Lincoln College, Oxford, and Founder of the Methodist Societies*, refused to believe John was capable of punishing Sophy because she had married another: "Though Mr. Wesley did not certainly see her married to another with perfect philosophy, it was not in his generous nature to allow his former affection to turn into resentment. . . ." But he argues that the affair could have been handled differently if John had been more Christlike.

"In the affair of Mrs. Williamson, he [John] stands perfectly exculpated from the base motives [with] which his enemies charged him," Mr. Watson states, "but in the first stages, it neither appears to have been managed with prudence, nor a proper degree of Christian courtesy. His enemies have sneered at his declaration that, after he left Georgia, he discovered that he who went out to teach others Christianity was not a Christian himself; but had he been a Christian in that full, evengelical sense, which he meant; had he been what he afterwards became; not only would the exclusion of Mrs. Williamson from the sacrament have been effected in another manner, but his mission to Georgia would probably

225

have had a very different result. . . . His spirit, though naturally frank and amiable, was not yet regenerated by that 'power from on high,' the first and leading fruits of which are meekness and charity."

But to return to Thomas' activities in the early stages of the feud. Not content to read aloud the personal passages in John's letters, he requested James Burnside, whose tenure at the Store, totaling and transcribing the accounts for the Trustees, covered two and a half years, to sign a certificate containing three heads: "(1) that Mrs. Williamson had been ten months past as constant a communicant as any others; (2) that he could conceive of no reason why she should be repelled; (3) that she was and had been of an unblamable behaviour."

James refused, explaining to John later that he "could not sign it with a safe conscience knowing it to be false." John assured him he had behaved in the only honorable way, the first article, particularly, being shamelessly untrue, for by actual count Sophy had omitted communicating nine times in three months.

James, alas, paid the price of his convictions. Thomas discharged him with the warning that he need never expect another favor from him.

Thomas was also busily exerting "his utmost power and art and application" to influence the persons who would form the Grand Jury at the next meeting of the Court. "He was talking with some or other of them day and night," John was told. "His table is open to all." "Whatever they pleased to have from the stores was delivered." "Old misunderstandings were forgot." "And nothing was too much to be done or promised to those who a week before could not procure a morsel of bread."

John, too, was extremely busy and increasingly agitated. He, who was usually so meticulously neat, was so wrought up that he spilled ink on a page of his Diary. He was driven to explain . . . and explain . . . and explain why he had turned Sophy away from the Table. He read the "case" in the open congregation after evening prayers; another evening he read it to Margaret Burnside's class; one day he read it to a number of friends—Mr. How, Mr. West, Mr. Vanderplank, and other members of his parish; and still another day he read it to Mrs. Fallowfield and Mrs. Vat, also parishioners.

Could it be that he was trying to bolster his own belief that he had done the right thing? Even his prayers indicate he was suffering the agonies of the unsure, the doubtful, the wretched. He noted in his Diary that one afternoon he offered "a special prayer for Mr. Causton and Miss Sophy," and just five days later he reported: "In the afternoon, remembering the former kindnesses of Mr. Causton and Miss Sophy, I was strongly moved to pray for them with all my might, with earnest cries and many tears."

The Court met on Monday, August 22, and, as had been customary ever since Thomas had been First Bailiff, the eight tithingmen on duty stood at attention at the main entrance of the building. Recorder Christie announced that the Court was now in session. Thomas immediately jumped to his feet and plunged into an impassioned charge to the Grand Jurors, though as yet they had not even been sworn in. "Beware of spiritual tyranny!" Thomas exhorted them. "Oppose this new authority which would usurp your conscience. I charge you to maintain your rights and privileges and not to suffer any person to infringe on your liberty and usurp your legal authority."

Then, one by one, as their names were called, the members of the Grand Jury came forward, swore on the shiny black, leather-encased Bible securely chained to the table, then lowered their heads and brushed the sacred book with their lips. The number of jurors had been increased from the usual fifteen to thirty-nine. John was confident that the First Bailiff had schemed to have the panel enlarged so that by their greater number they would be emboldened to take action that a fewer number might not have the cour-

227

age to take. They had already sided against him, he felt sure. Some were his avowed enemies, some were the Church of England's avowed enemies, and some, he suspected, were prejudiced against him because of the First Bailiff's underhanded work. Furthermore, they were a polyglot crew. One was a Frenchman who did not understand English; one, a Papist; one, a professed infidel; three were Baptists, and sixteen or seventeen were Dissenters.

The jury seated, Sophy's affidavit was read by Recorder Christie:

"Province of Georgia, Savannah Ss

"Sophia Christiana Williamson, the wife of William Williamson of Savannah aforesaid, maketh oath that about twelve months since she was committed to the care of Mr. John Wesley, the missionary residing in this Province, by her relations, which care the said John Wesley discharged with a great deal of seeming fidelity for two or three months.

"And this Deponent further saith that, after the said three months, the said John Wesley began to use his endeavours to alienate the affection of the said Deponent from her said relations; and often in very pathetic terms urged to her the necessity of her forsaking them and leaving their house in order to cohabit with him———"

John must have drawn in his breath sharply and cried inwardly, "Jesu! Jesu! O, Jesu, what a damnable lie!"

"———insinuating," the Recorder continued, "that she never could make so good a progress to salvation while she lived with them as she could if she lived wholly with him.

"And this Deponent further saith that the said John Wesley, finding all the aforesaid arguments and persuasions ineffectual, he, the said John Wesley, frequently made several overtures of marriage to the Deponent without acquainting her relations thereof, as they have informed this Deponent. And the better to induce this Deponent thereto, he, the said John Wesley, often alleged that he could easily alter anything in his way of life that was disagreeable to her; though he, the said John Wesley, had always prescribed to this Deponent the same way of life he then led as the only means of obtaining salvation; to corroborate which he always added that he endeavoured to imitate the primitive fathers, who were strict imitators of the life of Christ."

There were some grains of truth in this, John must have admitted to himself. John had, indeed, endeavored to imitate the primitive fathers whom he felt were strict imitators of Christ, and he had encouraged Sophy to lead the life he led as the only means of obtaining salvation. But was there anything culpable in that?

"And this Deponent further saith that the said John Wesley further added that whereas he had no settled habitation, and in this regard Deponent might not like his present wandering way of life, he would procure to himself the settlement of Savannah; and used other arguments which this Deponent cannot at present recollect, whereby he gave this Deponent to understand that he would lay aside his former intentions of going among the Indians, in case this Deponent would approve of him for a husband.

"And this Deponent further saith," the Recorder droned on, "that about three days before her marriage with the said William Williamson, the said John Wesley came to this Deponent and urged very much to know whether this Deponent had not been overpersuaded or forced to agree to the said marriage, and whether it might not still be prevented. Adding again that if there was anything in his way of life— by which he gave this Deponent to understand he meant fasting and the other severe mortifications which he, the said John Wesley, and she, this Deponent, by his instruction, had then strictly practiced for about six months—which she, the said Deponent, had any dislike to, he, the said John Wesley, would make all these things easy to her, in case she would consent to marry him.

"And this Deponent further saith that ever since her marriage with the said William Williamson, he, the said John

Wesley, hath taken all opportunities, in her husband's absence, to persecute this Deponent and to force his private discourses to her, wherein he hath often terrified her with the danger her soul would be in if she did not continue to spend her time and converse with him, the said John Wesley, in the same manner she did before marriage.

"And this Deponent further saith that particularly about three months since . . ."

John did not need to be reminded of the occasions "three months since" when he had talked with Sophy after she was wed. They were as fresh and painful to him now as on the days they had taken place.

At last it was over. Quickly John got to his feet and said he would like a copy of the affidavit.

Before the Recorder could answer, Thomas announced, "Parson, you can get a copy from any of the newspapers. I'm going to see to it myself that it is printed in all of them immediately."

John must have been horrified. Did Thomas mean the London papers as well as the South Carolina *Gazette?* Would all his old Oxford and London friends and acquaintances read this unfair, one-sided, biased account of his relations with Miss Sophy?

Next the Court delivered to the Grand Jury a List of Grievances, but it was eventually laid aside, "perhaps not so much for the notorious falsehoods of many parts," so John wrote, "as for the extreme uncouthness of the whole."

During the week of investigation, following the presentation of the affidavit, the Grand Jury interviewed many witnesses, but only three of them, according to John, threw any additional light on the case. Under questioning behind closed doors, Sophy, who was the first witness, reaffirmed the accusations, but added that she had had no objections to John's conduct before her marriage. Thomas followed and admitted that he would have given his niece's hand to the parson if he asked for it, and Martha, who was summoned next, testified that it was at her request that John had written Sophy the letter of July 5 in which he had set out what he disliked in her behavior.

After a long array of witnesses, the Grand Jury studied the letters and papers pertaining to the matter, deliberated for almost a week, and then delivered two Presentations, containing indictments against John, spelling his name Westley.

The first Presentation contained two True Bills. In the first, John was indicted because "he, the said John Westley, did, after the twelfth day of March last, several times privately force his conversation to Sophia Christiana Williamson, contrary to the express desire and command of him, the said Williamson" and "did likewise write and privately convey papers to the aforesaid Sophia Christiana Williamson."

In the second True Bill, he was indicted for refusing her the Sacrament of the Lord's Supper, "to the great disgrace and hurt of her character; from which proceeding we conceive that the said John Westley did assume an authority contrary to the laws established, and to the peace of our Lord the King, his crown and dignity."

The next set of Presentations roamed far afield from the Williamson case. It contained True Bills against John for failing since his arrival in Savannah to "emit any Public Declaration of his adherence to the Principles and Regulations of the Church of England"; for dividing "on the Lord's Day the Order of Morning Prayer, appointed to be used in the Church of England"; for refusing "to baptize otherwise than by dipping the child of Henry Parker . . . unless the said Henry Parker or his wife could certify that the child was weak and not able to bear dipping," adding to his refusal "that unless the said parents would consent to have their said child dipped, it might die a heathen"; for refusing the Lord's Supper to one William Gough, "saying he heard the said William Gough was a 'Dissenter' "; for refusing to read "the office of the Burial of the Dead over the body of Nathanael Polhill only because the said Nathanael Polhill was not of the

231

said John Westley's opinion"; for "presumptuously" calling himself "Ordinary of this place, assuming thereby an authority which we apprehend did of no right belong to him"; for refusing to allow one William Aglionby "to stand Godfather to the child of Henry Manley giving no other reason than that the said William Aglionby had not been at the Communion Table" and, lastly, for baptizing the child of Thomas Jones, "having only one Godfather and one Godmother."

The True Bill accusing John of calling himself "Ordinary" is quite mystifying. He did not comment on it in his Diary or Journal; but, as Editor Curnock suggests, if he did refer to himself by that title, he might have adopted it from the Moravians, who called their benefactor, Count Zinzendorf, "Ordinary."

(Twelve of the jurors took issue with nine of the ten True Bills and later prepared a minority report for the Trustees.)

When the Court sat again on September 2, John appeared and spoke: "As to nine of the ten indictments against me, I know the Court can take no cognizance of them, they being matters of an ecclesiastical nature, and this not being an Ecclesiastical Court. But the tenth, concerning my speaking and writing to Mrs. Williamson, is of a secular nature; and this, therefore, I desire may be tried here, where the facts complained of were committed."

John later reported, "The Court made little answer, and that purely evasive in which for the present I acquiesced."

But in the afternoon he moved the Court for an immediate trial on the one indictment that he claimed it had a right to hear. He argued most earnestly, "I ask for this trial so that those who were or might be offended may clearly see whether I have done any wrong to any one or whether I have deserved the thanks of Mrs. Williamson and Mr. Causton and all his family."

Again he was put off, this time indefinitely. Now that Thomas had succeeded in having John indicted on those ten counts, he was evidently at a loss as to how to proceed. His fear of the displeasure of the Trustees was very real. Suppose the Court tried John and found him guilty—what then? Suppose they fined him a sum they considered adequate to the crime that he was unable to pay, and so had to be locked up?

John was in an even more wrought-up state than the First Bailiff. Indeed, he was so highly nervous he was seized with a violent flux, which so weakened him before one evening service he "had much ado to get to church."

But worse than the flux was the humiliation he suffered because of the appearance in Savannah of the Reverend Mr. Dison, chaplain to the Independent Company of soldiers stationed on St. Simons, who announced that he had been summoned to perform the church services and would "begin so to do the next day by reading prayers, preaching and administering the Sacrament." The doubtful morals of the chaplain added insult to injury. Charles Wesley, during his stay at Frederica, "had formed a low estimate" of Dison and had passed his opinion on to John.

When the first bell rang the next morning to alert the parishioners of the approaching hour of worship, John hurried to his desk and penned the following curt note:

"To the Magistrates of the Town of Savannah.
"Aug. 8, 1737.
[It was actually September, but John apparently was too unnerved to know the month.]

"Gentlemen,
"If you are not apprised that Mr. Dison intends this day publicly to perform several ecclesiastical offices in Savannah, and, as he says, by your authority, I do now apprise you thereof, and am, Gentlemen, your humble servant. J.W."

Delamotte delivered the letter to Recorder Christie. "However," so John reported in his Journal, "at ten the bell rung again, and Mr. Dison entered upon his office, by reading

233

prayers and preaching in the church to Mrs. Causton (Mr. Causton being walked out of town), Mr. Williamson, Mrs. Williamson, and eight or ten more. He told the congregation he should do so every Thursday; that he had intended likewise to administer the Lord's Supper, but some of his communicants were indisposed; and that he would administer Baptism also to as many as he was desired."

In the face of this humiliation to John, Delamotte suggested that John should now return to England to remove the representations that might be spread about him. How exceedingly tempting the idea must have been to John! To be beyond the jurisdiction of the insensitive, ignorant Magistrates; to turn his back on his bitterly divided congregation; to put an ocean between him and Sophy's angry, accusing eyes!

But was it the right thing for him to do? In his overwrought state he could not decide; he felt he needed God's guidance. So he opened the Bible at random and blindly pointed his finger at a verse. It read, "But the same servant went out and found one of his fellow servants which owed him a hundred pence and he laid hands on him and took him by the throat, saying, 'Pay me what thou owest.' " John was shocked. It revealed nothing, absolutely nothing, concerning his problem.

He chose a second verse. It advised, "Cast out the scorner, and contentions go out, yea strife and reproach shall cease." This, too, he felt, was not relevant to the course of action he should follow, but it did, he decided, prophesy the events that were to come to pass in Savannah.

Giving up on sortilege for the time being, he sought the advice of his friends. All of them counseled against his leaving Georgia, declaring it was more suitable to his calling as a minister to remain in Savannah and commit his cause to God than to hasten to England to justify himself.

John submitted to their counsel; however, when the days lengthened into weeks and the weeks into months without the case coming to trial, he grew more restless and tense and once more consulted with his friends. Did they not by this time believe it was God's own will for him to return to England? he asked pleadingly. The reason he had left England, he pointed out, "had now no force, there being no possibility as yet of instructing the Indians." Nor had he "as yet found or heard of any Indians on the continent of America who had the least desire of being instructed.

"And as to Savannah," he continued passionately, repeating the argument he had given before, "having never engaged myself, either by word or letter, to stay here a day longer than I should judge convenient, nor ever take charge of the people any otherwise than as my passage to the heathen, I look upon myself to be duly discharged therefrom by the vacating of that design."

Finally, he argued, he could do more service to the "unhappy people" of Savannah if he were in England than he could do in Georgia "by representing, without fear or favour to the Trustees, the real state the Colony was in."

This time, "after deeply considering these things," his friends were unanimous that he should go, though not yet. He was disappointed, but again he bowed to their decision, even consoling himself with the thought that no doubt when the time was ripe God would "make the way plain" before his face.

In a supreme effort to ease his tormented mind and heart, he worked feverishly, zealously, continuously. He even became an itinerate preacher, as did so many of his followers in the early years of Methodism. He read prayers in French to the French inhabitants of the village of Highgate, and in German to the Germans in the village of Hampstead, and on Sundays he kept the fullest schedule of his life. He read the first English prayers in his own church from five until six-thirty (the Reverend Mr. Dison evidently commuted only on Thursdays to Savannah); Italian prayers to a few Vaudois at nine o'clock; conducted the second service for the English, including the sermon and communion, from ten thirty to twelve thirty, and then French services for the French of Savannah at one o'clock. At two he catechized the children. At three he held another English service, and when this was over, he joined as many people as the parlor of the parsonage would comfortably hold in reading, praying, and singing. Then at six he attended the evening service of the Moravians, but not as a teacher. For this one hour he became what he termed "a learner."

Once, at the morning service of his own parishioners, he subtly compared his persecution by the Magistrates to that of the apostle Paul, when led before Claudius Lysias, the chief captain in Jerusalem. Colonel Stephens sent the details of the occasion to the Trustees:

"Sunday, Nov. 13. Mr. Wesley preach'd on these words, Is It Lawful to give Tribute unto Caesar or not? from whence he discoursed largely on the duties of the Magistrates in their several Ranks and Degrees, and the Obedience due from the People; setting forth how far it was, nevertheless consistent with Christian Liberty, for People to insist upon their Rights, when they found themselves oppressed by inferior Magistrates exercising a discretionary Authority, which exceeded their Commission; as an Instance whereof, he laid down St. Paul's Behavior when the chief Captain had him before him, and how apprehensive the chief Captain was, of his having gone too far, as it is related in the twenty-second Chapter of the Acts. . . .

"The congregation was very thin again, which I was sorry to see; but I found that the Magistrates and many of the principal Inhabitants of late had wholly absented themselves from Church, nevertheless, I thought it my Duty not to abstain from the public Worship, whatever Failings the Minister might have, which in Time would be more fully known, whether more or less grievous, but at present represented in a bad Light by too many."

If the zealous Secretary was present at the service at which

236

John broke down completely and was unable to proceed with his sermon, he neglected to tell the Trustees about it. That pathetic hour went unrecorded until forty-nine years later when John, writing of the tragic dénouement of his romance with Sophy, recounted that in the course of a service he read the first half of the verse of Scripture, beginning, "Son of man, behold, I take away from thee the desire of thine eyes with a stroke," and, having read it, "I was pierced through as with a sword and could not utter a word more." Then, from the perspective of almost half a century he added, "But our comfort is, He that made the heart can heal the heart."

Once more John consulted with his friends about his desire to return to England and this time they agreed the hour had come. Immediately he went to inform Thomas of his plans. "I do not think it proper for a hinderer of the public peace to stay in the place where he is so," he told him with bitter irony. Then he posted an advertisement in Percival Square: "Whereas John Wesley designs shortly to set out for England, this is to desire those who have borrowed any books to return them as soon as they conveniently can to John Wesley."

Referring to this notice, Colonel Stephens noted on Nov. 24, 1737, he "was a little surprised to hear that Mr. Wesley had fixed up a public advertisement signifying his Intent of going soon for England."

And two days later he further reported: ". . . read a public Advertisement fixt up in the Common Place by Mr. Williamson and signifying That whereas Mr. Wesley had given public Notice of his Intention to go soon for England, he did hereby notify that there was a Cause depending in this Court where he had brought his Action against the said Mr. Wesley for 100 l Damages; and therefore, if anyone should aid and assist Mr. Wesley in going out of the Province, he would prosecute such Person with the utmost Rigour."

Then three days later the Colonel wrote: "Tuesday 29th.

237

Mr. Wesley continued in his Resolution of going forthwith to England, and Friday was given as the Day of his Departure."

A fairly heart-tugging note appears in John's Journal at this point. As an employee or apointee of the Trustees, he had to apply to Thomas for money to pay his passage to England. Whether Thomas gave it or not, John thoughtlessly did not say. He did say, however, that at ten o'clock on the morning of December second, when he was all packed and ready to sail on the noon tide for Port Royal, South Carolina, he was summoned by the Magistrates and informed that he could not leave the Province until he had answered the allegations against him.

His piercing eyes flashed fire as he answered, "I have appeared at six or seven Courts successively in order to answer them. But I was not suffered so to do, when I desired it time after time."

Then the Magistrates announced that nevertheless he was forbidden to go unless he gave security to answer the allegations in the Savannah Court. How John must have fumed inwardly! How could he post bond to appear in a Georgia court if he was to be in England? Still he questioned calmly, "What security?"

After the Magistrates consulted about two hours, Recorder Christie presented him with a "kind of bond," ordering him, under a penalty of fifty pounds, to appear at Court when he should be required.

Before John could protest, the Recorder added, "But Mr. Williamson, too, has desired of us, that you should give bail to answer his action."

John replied heatedly, "Sir, you use me very ill, and so you do the Trustees. I will give neither any bond nor any bail at all. You know your business, and I know mine."

That afternoon the Magistrates published an order requiring all the officers and sentinels to stop John from leaving the

238

Colony and forbidding any person to assist him in making his escape.

The action did not faze him. He realized that now he must leave no matter what hindrances were put in his way. Any delay would only serve to make his situation more desperate. As he wrote in his Journal, "Being now only a prisoner at large, in a place where I knew by experience every day would give fresh opportunity to procure evidence of words I never said, and actions I never did, I saw clearly the hour was come for me to fly for my life."

So that night around eight o'clock, when the evening prayers were over, he hurried through the cold December darkness to the foot of the Bluff. The Burnsides and Delamotte were there waiting to bid him farewell. Margaret pressed a warm loaf of gingerbread and a pint of rum into his hands. Then John stepped quickly into a rowboat, already occupied by three crouching, muffled figures whose character, judging from Colonel Stephens' account, was not much better than that of the thieves on the Cross:

"Dec 3 1737:

"Notwithstanding all the precaution that was taken, it was known this morning that Mr. Wesley went off last night and with him Coates, a Constable, Gough, a Tythingman, and one Campbell, a Barber," he recounted. "This surprised most people (even many of those who wished him best) that he should take such Company with him; for there scarce could be found men more obnoxious. Coates especially was and had been a long while one of the principal Fomenters of Mischief, a busy Fellow, always taking upon him a[s] Advocate and Pleader for any Delinquent, going from House to House with idle stories to fill People's Heads with Jealousies and distinguished himself for a most inveterate opposition to all Rules of Government. Moreover he was greatly accountable to the Trust on divers Articles as well as indebted to many people; And to add to all this he never improved one Foot of Land

239

since he came to the Province or built any Thing More than a very mean Hut. Gough was also a very idle Fellow, pert and impudent in his behavior, always (of late) kicking against the Civil Power, and making it his business to enflame a Sedition. He likewise had little to shew of any Improvement, more than setting up a Shell of a House, which he never near finished, though (if I'm rightly informed) he had received considerable favours to enable him; and now went off in many people's Debt, leaving a Wife and Child behind, who even in this forlorn State scarcely grieve at his Absence, since he used to beat them more than feed them. Campbell was an insignificant loose Fellow, fit for an[y] Leader who would make a Tool of him; and all the visible Motive at present to be found for his going off was in so doing to escape his Creditors.

"As I was always ready and willing, in conversation or otherwise, to make allowance for Mr. Wesley's failings in policy, and was careful not to run hastily into an entire belief of all I heard laid to his Charge, I was now asked by divers in a sneering way what my Sentiments were of him, which indeed puzzled me. 'Noscitur ex sociis' [One is known by his companions] was the common byword; and all I had to say was that he must stand or fall by himself, when his Cause came before the Trustees."

John made no written comment about his companions. He simply noted a bit wistfully: ". . . the tide then serving, I shook the dust off my feet, and left Georgia, after having preached the gospel there (with much weakness indeed and many infirmities) not as I ought, but as I was able, one year and nearly nine months."

SIXTEEN

Twenty days later, when John went on board the *Samuel* at Charles-Town for the return voyage to England, his heart was as heavy as an anchor buried in mud. He had struggled nobly those last weeks in Savannah to keep his countenance serene, but his spirit was crushed.

The pain was mostly in his mind and bruised heart when he first came aboard; but two days later, on the morning of December 24, as the frail little ship unfurled its sun-stained sails, he also became bodily ill. He was more nauseated than he had been during the 112 stormy days of the westward passage. Indeed, his stomach was so queasy and his head so dizzy, he had to lie flat on his back for almost twelve hours.

He did not, however, blame his illness on his dejected state. He told himself he had been eating too "delicately" at the table of the ship's master, a Captain Percy. So he went back to his usual exceedingly plain diet, consisting mainly of bread, cheese, and water, and shortly his body felt at ease.

But not his morale. The most serious cause of his depres-

241

sion was his fear—not of losing his life as had been the case several times on his way to Georgia, but fear of losing his faith in God. The rock of his belief had been shattered by the cruel blow of Sophy's defection. When she turned her back on him, his sure hold on salvation had been loosened. For some time he refused to face the appalling truth, but four days after sailing, he groped for the truth in these words:

"Finding the unaccountable apprehensions of I know not what danger (the wind being small and the sea smooth) which had been upon me for several days, I cried earnestly for help. . . ." Then, a day or so later, he confessed that "being sorrowful and very heavy," he was utterly unwilling to "speak close" to any of his "little flock (about twenty persons)" and that he could not speak to the sailors, though he went several times to do so.

Sad, despondent words for the usually confident, zealous John. What furious pacing of the little forward deck he must have done! Around and around that cramped, swaying space he went, oblivious of the wintry gales, the coiled ropes, the muddy anchor, the gangplank, the chests, the hogsheads of turpentine. . . . Did he hold in his hands the opened Testament, reading mindlessly the same passage again and again? Did the fair face of Sophy swim between his eyes and the wind-whipped pages?

Yet, as the voyage continued, he spilled into the Journal a much more poignant passage of capitulation of all he had held sacred. On Saturday, January 8, of the new year, he wrote from the "fullness of his heart":

"By the most infallible of proofs, inward feeling, I am convinced:

"1, Of unbelief, having no such faith in Jesus Christ as will prevent my heart from being troubled; which it could not be, if I believed in God and rightly believed also in Him:

"2, Of pride, throughout my life past; inasmuch I thought I had what I find I have not:

242

"3, Of gross irrecollection; inasmuch in a storm I cried to God every moment; in a calm, not:

"4, Of levity and luxuriancy of spirit, recurring whenever the pressure is taken off . . ."

But even after putting down in black and white this pathetic confession, he did not stop searching his heart and mind for the real facts about himself. He no longer knew what kind of man he was. The security he had always had—not only in his sure salvation, but in himself as a decent human being—was lost. Whether he searched for the facts leaning listlessly, hour after hour, on the dipping and rising rail, staring sightlessly at the shuffling sea, he did not say, at least on paper. Or whether he searched on his knees in the dim recesses of his windowless cabin, debating with his now distant God, we have no way of knowing.

We do know, however, that he never stopped seeking the basic core of his being. Until the very hour on February 1, when the *Samuel* rode safely into the Downs, he continued to judge with bitter frankness his thoughts, his emotions, and his actions.

"It is now two years and almost four months [John is including those many weeks on the westward voyage on the *Simmonds*] since I left my native country, in order to teach the Georgia Indians the nature of Christianity," he wrote. "But what have I learned myself in the meantime? Why, what I least of all suspected, that I, who went to America to convert others, was never myself converted to God. 'I am not mad,' though I thus speak; but 'I speak the words of truth and soberness'; if haply some of those who still dream may awake and see that as I am, so are they.

"Are they read in philosophy? So was I. In ancient or modern tongues? So was I also. Are they versed in the science of divinity? I too have studied it many years. Can they talk fluently upon spiritual things? The very same could I do. Are they plenteous in alms? 'Behold I gave all my goods to feed the poor.' Do they give of their labour as well as of their substance? I have laboured more abundantly than they all. Are they willing to suffer for their brethren? I have thrown up my friends, reputation, ease, country; I have put my life in my hands, wandering into strange lands; I have given my body to be devoured by the deep, parched up with heat, consumed with toil and weariness, or whatsoever God should please to bring upon me. But does all this—be it more or less, it matters not—make me acceptable to God? Does all I ever did or can know, say, give, do or suffer, justify me in His sight? . . .

"This, then, have I learned at the ends of the earth—that I 'am fallen short of the glory of God'; that my whole heart is altogether corrupt and abominable; and consequently my whole life (seeing it cannot be an 'evil tree' should 'bring forth good fruit') that 'alienated' as I am from the life of God, I am 'a child of wrath' and heir of hell. . . ."

Could he have abased himself more? Could he have expressed with greater poignancy his humility, his frailty, his consciousness of total failure? Still he was not ready to surrender. Though convinced he was a lost soul, a sinner, an outcast from the throne of God, he continued to wrestle with the Lord in prayer. He cried from his heart:

> O, grant that nothing in my soul
>   May dwell but Thy pure love alone!
> O, may Thy love possess me whole,
>   My joy, my treasure and my crown!
> Strange fires far from my heart remove,
>   My every act, word, thought, be love!

Indeed, all that John wrote in those early weeks of 1738 bears out the truth of his own statement that he made many years later: "God humbled me and proved me and showed me what was in my heart." Those twenty-one months in England's Thirteenth Colony were most assuredly John's sojourn in the wilderness. As the Reverend Mr. Moore declared in his biography, ". . . he [John] was, as every minister of Christ is, in some sense and degree 'led into the wilderness to be tempted'. . . . And, indeed, he always considered the American Mission in that point of view."

It is indisputable that John came out of Georgia a changed human being. Historian Abram Lifsy, describing him during those months of the return voyage, wrote: "His Journal indicates he was profoundly disturbed. The depth of his soul had been turned up in the passionate turmoil in Savannah. The old Wesley had been shattered. A new Wesley was struggling to be born." Then, in another passage, he said, "The affair with Sophy brought the whole system [John's ministry] down with a crash. He was beset with neurotic fears, by unaccountable apprehensions of he knew not what dangers."

Robert Wright, in his biography of John, summed up the result of the Savannah experience thusly: "There has never been a more remarkable transformation of character than that of the self-sufficient, arrogant young priest into the subsequent reviver of our church."

But the most detailed discussion of John's state of being on leaving Georgia has been made by Dr. Doughty. In *John Wesley, Peacher*, he wrote:

"Whatever Wesley may have learned or failed to learn in Georgia, he had come very near to that self-knowledge which some have held to be the *summum bonum* of human wisdom, and he was appalled to the point of despair. He had practiced the Christian virtues almost to perfection and exceeded in deeds of kindness and charity. He had played the part of the model parish priest, rigorously self-exacting in the performance of every duty and expecting complete co-operation from his parishioners. . . . All had ended in confusion, heartburnings, hatred and—flight. His natural pride had been wounded; his self-confidence severely shaken; and the demon of despair was seated at his elbow. Atlantic storms were raging around him but there was a more devastating storm within."

And a few lines further on, Author Doughty compared John to a "Mourner Convinced of Sin," whose lament in the Methodist Hymnal goes this way:

> In the wilderness I stray,
> My foolish heart is blind
> Nothing do I know; the way
> Of peace I cannot find.

There were contributing causes, as we have seen, that unhinged John's belief in himself and in Christ and convinced him that he must begin anew to try to find salvation; but Sophy was the chief instrument. Musing over several "ifs" in John's life, Historian Wearmouth argues: "If, perchance the High Church missionary to Georgia in 1735 [actually 1736–1737] had succumbed to the attractions of Sophia Hopkey, married her as his natural impulses prompted, made a home of her uncle's estate in accordance with that gentleman's wish, there can be no doubt that Methodism, an acorn planted at Oxford, would never have grown into a tree of marvelous stature." In 1945, at the time Wearmouth's history was published, the "tree of marvelous stature" had already grown to thirty million Methodists "in most parts of the inhabited globe." In Europe, Africa, Asia, the Americas, China, India and in every section of the British Empire there were and are people "who accept Westley's doctrine and follow his methods."

Biographer Tyerman also indulges in this game of "Ifs." "Though the courtship of young people is an ordinary, commonplace sort of thing," he writes, "inconceivable great events were dependent upon the result of this [of Sophy's and John's]. . . ." ". . . supposing the courtship had ended in marriage, is it likely that we should have ever heard of Wesley at Bristol, Kingswood, Kensington Common, and Moorfields? Is it likely there would ever have been any 'United Societies of the People called Methodists'? Should we have ever heard of either the Methodism of the past or

246

present? . . . for had John Wesley married Sophia Christiana Hopkey, the probability is that instead of returning to England and beginning the greatest religious revival of modern times, he would have settled in Georgia and, like another Xavier, have spent a most spiritual and devoted life in converting Indians and other kinds of heathen. . . . Wesley's courtship in Georgia was pregnant with infinite momentousness. . . ."

Pursuing Dr. Wearmouth's and the Reverend Mr. Tyerman's "ifs" with one of our own: If there had been no Sophy, John more than likely would not have waited sixteen years to marry a wealthy widow, Mary Vazeille, who, before she deserted him, made his home life so miserably unhappy that it encouraged him to become "the traveller-evangelist" instead of a "stay-at-home" parson. For more than fifty years John traveled across the length and breadth of Britain, covering an average of at least forty-five hundred miles a year, though roads were almost nonexistent and transportation all but impossible.

Yes, Sophy was the turntable that helped so amazingly to switch him completely about and set his feet on the track leading to the experience that, on May 24, 1738, revolutionized not only his life, but the history of England and, through the Evangelical Revival, the history of the Christian world.

He described that experience simply in his Journal:

"In the evening I went very unwillingly to a society in Aldersgate Street, where one was reading Luther's preface to the Epistle to the Romans. About a quarter before nine, while he was describing the change which God works in the heart through faith in Christ, I felt my heart strangely warmed. I felt I did trust in Christ, Christ alone for salvation; and an assurance was given me that He had taken away my sins, even mine, and saved me from the law of sin and death."

BIBLIOGRAPHY

Anderson, J. R. "The Genesis of Georgia: An Historical Sketch,"
Georgia Historical Quarterly, vol. 13 (1929), pp. 231–83.

Arthur, T. S., and W. H. Carpenter. *History of Georgia* (Philadelphia: Lippincott, Grambe & Co.; 1852).

Baker, Frank. "John Wesley and the Imatatio Christi," *Quarterly
and Helborn Review*, vol. 166 (London, January 1941), pp.
74–87.

Barrow, Elfrida De Renne, and Laura Palmer Bell. *Anchored
Yesterdays* (Savannah, Ga.: Review Publishing and Printing
Co.; 1923).

Birrell, Augustine. "John Wesley," *Empire Review* (London,
July–December 1925).

Bourne, George. *The Life of the Reverend John Wesley* . . .
(Baltimore: privately printed; 1807).

Bowen, Marjorie. *Wrestling Jacob* (London: Butler & Tanner,
Frome and London; 1938).

Brailsford, Mabel Richmond. *A Tale of Two Brothers, John and
Charles Wesley* (New York: Oxford University Press; 1954).

Brash, W. Bardshy. "Wesley's wit and humor," *London Quarterly Review*, series 5, vol. i (1921).

Bruce, Henry. *Life of General Oglethorpe* (New York: Dodd, Mead and Company; 1890).

Candler, Allan D., and Lucian Lamar Knight, eds. *Colonial Records of the State of Georgia*, vols. 1–5, 20–3, 27 (Atlanta, Ga.: Franklin Printing and Publishing Company; 1904–16).

Carroll, B. R. *Historical Collections of South Carolina* (New York: Harper & Brothers; 1836).

Charlton, Walter Glasco: *The Making of Georgia: Oglethorpe, Two Addresses* (Savannah, Ga.: Society of Colonial Dames; 1902[?]).

Church, Leslie Frederick. *Knight of the Burning Heart* (London: Epworth Press; 1938).

Clarke, Adam. *Memoirs of the Wesley Family* (London: Bangs; 1824).

————. *Collections of the Georgia Historical Society*, vols. 1–4, 13 (Savannah, Ga., 1840–59).

Coke, Thomas, and Henry Moore. *The Life of the Rev. John Wesley* . . . (London: G. Paramore; 1792).

Cooper, Harriet C. *James Oglethorpe: The Founder of Georgia* (New York: D. Appleton and Company; 1904).

Cooper, Joseph. *The Love Stories of John Wesley and Other Essays* (Boston: R. G. Badger; 1931).

Coulter, E. Merton. "When John Wesley Preached in Georgia," *Georgia Historical Quarterly*, vol. 9 (December 1925), pp. 317–51.

————, and Albert B. Saye. *A List of Early Settlers of Georgia* (Athens, Ga.: University of Georgia Press; 1949).

Curnock, Nehemiah. *The Journal of the Rev. John Wesley* . . . , vols. 1–8 (London: Epworth Press; 1938).

Doughty, William Lamplough. *John Wesley, Preacher* (London: Epworth Press; 1955).

————. *John Wesley, His Conferences and His Preachers* (London: Epworth Press; 1944).

Du Bose, Horace. *A History of Methodism*, vol. 2 (Nashville, Dallas, Richmond: Publishing House of the M.E. Church South; 1916).

Egmont, John Percival. *Diary of Viscount Percival, Afterwards*

250

First Earl of Egmont, 1730–1747, 3 vols. (London: H.M. Stationery Office; 1920).

Estill, Eugenia. *James Oglethorpe in England and Georgia* (Charleston, S.C.: Southern Printing & Publishing Co.; 1926).

Ettinger, Amos Aschbach. *James Edward Oglethorpe, Imperial Idealist* (Oxford: Clarendon Press; 1936).

Faris, John T. *Romance of Forgotten Towns* (New York: Harper & Brothers; 1924).

Fitchett, W. H. *Wesley and His Century, a Study in Spiriual Forces* (Cincinnati: Jennings & Graham; New York: Eaton & Mains; 1907).

Fries, Adelaide L. *Moravians in Georgia, 1735–1740* (Raleigh, N.C.: privately printed; 1905).

Gamble, Thomas. *The Love Stories of John and Charles Wesley* (Savannah, Ga.: Review Publishing and Printing Co. Inc.; 1927).

Gladstone, James Patterson. *The Life and Travels of George Whitfield, M.A.* (London: Longmans, Green and Co.; 1871).

Gordon, Peter. *The Journal of Peter Gordon, 1732–1735*, ed. by E. M. Coulter (Athens, Ga.: University of Georgia Press; 1963).

Green, Richard. *John Wesley, Evangelist* (London: Religious Tract Society; 1905).

———. *The Work of John and Charles Wesley* . . . (London: C. H. Kelly, 1896).

Hampson, John. *Memoirs of the Late John Wesley* . . . (Sunderland: privately printed; 1791).

Harden, William. *The History of Savannah and South Georgia* (Chicago: Lewis Publishing Company; 1913).

Harris, John. *A Complete Collection of Voyages & Travels*, vol. 2 (London; 1748).

Hendrix, Eugene R. "Wesley's Original American Journal," *Methodist Review*, vol. 83 (New York, July 1903), pp. 513–23.

Hoole, Elijah. *Oglethorpe and the Wesleys in America* (London: R. Needham; 1863).

Ingham, Benjamin. *Diary*, in Phillips (manuscript) collection (University of Georgia).

Jackson, Thomas. *The Life of the Rev. Charles Wesley, M.A.* (London: John Mason; 1841).

Jones, Charles C., Jr. *History of Savannah, Ga., from Its Settlement to the Close of the Eighteenth Century* (Syracuse, N.Y.: D. Mason & Co.; 1890).

Johnson, Amanda. *Georgia as a Colony and State* (Atlanta: Walter W. Brown Publishing Co.; 1938).

Kelly, Charles H. *Wesley the Man, His Teaching and His Work* (London: C. H. Kelly; 1891).

Knight, Lucian Lamar. *Georgia's Landmarks, Memorials and Legends* (Atlanta: Byrd Printing Company; 1913).

Lee, F. O., and J. L. Agnew. *Historical Record of the City of Savannah* (Savannah, Ga.: J. L. Estill; 1869).

Lipsky, Abram. *John Wesley, a Georgia Portrait* (New York: Simon & Schuster; 1923).

Maser, Frederick. "The Early Biographers of John Wesley," *Methodist History*, vol. 1 (January 1963).

Mereness and Dennison, eds. *Travels in the American Colonies* (New York: Macmillan; 1916).

Mitchell, Frances Letcher. *Georgia Land and People* (Atlanta: Franklin Printing and Publishing Co.; 1900).

Moore, Francis. "A Voyage to Georgia begun in the year 1735," *Collections of the Georgia Historical Society*, vol. 1 (1840–59), pp. 79–152.

Moore, Henry. *The Life of the Rev. John Wesley, A.M.* (New York: Methodist Episcopal Church; 1792).

Naylor, John. *Charles Delamotte, John Wesley's Companion in Travel, Labour and Affliction* (London: Epworth Press; 1938).

Newman, Henry. *Salzburgers Letterbooks*, transcribed and ed. by George Fenwick Jones (Athens, Ga.: University of Georgia Press; 1966).

Oglethorpe, James. "Letters from General Oglethorpe to the Trustees of the Colony of Georgia and others, 1735–1745," *Collections of the Georgia Historical Society*, vol. 3 (Savannah, Ga.: 1840–59), pp. 1–156.

Parker, Percy L. *Heart of John Wesley's Journal* (New York: Fleming H. Revell Company; 1902).

Pennington, Edgar Legare. "John Wesley's Georgia Ministry,"

reprinted from *Church History*, vol. 8 (Chicago: University of Chicago; September 1939), pp. 231–55.

Phillips Collection of Letters, etc., mostly in manuscript at the University of Georgia.

Reck, Philip Georg Friedrich von. *An Extract of the Journal of Commissary von Reck* . . . (London: Society for promoting Christian Knowledge; 1734).

Simon, John Smith. *John Wesley and the Advance of Methodism* (London: Epworth Press; 1925).

Smith, George Gilman. *History of Georgia and Georgia People —1730–1860* (Macon, Ga.: G. G. Smith; 1900).

South Carolina *Gazette* (Charleston, S.C., 1732–8).

Southey, Robert. *The Life of Wesley and the Rise and Progress of Methodism* (London: privately printed; 1820).

Spalding, Thomas. "Sketch of the Life of Gen. James Oglethorpe." *Collections of the Georgia Historical Society*, vol. 1 (Savannah, Ga., 1840–59), pp. 239–95.

Stephens, William. "A Journal of the Proceedings in Georgia, beginning October 20, 1737," *Colonial Records of the State of Georgia*, vol. 4 (Atlanta: Franklin Printing and Publishing Company; 1906).

Tailfer, Pat, and Hugh Anderson, Dr. Doughlass, and others. "A True and Historical Narrative of the Colony in America, etc." *Collections of the Georgia Historical Society*, vol. 2 (Savannah, Ga., 1840–59), pp. 163–263.

Telford, John. *The Life of John Wesley* (New York: Eaton & Mains; Cincinnati: Curtis & Jennings; 1898).

———. "Wesley in Training," *London Quarterly Review* (London, January 1929).

True . . . , a pamphlet (London: G. Paramore; 1792).

Tyerman, Luke. *The Life ad Times of the Rev. John Wesley, M.A., Founder of the Methodists* (New York: Harper Brothers; 1878).

———. *The Life of Rev. George Whitefield*, 2 vols. (New York: A. D. F. Randolph Company; 1877).

———. *The Oxford Methodists; memoirs of the Rev. Messrs. Clayton, Ingham, Gambold, Hervey and Broughton, with biographical notice of others* (New York: Harper Brothers; 1873).

Urulsperger, Samuel, ed. *Detailed Reports of the Saltzburger Emigrants Who Settled in America*, 2 vols. (Athens, Ga.: University of Georgia Press; 1968).

Wade, John Donald. *John Wesley* (New York: Coward-McCann; 1930).

Wakeley, Joseph Beaumont. *Anecdotes of the Wesleys: Illustrative of their character and personal history* (London: Hodder & Stoughton; 1870).

Watson, Richard. *The Life of the Rev. John Wesley, Founder of the Methodist Societies* (New York: B. Waugh and T. Mason for the Methodist Episcopal Church; 1836).

Wearmouth, Robert F. *Methodism and the Common People of the Eighteenth Century* (London: Epworth Press; 1945).

Wesley, John. *Letters of the Rev. John Wesley*, ed. by John Telford (London: Epworth Press; 1931).

———. *Mr. Wesley's Primitive Physic . . .* , 16th edition (Trenton, N.J.: Quelle and Wilson; 1788).

———. *An Extract of the Rev. John Wesley's Journal from His Embarking for Georgia to His Return to London* (Bristol: S. &. F. Farley; 1739).

———. *Psalms and Hymns for Sunday* (Charleston, S.C.: printed by Lewis Timothy; 1737).

———. *Standard Sermons*, ed. and annotated by Edward H. Sugden (London: Epworth Press; 1746, 1748, 1750, 1760).

———, ed. *The Sunday Service for Methodists in America* (London: Frys and Coachman; 1786).

———. *Works of the Rev. John Wesley*, A.M., vols. 1–14 (London: Wesleyan Conference Office; 1872).

White, George. *Historical Collections of Georgia* (New York: Pudney & Russell; 1854).

Whitehead, John. *The Life of the Rev. John Wesley . . .* (London: Stephen Couchman; 1793).

Wright, Robert. *A Memoir of General James Oglethorpe* (London: Chapman and Hall; 1867).